T0358541

The International Library of Sociology

THE PRICE OF
SOCIAL SECURITY

Founded by KARL MANNHEIM

The International Library of Sociology

PUBLIC POLICY, WELFARE AND SOCIAL WORK
In 18 Volumes

THE PRICE OF
SOCIAL SECURITY

by
GERTRUDE WILLIAMS

First published in 1944 by
Routledge

Reprinted 1998, 2000, 2002
by Routledge
2 Park Square, Milton Park, Abingdon, Oxon, OX14 4RN

Transferred to Digital Printing 2007

British Library Cataloguing in Publication Data
A CIP catalogue record for this book
is available from the British Library

The Price of Social Security
ISBN 0-415-17719-7
Public Policy, Welfare and Social Work: 18 Volumes
ISBN 0-415-17831-2
The International Library of Sociology: 274 Volumes
ISBN 0-415-17838-X

Publisher's Note
The publisher has gone to great lengths to ensure the quality of this
reprint but points out that some imperfections in the original
may be apparent

CONTENTS

v

FOREWORD

ANY writer who deals with contemporary events is faced with the danger that the scene may have changed between the completion of the book and its publication. This danger is increased at the moment because of the rapid course of events on the one hand and the inevitable slowing down in the pace of book production on the other. It is impossible, therefore, to try to bring up to date in every particular the account of war-time labour controls given in Chapter IV; it must stand as a description of those controls at the time the book was finished—that is, in August, 1943. I am the more ready to do this as this book is not concerned primarily with war-time practices in the organisation of the labour market. Indeed, my only purpose in analysing these was to see what light they throw on the post-war problem of increasing occupational mobility, and as labour resources were so fully mobilised by the summer of 1943 any very startling or revolutionary developments in policy are unlikely.

As I was employed in the Man Power Division of the Ministry of Labour and National Service during part of the time covered by Chapter IV, it may be as well to point out that all the information given is taken from published sources. But I am glad to have this opportunity of expressing my gratitude to all the officials with whom I came into contact for the kindness and patience with which they helped me to appreciate something of the nature of administrative problems. I owe a great deal to the many friendly discussions I enjoyed, as well as to the good fortune of being able to play a part in the first experiment in total mobilisation.

GERTRUDE WILLIAMS.

BEDFORD COLLEGE,
  LONDON.
    October, 1943.

CHAPTER I

LABOUR MOBILITY AND IMPERFECT COMPETITION

I

SYNOPSIS OF CHAPTER

1. Changes in production necessitate a perpetual shifting in occupational distribution. Improved techniques economise labour and release workers for other jobs, but unless the released workers do, in fact, transfer to the other forms of work, the effect of the new techniques on increasing wealth and raising standards of living is not fully realised.

2. Legally there is freedom of choice of employment and in theory wage differentials direct labour into the channels where it is most needed ; but there are many social and psychological obstacles to be overcome.

3. Geographical industrial specialisation adds to the difficulties of occupational transfer.

4. Changes in the relative sizes of industries are usually brought about more by natural wastage and by the movement of new recruits to wage-earning than by the transfer of adults. But young people do not always enter the growing industries, owing to ignorance, lack of necessary education and faulty guidance.

THE last census before the war showed that there were in this country nearly 19 million people who were " gainfully occupied ", i.e. who were doing various jobs for which they received payment. In this total was included every kind of worker from the lowest unskilled grade to the highest levels of manipulative dexterity, mental ability and creative energy. Not all of them were employed in the ordinary sense of the word. A small proportion (less than 7%) acted " on their own account ", i.e. they employed themselves as owners of businesses, shopkeepers, doctors, jobbing gardeners, etc. ; and the income they made depended on their ability to find a market for what they had to offer. But the remainder were working on some form of contract of service. Some employer—it might be a private individual or a company, or the State—was prepared to pay them for their work. This wide comprehensive group had no homogeneity either as regards work or payment. The unskilled casual labourer, earning his shilling an hour, and the manager of a big business, drawing his four-figure salary, were equally included ; all that they shared in common was that they received payment from somebody else who, presumably, found it worth while to pay for their services.

From a closer examination of these census figures we could get some idea of the various branches of work in which this huge total was employed. We would find, for example, that while there were over a million employed in mining, there were only about a quarter of that number in the woodworking industries. About half a million got their living in agriculture and less than 200,000 in " sport and entertainment ". These are broad categories and include within themselves very many subdivisions of sharply differing types of work. The cowman, the shepherd and the ploughman require different kinds of skill, knowledge and experience, yet all are agricultural workers ; the man who takes the gate money at the football field and the man who kicks the ball both get their living from " sport and entertainment ", but their occupations are not identical ; the engine driver and the porter are both employed by the railway company but they could not readily do each other's work. And we should need, therefore, to look at all these occupational sub-divisions to get any idea of the sorts of work that people do for their living.

If we examined some earlier censuses the picture of the working life of the community that we should get would present many similar features but quite different details. Some of the groups in the industries and sub-divisions would be larger than in the later census, others much smaller. There would be no mention in the earlier tables of new groups that appear in the later, for example, the motor-car and radio and cinema industries. Some that loomed large in the earlier picture would be seen to have shrunk later on to very small proportions, for example, wheelwrights and harness makers.

A series of such statistical pictures followed over a period of years shows that the men and women who make up the working community are not permanently split up into trades but that there is constant ebb and flow, swelling the size of some industries and reducing that of others. Some of these movements are of only temporary significance and are the response to a sudden need. If a ship springs a leak all hands are called to man the pumps, though they will return to their usual work when the crisis is over. And similarly during a war there is an enormous shift in occupations. But when the war is over the number engaged in national defence or in making munitions shrinks again to whatever is considered necessary for safety in peace-time. If we discount these sudden temporary movements we find that most of the shifts are fairly enduring in character and show certain definite trends, so that a pattern gradually emerges out of the shifting kaleidoscope.

Every human community, whatever its social or political organisation, is faced with the same fundamental economic problem—the difficulty of reconciling its limited powers of production with its ever-widening and seemingly insatiable wants.

Productivity is governed by certain factors which may relax their pressure but which never abandon their ultimate control. The first of these is the quantity of available material resources, for while man can show great ingenuity in the use to which he puts the gifts of nature, he is completely at a loss unless he has something to work on. The most cunning farmer cannot grow crops without soil and water ; the most intricate and delicate piece of mechanism has to start out in life as a lump of ore ; beautifully woven and coloured fabrics need fibre which has to be grown whether the thread is spun by the silkworm or the industrial chemist. In fact, all that mankind can do is to change the shapes of things that nature has given him, or to move them from a place where they are of no use to him to somewhere else where they can be made to serve his needs.

But natural resources alone would be of no great value in satisfying wants without the human labour and human ingenuity to make use of them. Even the simplest of societies—the food-gatherers—are bound to expend a considerable amount of physical energy and sleuthing prowess if they want to collect sufficient food to remain alive, even if they have the luck to be placed in a particularly favourable environment. But for the most part the human factor plays a much more important part than this. Crops have to be grown and animals domesticated ; tools must be devised for transporting and shaping raw materials ; organised co-operation has to be evolved for distributing goods to where they are wanted. So that the power to make use of natural resources is consequently limited by the human energy available and by the amount of knowledge that has been acquired. At any given moment, there are only so many people capable of work ; some are too old, some too young, some too ill or feeble to take their share. And those who are able to work cannot go on working for twenty-four hours a day. Some time must inevitably be spent in sleep and recuperation. It follows then that even if the fullest possible use is made of the knowledge that has been accumulated and of the powers of organisation that have been developed, there must be a limit to the total of what can be produced at that time. That total is, of course, not a fixed amount. It is continually being increased as man restlessly experiments and learns more of the nature of his physical environment and inherent potentialities. But at any time the limit is there and compels men to choose between alternatives which conflict with one another. We decide, for example, to build a cinema. We have to realise that we cannot use the same materials and the same labour to build a school. One or the other—not both. If we satisfy one desire it must, necessarily and inevitably, be at the cost of forgoing the other. That is the basic economic problem that confronts humanity. We can satisfy more wants only by increasing our total production—by locating further supplies of material, or by finding new uses for natural resources that were previously considered worthless or inaccessible, or by making use of those resources with a greater economy of human effort. Despite the immense development in our capacity to produce we have never managed to catch up with our needs. For human wants, unlike our productive powers, are not limited. As far as it is safe to judge from the history of the human race there is no conceivable boundary to our wants. Moralists may preach of the value of the " simple life " and may urge us to content ourselves with modest standards so that time and energy given to the pursuit of material luxury may be devoted to cultural or spiritual ends. This does not in any sense change the nature of the problem. Wants are no less in conflict with one another if one is for a material object and the other for a non-material. A man who demands more leisure whether to lie on his back in the sunshine, or to wrestle with the problems of his soul, or to be a member of the City Council, or to learn to play the violin has necessarily to forgo the other things that he might have been doing, and the wants that he might have been satisfying, if he had occupied himself differently during those hours. A community may decide, as we in this country have been doing in the last couple of decades, that leisure for the enjoyment of personal and individual interests is of such value that it is worth the sacrifice of a certain amount of material production. What it has no power to decide is that it will have both the extra leisure and the extra material production, unless at the same time it discovers such measures for economising human labour as to increase the total amount of production. It may well be that our happiness will be drawn from more enduring sources of satisfaction if we learn to prefer to listen to a symphony concert to having an extra suit of clothes or drinking more beer. But the basic economic choice remains the same. All it means is that we prefer to use a larger proportion of our material and human resources on educating musicians, making musical instruments, building concert halls and radio sets, on the one hand, and a smaller proportion on the textile industries and stores, or in brewing beer and in building public-houses on the other.

As a matter of experience, we find that there has been a very marked degree of similarity in all societies with regard to the relative prominence given to different kinds of wants. Each community shows its own variations in the emphasis it lays on particular *methods* of satisfying wants, but on the whole the broad development as regards *categories* of wants has been the same. The East may satisfy its hunger with rice and the West with wheat, but in both hemispheres food is urgently demanded as the prime necessity. So long as our productive capacities are in the crudest stage of development the greater part of our time and energy must be taken up with supplying ourselves with food and shelter. But as we gain more knowledge and skill in exploiting our environment elementary hunger is more easily satisfied and labour is released which can be put to other uses. Even the greediest among us soon finds that a ceaseless concentration on the same food begins to pall and long before that point in satiety has been reached, has attempted, at least, to introduce some variety into his diet. We turn from " filling " foods such as rice or potatoes in favour of meats and poultry, fruits, vegetables and dairy produce. Even so, the human stomach is of very limited capacity, and when, as Bishop Blougram says, " . . . body gets its sop and holds its noise ", all kinds of other wants get a chance to make themselves felt. Houses are more carefully built and more elaborately equipped, with rooms specialised to various uses. Instead of eating, sleeping and cooking in the same room, one part of the house is furnished with beds and cupboards, another with stoves and cooking utensils, another with tables and chairs, pianos and bookshelves, another with bath and washbasin and a complicated system of water-pipes, and so on. Roads are built and systems of drainage and sewerage contrived. All this makes a demand, quite apart from the building itself, for a whole host of manufacturing industries, engineering, furniture, upholstery, decoration, etc.

The next stage in a rising standard of living shows itself in two different ways. On the one hand, personal taste and individual idiosyncrasy have more scope. The ways in which the basic needs for food and clothing are satisfied are dictated, in general, by the customs of the country in which we live. We are led to this partly by the fact that it requires a great effort to break away continually from the traditional pattern of living in which we have been brought up and which we see going on around us. But, also, the things which are made to satisfy large and popular demands can be produced on mass production lines and are, therefore, cheap to buy. But as we grow richer we can build on this common foundation a superstructure which is designed to suit our individual fancy. Some of us may decide to have our clothes made to measure instead of buying them from the peg, others prefer to pay somebody else to cook the dinner or dust the rooms, others buy more books or go oftener to the cinema or listen to concerts or save up for a holiday abroad. Consequently, more people are drawn into the activities which provide all these amenities, personal service, travel, entertainment, etc.

The second way in which a higher standard of living shows

itself is by the development of the network of institutions which are essential to a well-organised community life. Law and medicine, banking and commerce, educational facilities, the fine arts, public administration begin to play a more important rôle and to draw a larger proportion of the population into these employments.

In all countries, therefore, economic progress has shown itself first in a reduction in the number of people engaged in the primary industries of agriculture, forestry and fishing, and an increase in those employed in mining, manufacture and building —the secondary industries. As wealth has continued to increase, a larger proportion of the income of the community has been spent on the third type of want—personal services of one sort or another. With the improvement in communications, much of a country's demand for manufactures may be satisfied by imports from other countries, but such activities as those of the professions, public administration, finance and personal services must necessarily be carried on close to their market. Consequently, every country with a rising standard of living has a growing proportion of its population employed in these tertiary occupations. Mr. Colin Clark has estimated the numbers engaged in different activities in many different countries and has shown the close correlation between increasing wealth and occupational distribution. In China, for example, where the standard of living is extremely low, 75–80% of the population are primary producers, whereas in Australia and New Zealand— both of which are countries which we think of as predominantly agricultural—only 25% are so engaged and nearly half of the working population is employed in tertiary industry.[1]

The changing emphasis of demand does not of itself, however, give a complete picture of the variations in employment. New wants can be satisfied because old wants can be more easily met. It is only because new techniques can be introduced into the old industries that labour and materials are released for new purposes. Australia and New Zealand can employ so large a proportion of their man-power on tertiary production because the 25% engaged in agriculture are using new methods and new knowledge. So that even those who remain in an industry do work which is very different in nature from that of their predecessors. Land is still ploughed, but it is ploughed by a mechanical tractor instead of a man with two horses. Milk is still made into butter and cheese, but it is no longer the farmer's wife or the dairymaid but the factory worker who converts it. The modern lorry-driver needs to know a great deal about internal combustion engines and nothing about horses. In manufacturing industries, mechanical cranes replace human

[1] Colin Clark, *Conditions of Economic Progress*.

muscular power and highly skilled processes are broken down into a number of comparatively simple gestures, each of which can be copied by a machine. The completely unskilled labourer, with nothing to offer but his strength, comes to be of less value to production, but so too does the highly skilled worker, trained to adapt his accumulated experience to a series of varying jobs. In the most highly developed manufacturing industries, the general occupational pattern tends to consist of a small nucleus of very skilled workers, a decreasing number of unskilled and a large and expanding body of semi-skilled.

But this does not mean that skill, initiative and experience are of no further value in production. The same factors which eliminate the need for them in one type of activity tend to widen their scope in others. Commerce and the professions, administration and the arts, require personal qualities for which no substitute has yet been found. These offer a field for the worker of quality, and though the training and experience they demand are different from those that were required in manufacture, the opportunity they afford is even wider in extent.

This ceaseless movement does not go on at an even pace. Sometimes new ideas and inventions hang fire and for a long time no practical use is made of them. At other times the world moves so quickly that we seem to be living in one of H. G. Wells's scientific romances. War is a great forcing house in this respect. The shortage of everything that is wanted—raw materials, labour, machinery, transport—lends an increased urgency to research and there is much greater readiness to try out new ideas. Methods which would remain in the experimental stage for years in peace-time become universal practice in as many months of war. So much inventive genius is now concentrated on making two tanks grow where one grew before that there is little doubt that the decade after the end of this war will see at least as marked an industrial revolution as did the years following 1918. As far as it is possible to prophesy now it seems that in the future we shall look to the industrial chemist for a large part of our raw materials. Plastics, unbreakable glass, chemical rubber, synthetic textiles, are likely to revolutionise our manufacturing industries and to necessitate a largely different occupational pattern from the one with which we were familiar before the war.

There is, then, no distribution of the working population between the various productive activities which represents the optimum use of our resources for more than a very short space of time. New knowledge and new opportunities are perpetually altering the amount of labour required to produce a desired result, and a changing emphasis in demand is perpetually altering the results desired. These changing demands and techniques involve an incessant shifting of workers between occupations and industries. How is this shift achieved ? Who decides that there shall be more electrical engineers and shop-assistants and fewer coal-miners and cabbies ? How rapidly does the change-over from one job to another take place, and what forces help or hinder it ? These questions are important because human labour is' the most productive asset in the world and it is only by making the best use of it that humanity is able to provide for itself the wealth of varied goods and services that it has come to want. For this to be accomplished two essential conditions must be fulfilled. Firstly, men and women must be employed in those industries which produce the things the community wants and in the proportions it wants them. Secondly, there must be a quick and sensitive response to changes in demands and in techniques. Of these two essentials, the second is much more difficult to attain than the first. If industrial methods " stayed put " for some time men and women would gradually find themselves squeezed out of the less essential jobs and into those in which they were more needed. It is, however, the dynamic character of economic life that presents the knottier problem for solution. There are very strong forces operating to keep workers where they are and to slow down the movement from occupations in which changes in technique have made the numbers excessive. The effect of such sluggishness is to throw away the benefits offered us by improved methods. By preventing the best use of our material resources it keeps the standard of living at a lower level than it need be.

The peculiar nature of the economic and social problems with which we were confronted in the period between the two wars has done much to divert attention from the importance of this factor and to lay undue emphasis on less fundamental elements in economic welfare. From many of the fashionable slogans that gained currency during the last two decades, the unwary might justifiably have drawn the conclusion that the fundamental economic dilemma of reconciling limitless needs with strictly limited powers of production had been solved, and that all that remained for us to do was to adjust ourselves to our fortunate circumstances. " The Age of Plenty " was, probably, the most popular sobriquet for our pre-war world. The burning of Brazilian coffee and American hogs was mistakenly interpreted as an indication that the world could produce actually more than anybody could possibly want, not for what it really was—a serious misdirection of productive power that was badly wanted elsewhere. The writers and publicists who focused attention so exclusively on distribution problems have done a great disservice, and have fostered an unwarranted and false optimism which may prove one of the most serious obstacles to the attainment of the end they had in view.   Criticism of these writers must not be taken to imply disagreement with the ideals which inspired them.   An economic machine which continually gets clogged up and throws millions into disastrous poverty, destroys that stability which is the essential foundation of a good social organisation. There is no doubt of the urgency of the problem that this offers for solution, and of the importance of devising such controls as will prevent the constant recurrence of these breakdowns.   And equally the gross inequality in wealth which has been the outstanding characteristic of our society must be condemned on many counts—social and political as well as economic.   We have learned during the stresses of war that when necessaries are scarce in supply, it is better for all to have a modest ration than for some to gorge while the remainder go hungry.   It is a lesson that is capable of extensive peace-time application.

The reform of distribution is a vital and pressing matter, but we cannot meanwhile console ourselves with the thought that the production problem is solved.   The fact of the matter is that we are not living in an Age of Plenty and we never have been, and, as far as we can prophesy, there is no likelihood that we shall be doing so in any future sufficiently near for us to concern ourselves with it.   The world is still extremely poor. The total of what was being produced before the war was not enough to provide more than the barest living for the population of the world.   In most countries it was barely sufficient to keep people alive.   It is true that in some areas there was marked unemployment and that if everybody had been fully employed more could have been produced.   But even if productive effort had been used to the utmost the net result would not have been very different.   Even in the richest countries, such as U.S.A. and Canada, the average amount produced by each member of the " working population "[1] was only £270 a year, and each of these individuals had, on the average, $1\frac{1}{2}$ persons to support in addition to himself.   In all but the four or five wealthiest countries, the average was very far below this amount : in China, for example, £20 a year, in British India, £40.   When we remember that out of these meagre totals had to be provided all the elements of communal living—national defence, the maintenance of law and order, roads, schools, etc.—it will be seen that the average amount we had to live on could hardly be called plentiful in even the richest countries and, in the majority, represented the barest subsistence.

[1] " Working population " is here used in the widest sense to include all persons earning a living in any capacity.

If we compare our present production achievements and the possibilities that are known to exist in the immediate future, with the poverty of a hundred years or so ago, we can justly be proud of the distance we have travelled.   But if we take as the criterion of our success the amount that is needed to supply everybody with the necessaries for a modest but healthy standard of living, we are a good deal more humble.   There are some spots that are brighter than others—notably this country and America—but even by contemporary standards of the minimum requirements for a decent and healthy life, the world as a whole is lamentably poor ; and our present standards are themselves fairly conservative.

Such terms as " poverty " and " necessaries of life " have meanings that are relative to the stage of economic development that has been reached.   Experience shows that our ideas of the constituents of an acceptable minimum are largely governed by our productive capacity.   Our grandfathers would not have included a dwelling with water laid on and with hygienic sewerage as an absolute essential for decent living, but we do.   And there is no doubt that many of the things which we look upon as pleasant amenities—things which add comfort but which can be dispensed with without serious loss of health or efficiency—will be considered by the next generation to be essential elements in a standard of living permissible in a civilised community.   For example, widening opportunities for the industrial employment of women lend a new urgency to the demand for labour-saving devices in the home.   Electric washers and vacuum cleaners are now beyond the purse of the masses ; but if improved technique and new raw materials bring down their cost of production sufficiently to allow of the creation of new domestic habits, they will come to be thought of as part of the normal equipment of a home, much as flush plumbing is now.

The war is likely to have a good deal of influence in determining our demands for the future.   We now have a fair amount of knowledge of the ingredients of a healthy diet, and much public effort has been spent in persuading people to change their traditional habits.   Food has become one of the most absorbing and interesting topics of conversation, and the need to make use of what can be got or go hungry has broken down resistance to change.   If this situation lasts for any length of time, new ideas of food values and new methods of cooking will have time to gain wide acceptance and will effect radical changes in public demands.   Such a change in practice might have an appreciable effect on the cost of a minimum healthy diet.

It requires, indeed, a very real effort of the imagination to appreciate that such a term as " minimum standard of living " changes its content with every generation. We come to take for granted so quickly the things with which we are familiar that we assume that life cannot be different. There is probably no part of our habitual expenditure in which such a rapid revolution in standards has taken place during the last twenty or thirty years as in clothing, though we are now so accustomed to the attractive appearance of working women that we rarely remember how new the situation is. Early in the present century, few women of the wage-earning class would have aspired to more than one " best " dress in addition to working clothes whose only merit was that they were neat and tidy. As the " best " dress had to last for many years, it had to abandon any pretensions to fashion ; it had to be made of durable material and in a style that would not date too much. The introduction of rayon and the reorganisation of the clothing industry on large-scale factory lines have combined to change all this. The working girl of to-day follows fashion as readily as the duchess. With rayon underclothes and dresses, which are cheap enough to be discarded when fashion dictates, and which are quickly and easily washed, it needs a very trained and observant eye to detect indications of her social class in a woman's appearance. One would be hard put to it to say what are the *minimum* essentials in clothing. If we were to take simply physiological needs and the claims of decency, and if clothes were made of the most durable material irrespective of their effect on the woman wearing them, we should arrive at one standard. But if we were to take into account also the " imponderables ", the psychological need to express some choice, and the breaking down of social barriers by the blurring of class differentiation in clothing, we should arrive at something quite different.

Soon after the end of the last war, a Basic Wage Commission was appointed in Australia to assess, at prices then ruling, the weekly wage that could be taken to be a reasonable minimum. The Commission was instructed to base its estimate on the " normal needs of a human being in a civilised community ", and its findings are particularly interesting as showing the interpretation put upon this phrase by a representative group of people. (The Commission consisted of seven members, three nominated by employee organisations and three by employer organisations, Federal in character, with a distinguished lawyer as Chairman.) It is worth while to give the list of clothing which they considered should be included in this " basic wage " for the Wife :

Hats, best, 2 to last 2 years and another to last a year ; costume, winter, 1 to last 3 years and summer, 1 to last 3 years ; skirt, blue serge, 1 to last 3 years, tweed, 1 to last 2 years ; blouse, silk, 1 to last 2 years, voile, 1 a year, cambric, 3 to last 2 years, winceyette, 3 to last

2 years; camisoles, 4 a year; combinations, 4 to last 2 years; under-vests, woollen, 1 to last 2 years, cotton, 3 to last 2 years; bloomers, winter, 2 to last 2 years; nightdresses, 4 to last 2 years; underskirts, white, 1 to last 3 years, moreen, 1 to last 3 years; corsets, best, 1 to last 2 years, and another to last a year; dressing-gown, 1 to last 3 years; aprons, 4 a year; stockings, cashmere, 3 a year, cotton, 3 a year; handkerchiefs, 6 a year; gossamer, 1 a year; veil, 1 a year; gloves, silk, 1 a year, cotton, 1 a year; top coat, 1 to last 4 years; golfer, 1 to last 3 years; umbrella, 1 to last 3 years; shoes, best, 1 a year; second, 1 a year; slippers, 1 a year; repairs, best, 1 a year, second, 1 a year; sundries.   The cost was 10s. 9d. per week.[1]

It is obvious that the patient and conscientious enumeration by these seven men of the basic requirements of a woman in a civilised community draws its inspiration, not from physiological needs or claims of decency, but from cultural sources.   If the Commission had carried on its deliberations a few years later, " veil, 1 a year " would no longer have been included, nor, probably, would the " moreen " underskirt; but place would have been found for " camiknickers, rayon ", though I hesitate to estimate the number of such that they would have apportioned to Wife.   But the list they give would have filled the woman of twenty years earlier with longing, and astonishment that such luxury could be considered to be basic needs.   Such a general rise in the standard of living as is indicated by this list of clothing had been made possible by changes in industrial technique and the development of mass production, and the enjoyment of such commodities had come rapidly to be thought of as " the normal needs of a human being living in a civilised community ".

Even so, when the basic wage had been calculated on this level, it was found to be more than the whole of the Australian national income—that is, if the whole produced wealth of the country, including all that ordinarily went to employers as profits, had been divided equally amongst employees it would not have been sufficient to yield the necessary amount that the Basic Wage Commission had set down as the " normal needs of workers in a civilised community ".   This points the moral that distribution is governed by production, that you must cut the coat according to the cloth, that your power to raise the general standard of living by changes in distribution has narrow limits.   A more equal distribution of wealth can ensure that nobody gets more than his fair share of what there is, but it cannot enable anybody to have a share of what does not exist.   And for there to be more to share it is not enough that the industry of the moment should be well organised and efficiently run.   It is equally important that people should be quick to seize the opportunities given them

[1] A. B. Piddington, K.C., *The Next Step. A Family Basic Income*, p. 8.

by improved techniques and new knowledge. It is necessary, that is to say, for labour to be fully and continuously mobile.

II

In peace-time there is no authority which compels a man to do one job rather than another. Theoretically he is completely free to enter any employment which attracts him and for which he can find an employer. He is equally free to change his mind if he thinks it to his interest to do so. All he need do is to give in the customary notice to his employer and try his luck elsewhere. In a price economy we leave it to movements in prices to guide productive resources along the channels where they are needed. If price rises, there is evidence that more of that commodity is wanted, and the hope of making a profit out of the higher price induces a larger supply to be forthcoming; if price falls, some disappointed producers cut down the scale of their production and turn their attention to a more attractive enterprise. In the field of employment wages, the price of labour, are supposed to act in this way as a fingerpost to the direction in which workers should move.

The employer's need for workers is what the economist calls a " derived demand ". He wants them for the part they are to play in a co-ordinated enterprise, the joint product of which will be a quantity of goods or services for which the public (or so he hopes) will be prepared to pay a certain price. His eagerness to obtain the workers' co-operation—and consequently the wage he offers—is governed by his expectations of the market for his goods. If there is an increasing demand he may need to offer higher wages to attract a larger number of workers to him; but the very necessity for this will probably induce him to try out alternative methods by which he can make greater use of workers of a lower grade or economise in the total amount of labour he requires.

For their part, workers are more likely to offer themselves to the employer who makes the most favourable bid for their services; and they are, therefore, gradually drawn into those businesses which produce the goods most keenly demanded by the public and in which their aptitudes provide the most economical technique.

There is here an assumption that the workers can calculate the rival attractions of entering difficult occupations by comparing the rates of pay they will receive for different jobs. But such a comparison is not in practice so easy to make. " Wage rate " is not a term which is capable of precise definition and which has the same meaning in all contexts. In the building industry, for example, wages are fixed on an hourly basis ; in some occupations, such as teaching, they are reckoned as a yearly salary ; in others, such as the clerical, they are weekly. Miners are paid by the shift and dockers by the half-day. In a great many trades wages are calculated on a piece-work basis and vary with the output of each individual worker. There is nothing here that is comparable.

The employee is not, however, primarily concerned with the wage rate. What influences him are the earnings he makes at his work, and here comparison is even more difficult. It is true that wage rates and earnings are directly connected with one another, but there is no ratio between them that is constant in all trades or even, for that matter, in the same trade at all times. Building cannot be carried on in bad weather and builders must expect a good deal of intermittent unemployment during the winter months. But just how much interruption there will be depends on the severity of the season and the part of the country in which the work happens to be carried on. A teacher's employment, on the other hand, is generally permanent. It would be rare for a teacher to be unemployed even if the number of children in his school declined seriously : he would more probably be transferred to another school without any break in his salary. Clerks and shop assistants have less security of tenure than teachers, but much more than builders. In a great many trades there are marked seasonal fluctuations and the employee's earnings may be lowered during one part of the year by slack employment, and increased during another by overtime. In some types of work there are expenses that have to be met. The skilled joiner is expected to provide his own bag of tools which may be very costly ; the waiter and the domestic servant must equip themselves with occupational uniform ; the teacher and the clerk are expected to wear, during working hours, clothes which are suitable to their social status, while, on the other hand, the skilled engineer can work all day in dungarees and keep his good suit for his leisure time. Similarly there are other trades to which quite good perquisites are attached. An agricultural labourer, for example, often gets the use of a cottage at an exceptionally low rent ; in couponless days, the domestic servant may be given her mistress's slightly worn clothes ; the shop assistant is often allowed to buy from the store at wholesale prices ; the teacher may get his children admitted to schools and colleges at reduced fees ; and so on.

With so many variable factors to take into account it is not possible to arrive at any sound basis of comparison of the incomes in different occupations. And if it is difficult for the detached observer to do so, it is very much more difficult for the worker who can get only a very restricted and distorted view of the situation.

Yet, even though we cannot get an exact idea of the earnings of grades that seem to lie fairly close together on the economic scale, we can see that there are many which are widely separated from one another. It may be impossible to decide whether the income of a motor engineer is, on the average, more or less than that of a woodworker or a tailor; but there is no doubt whatever that it is much less than that of a doctor or a solicitor, and considerably more than that of an agricultural worker or an unskilled labourer. At the end of 1936 (the last year for which complete figures have been published) the average weekly earnings of men employed in motor engineering were 65s. 9d.,[1] of woodworkers engaged in house and shop fitting, 63s. 4d.,[1] and in tailoring, 67s. 6d.[2] At the same time the weekly wages of agricultural labourers ranged from 28s. 6d. in Merionethshire to 35s. in Middlesex, and the wages of unskilled labourers generally were about 48s.[3] It is not possible to be as precise as this in respect of doctors and solicitors because, as " one-man businesses " they have no standard rate. But

> There is no reason to doubt that a fully employed panel doctor in a populous area, using half his time for panel and half for private patients, can make £1,400 per annum free of expenses (quoted from the Royal Commission on the Civil Service, 1929–30, p. 55).
> . . . Of solicitors it is said that a university man should earn £1,000 after ten years and £2,000 at the age of forty.[4]

The doctor and solicitor need a long and expensive education during which period they must be maintained. But if we were to reckon the total costs involved in " producing " them, we should not find that the capital invested in them was sufficient to account for a difference in earning capacity between £1,400 to £2,000 a year and round about 65s. a week. The motor engineer, the woodworker and the tailor must spend several years on low wages while they are learning their jobs but this again is not enough to account for the difference in earnings between 65s. a week and 48s.

The fact is, of course, that it is only a legal fiction that there is complete freedom of choice of occupation. The individual is not only ignorant of the earnings obtainable in different jobs but he is unable to do much about it even when he finds out. An electrical engineer cannot suddenly become a newspaper compositor overnight. It is possible that the two kinds of work

---

[1] *Abstract of Labour Statistics* (1922–36), Cmd. 5536, 1937, p. 104.
[2] Ibid., pp. 78–9.   [3] Ibid., p. 76.
[4] A. M. Carr-Saunders and P. A. Wilson, *The Professions*, pp. 460–1.

require the same degree of mental alertness and manipulative dexterity, but by the time that a man has become adult his capacities have become too narrowly canalised to be easily diverted. At the age of 16 a boy of ability might have hesitated as to which of the two industries he should enter and might have proved equally adept at either. But having once made his choice he has to stick by it. It is true that the number of highly skilled jobs is diminishing and that the clear lines of demarcation between trades have become much more blurred than they used to be. But even though the great body of work can be classed as semi-skilled there are few processes in the manufacturing industry which require no training at all. The time taken to acquire full speed may be anything from three weeks to three months, but it is enough to act as a barrier to the worker whose hesitation to try something new is increased by the fear that he will be the first to be turned off if the new trade gets slack. If he had lost his job in his old trade and had little chance of being reabsorbed he would be more prepared to try. But as long as his usual job is open to him, the difference in earnings' would have to be very marked to make it worth his while to take the plunge and change.

Man is not entirely an economic animal and there are many other factors to be taken into consideration, besides the wages to be earned. Some kinds of work are agreeable in themselves or are carried on in conditions that are attractive. The discrepancy between the wages of agricultural labourers and urban workers has been so great over so prolonged a period that a considerable migration from country to town has taken place, but it is probable that the shift would have been even more pronounced and certainly more rapid had it not been that so many men found it hard to tear themselves from the familiar routine and setting of the countryside despite the lowness of the wage to be earned there. While on the other hand the lure that took so many thousands to the town was not so much the chance of higher wages as the shops and cinemas and greater opportunities for social intercourse in the town. Similarly, one of the reasons that the supply of dock labour has generally been so ample, despite the insecurity attached to it, is that the work is done out of doors. In the food factories of London's Dockland there have often been openings for the type of worker who is usually employed in the docks, but the men found themselves unable to get used to working under a roof. Tastes differ so greatly that we cannot list jobs according to their relative agreeableness. Some take a lower wage in the town because they cannot bear the loneliness of the country, and others take a lower wage in the country because they hate the noise and crowds of the town. I remember once sympathising with a slaughterer's assistant on his job only to be met with an uncomprehending stare and the reply, " But I don't know what you mean. I like it." Since then I have always reminded myself of the subjective nature of tastes and have hesitated to rate any occupation as inherently more agreeable than another. But despite this there are certain jobs which have a wide appeal because of the social prestige that attaches to them. The strong pull exercised by the " black-coated " occupations is a conspicuous example. Now that wider educational facilities are open to all classes of the community, many new sections are able to get the necessary training for non-manual wage-earning work. Thousands of working-class parents have felt that their ambitions would be fully satisfied if they could get their sons and daughters settled as clerks, typists and shop assistants. Economic, as well as social factors, have undoubtedly supported this ambition. Earlier in the century clerical occupations had a much greater salary range than most manual jobs ; they were less standardised and provided many opportunities of promotion for the young man of ability. In some respects, the security they offered was an even greater bait than the actual salary, though this security was not quite as great as it appeared on the surface. Clerks, it is true, were not as easily turned off during bad times as were the ordinary manual workers, but if they *did* find themselves unemployed they were likely to be out of work for a longer period, particularly if they had already reached middle age. The rapid influx of workers into these trades has brought down their earnings in many cases below that of factory employees. The expansion in the size of the productive and commercial unit has standardised their work and narrowed, though not destroyed, their chances of promotion. Yet, in spite of this, the social prestige attached to these jobs is enough to persuade a very large proportion of working people to choose this type of employment in preference to better-paid manual work. The white collar and black coat are outward symbols of respectability. To be addressed politely as *Miss* Smith or *Mr.* Jones implies that you have gone up a step in the world and is considered well worth the loss of more material comforts. Unless there is a shift in social values, men and women in the non-manual jobs will continue to resist the inducement to change to better-paid manual work, even if other practical obstacles could be overcome.

It would be interesting to speculate how far domestic service has become unpopular because of its downward slide in the social hierarchy. Throughout the last century domestic service was still regarded as the most respectable female occupation and all parents, but those of the lowest ranks, were generally unwilling to let their daughters go into factory work. This bias was beginning to be less marked already before the last war, principally on account of the higher standard of cleanliness and the general amenities that were being introduced into the newer factories ; and as the wages of domestic workers were extremely low, it is no matter for surprise that thousands grasped the chance of earning a better living in the many new industries that were opening their doors to women. The war, with its urgent need for women's labour, accelerated this process and made factory employment both normal and financially attractive. This had its repercussions on domestic service and by the end of the war the competition of alternative employments had not only forced up the wages of domestic servants but had largely revolutionised their conditions. Before the outbreak of the present war, in most of the big industrial centres, a competent maid had her choice of jobs at 20s. a week, clear of all her living expenses. This compared more than favourably with the 30s. 3d. which was the average weekly wage of women workers in the textile industries, or the 32s. 8d. of the clothing industries, or 31s. 1d. of the engineering, or 32s. 1d. of the food trades.[1] Yet so unpopular had domestic work become that there was everywhere an acute shortage of women prepared to undertake it. The factory women were, it is true, working for a well-defined day ; they had their evenings and Sundays free. No such generalisation can be made about domestic service because of the wide variation in practice that necessarily exists in a million separate households. All that can be said is that a much larger measure of personal freedom was coming to be commonly allowed than had been customary in the past. It yet, however, remains true that the maid is not considered as an equal member of the household ; and there are many serious problems in the adjustment of personal relations when class distinctions are maintained in so small and closely-bound a community. Forty or fifty years ago, when class demarcations were taken for granted, this particular difficulty had not to be surmounted. But in an age which is so consciously democratic and egalitarian as this both mistress and maid are raspingly aware of their undefined relationship. The general result of all this is that a woman who becomes a domestic servant often feels that she has " lost face " and, in fact, is so treated by her acquaintances who have gone into industry. In most recreational clubs for young women a very marked division will be apparent between the industrial and the domestic workers ; the former often refuse to mix with the latter because of their inferior status. It is doubtful whether any economically possible rise in pay would be sufficient to attract an appreciably larger number

[1] *Abstract of Labour Statistics* (1922–36), Cmd. 5556/1937, pp. 104–5.

of women into resident domestic jobs so long as this social rating lasts.

III

But in the majority of cases there is no question of the place of the industry in the social hierarchy and it is other factors which intervene to reduce a worker's willingness to change his occupation. Of these, one of the most important is the necessity that usually arises for a worker to change the locality in which he lives if he changes his occupation. The high degree of specialisation which is an outstanding characteristic of modern industry has a geographical as well as a functional aspect. While there are a number of activities such as building, retail distribution and personal service, which must inevitably be carried on close to their ultimate market, the majority of industries can establish themselves wherever they can be most economically sited. In the past, when most machinery was worked by steam power, industry was bound to settle as close as possible to the coalfields, so as to cut down the costs of transporting so heavy and bulky an article as coal. But, with the greater use of cheaply-carried electric power, other factors play a relatively more important rôle. Firms are now more inclined to choose sites in which suitable labour supplies are to be found or where a large urban population provides a market with an adequate capacity for absorbing their products. Sometimes there are particular environmental features, such as the lie of the land, the climate or the nearness to ports, which attract certain industries to a place. Sometimes the choice of site is purely fortuitous or solely of historical significance. But whatever the reasons which guided the decisions of the first firms to establish themselves, there are very strong tendencies for other businesses engaged in the same kind of production to group themselves around this nucleus. The concentration of an industry in one or a few centres allows of the introduction of many economies which are less practicable to a widely scattered industry. Firms specialise in detailed processes for the benefit of the whole industry ; organised markets are developed for raw materials, capital, labour and the finished product ; technical research can be carried on collectively ; subsidiary industries grow up to serve the specialised needs of the main industry and firms can be established to make use of its by-products. When such a localised industry expands there is a much greater likelihood that it will increase in the place where it is already established than that firms will be set up in new areas. It follows consequently that workers who are squeezed out of an occupation which no longer requires so much labour, or who wish to better themselves, must generally be prepared to change their homes as well as their trade, and this further necessity presents a serious obstacle to mobility.

We are employed as individuals but we live our lives as members of a social group—the family. If the need to change his locality affects one of the younger members of the family, the problem is not so serious. He may feel the separation keenly, but he realises that it is only forestalling a break that would anyway come with marriage. When, however, the father of the family finds himself faced with such a situation, the problem is not capable of any really satisfactory solution. If he decides to leave the family behind he has the expense of maintaining two homes in addition to the social and psychological disadvantages of such a separation. If he takes them with him, he forces on them many difficult problems of adjustment. It is possible that some members of the family are already in work and are not sure of being able to get such good' openings in the new place ; so that although the father's income goes up the family income goes down. Perhaps the children are well established in their schools and in the running for scholarships. The strain of settling down in new schools with, perhaps, different methods of teaching and new personalities may tip the balance and ruin the children's prospects of further education. Even if a house is available in the new district there is much expense involved in moving the household. Perhaps the present home has a garden in which the children can play out of danger and where part of the food can be grown, whereas the new home is in an area which does not allow of such amenities. With the wage-earning family, the insecurity of tenure of most jobs weights the scales still further against moving. There is no guarantee that the job will last long enough to justify the expense and dislocation involved. The man has a well-justified fear that if the firm to which he is going has a slack period, he will be the first to be sacked or " stood off " simply because he is a newcomer. And to be out of work in a town in which he is a stranger is a much more serious matter than to be unemployed at home. In his own neighbourhood he is known to many and probably respected as a decent, independent person. The shops at which he deals know that he was always ready to pay his debts after previous slack times and are prepared to give him a little credit. His foreman and his fellow-workers and neighbours give him a tip if they hear of a likely job he might try for, and are ready to speak on his behalf if there is a vacancy at their own works. Nobody knows him well enough to bother to do these services for him in a strange town, and he must rely solely on the Employment Exchange for his placing. Apart from all these economic considerations, it is not easy for a family to tear itself up by the roots and plant itself somewhere else. Each member of the family may have attachments to local groups. The father may be an elder in the church or a member of the choir, or, perhaps, a shop steward for the local branch of the trade union ; the younger ones may be leading lights in the local Boy Scouts or Girl Guides, or be in a football team or hiking club. It is probable that they may be able to take part in all these activities and more in the new district. But most of us are conservative in our attachments. It needs a severe wrench to cut oneself off from one's friends and loyalties, and it is not to be wondered at if most people hesitate for a very long time before taking the plunge.

The degree of geographical specialisation which has been reached in this country has also a rather less obvious psychological influence which hinders mobility between trades. In an area whose fortunes have long been bound up with the prosperity of a single outstanding industry, the inhabitants are so accustomed to assume that everybody will find their living in one occupation or another connected with it that the possibility of entering an entirely different industry does not come into their minds. They are inclined to take it as part of the natural order of things that they should go into coal or cotton or whatever the principal industry may be. They are familiar with its processes from childhood ; they are used to its jargon, and take it for granted that they, like their father before them, and their friends and relatives now, will earn their living by it. Any other industry carried on in another locality seems like a different world, and the thought that they might enter such a strange world does not easily suggest itself to them. In regions such as the Midlands, where there is a great diversity of industry, mobility of workers between them is much greater than, for example, in South Wales or Lancashire. This is not merely because workers can change their occupation without changing their home, but because they are less closely identified with a single industry and more familiar with the different kinds of work done in different trades.

IV

Very little statistical evidence exists of the rate and amount of movement into and out of industries, but from a limited investigation into new entrants into sample industries during the years 1927–31 it appears that an expansion of personnel depends much more on attracting new juvenile workers than on inducing older workers to change their occupation. Far from contributing towards the increase in the size of growing industries, adults (those between 18 and 64) failed to move even sufficiently to compensate for loss of workers due to death and retirement, and the whole of the increase was provided by juvenile entrants (those between 16 and 18). If this situation is general, it means that the obstacles to mobility are so great that it is to the new generation of workers that expanding industry must look, while the contraction of declining industry is brought about by the non-replacement of those employees who die or retire. This, in itself, necessarily involves a considerable time-lag in achieving an economic occupational distribution, but this time-lag is increased by the influence exercised by our social stratification on young people's choice of employment.

The high standard of education demanded as a prerequisite for entry to the liberal professions precludes all but a tiny minority from offering themselves for this kind of work. As the education is extremely expensive the principal selecting agent is money and not ability. The scholarship system provides a slender and precarious bridge by which outstanding members of the wage-earning classes may reach the gates of the comparatively well-paid professions, but these gates are effectively closed to the majority of those who would have both the ability and the desire to carry on the profession efficiently. The restriction of entry to the professions is most easily recognised because here a specific educational qualification is required, but similar bottlenecks are to be found all the way down the social and economic scale. There is a wide variety of occupations—generally of a non-manual type—in which a secondary education, whilst not a definite prerequisite, is a very decided advantage to the would-be entrant. But the vast majority of the population cannot afford to give their children a post-primary education without some financial assistance and, as the number of free places is strictly limited, only 7% of the elementary school population are admitted to the secondary schools without fees.[1] This means that only the cream of the non-fee-paying children have an opportunity of secondary education, while even those children who are only of average intelligence are admitted provided their parents are able and willing to pay the fees. In fact, an investigation made by Mr. J. L. Gray into the intelligence of school-children yielded, in his own words,

> two astonishing results. One is that when we compare children of equally high ability, seven fee-paying pupils will receive a higher education for every one free pupil. The other is that a child of inferior ability born with a silver spoon in his mouth has more than a hundred times the chances of receiving a higher education than a correspondingly dull child of the masses.[2]

Consequently the general mass of young people are prevented

[1] See on this subject, J. L. Gray, *The Nation's Intelligence*.
[2] Ibid., pp. 95–6.

from entering those industries which ask for more educational background than is given in the elementary school and are compelled to crowd into the jobs with more modest educational demands.   The resulting congestion in these industries with the comparative scarcity of entrants to the others brings about a more or less permanent disparity in relative earnings which can have little effect on labour mobility as long as the differences in educational opportunity remain as great as they are at present.

But it is not only the inequality in formal education that creates an obstacle to the free choice of employment.   A skilled trade demands a preliminary period of training which may last anything from three to seven years.   During this time the learner receives low wages which are certainly not enough, particularly during the earlier years, to pay for his keep.   Only the children of those parents who are prepared to make a very big sacrifice are able to enter such industries ; and many parents who would willingly make the sacrifice if they were able are compelled by pressure of economic circumstances to put their children to unskilled labour so that their higher immediate earnings may bring relief to the family budget.   On the whole, the children of the unskilled have much less chance of entering skilled trades than the children of skilled workers.   This is largely on account of the lower incomes of the unskilled.   But it is also in part accounted for by the general outlook of both parents and children. Generalisations which relate to whole classes of people can never hope to be accurate but it is fairly safe to say that unskilled labourers are less ready to appreciate the importance of training than are those who have themselves undergone it.   This varies, of course, not only with individuals, but also with the regularity of the father's work.   The more casual the employment the less willingness in general to put the child to skilled work even if it could be afforded..   The children also are less willing to be trained.   The adolescent worker who finds that his ex-school mates are earning good money in unskilled trades and have money to spend on the movies and dances chafes at the nominal earnings of his early years while learning a trade and is unwilling to go through with it.   Moreover, it is often difficult for an unskilled labourer to get his boy the chance of entry to a skilled job.   The foreman of a works is often ready to give a trial to the son or younger brother of one of the firm's own employees when he would not take on an unknown quantity, and the unskilled worker is less likely to have such personal contacts to help him.   A survey made by Dr. A. L. Bowley [1] into 30,000 working-class households in London, showed that whereas 36% of the

[1] A. L. Bowley.   Occupations of Fathers and Children. *Economica*, Nov. 1935.

sons of skilled workers entered skilled trades only 16% of the sons of unskilled workers followed skilled occupations, while 59% of the sons of unskilled fathers remained unskilled, leaving the remainder in the betwixt and between condition of the semi-skilled. Even where there is some movement out of the father's grade it does not usually carry the children very far along the social scale ; the children of the unskilled, that is, are more likely to go into semi-skilled processes than into skilled jobs, just as the children of skilled fathers are inclined to move up into black-coated occupations.

In all occupations, but particularly in the skilled, there is a very strong tendency for children to follow in their father's footsteps—partly because of the father's pride in his work but more because he is able to " speak for " his son and get him an opening soon after he leaves school. This means that young people very often go into industries which are declining and which will not be able to offer them regular employment during their manhood. Even the most careful and far-seeing parent could not, of course, foretell accurately which are going to be the growing industries during the next fifty years (the period during which his son can expect to be earning), but his limited vision and his eagerness to get his son placed in a job of which he has some knowledge combine to draw new entrants into industries which are already visibly declining. When the difficulty of movement for adults is remembered it will be recognised how serious an effect on occupational maldistribution may be exercised by this haphazard choice of employment and it becomes a matter of the greatest importance to see that young people get adequate guidance in their initial choice of a job.

There is at present a dual system for providing advice and help to boys and girls in search of work. Local education authorities have been empowered for over thirty years to set up Choice of Employment Committees for this purpose. In those areas in which the education authority does not make use of its powers, a special juvenile department is set up in the local Employ-ment Exchange under the Juvenile Employment Committee. In all cases the work is under the central supervision of the Ministry of Labour and the activities of the two types of committee do not differ to any appreciable degree. The aim of these agencies is to give to boys and girls some clear idea of the different indus-trial processes carried on in the locality so that they may know the alternatives that are open to them, and to advise them as to which jobs are likely to be suited to their individual capacities. Armed with the child's school record and his teacher's summing up of his qualities, on the one hand, and with information about industrial prospects from representative employers and Trade

Union leaders, on the other, the Committee advises the parents what jobs they should try and put their children into. It must be admitted, however, that as far as it is possible to collect evidence, it appears that children rarely get into the work they are advised to try for, and that the Committees themselves can do little more than bring together juveniles wanting work and employers in need of young labour. There is generally little difficulty for a child of fourteen in getting employment. The wage he gets is so small that he can usually move easily from one job to another without outside assistance, but the jobs seem to have little connection with one another, so that the experience gained in one is not of particular value to him in the next. Far from building up a fund of knowledge and experience the general run of work to which the young school-leaver is put stunts his developing powers and destroys the mental alertness, adaptability and curiosity that it has been the aim of the school to encourage. By the time that he reaches the age of 16 or 17 and can no longer hop lightheartedly from job to job he is eager to snatch at whatever is offered him that seems to offer reasonable pay. He cannot afford to concern himself with whether the industry is likely to expand or contract in the future, provided it can give him employment now.

It is estimated that only about a quarter of juvenile workers get their jobs through the help of the statutory bodies and that only a small minority find their way into the kind of work recommended by the Committee advising them. But it is doubtful whether a better occupational distribution would be achieved if a larger proportion of adolescents were placed by the Committees. So much of what the future holds in the way of industrial development is not and cannot be known to the Committees. Who, for example, would dare to say at this moment how rapidly the new plastic industries are likely to develop and what kinds of employment they will offer ? Which Committees would have been able to foresee the rise of rayon and the motor-car and electrical engineering industries to their present stage and would have risked steering large numbers of young people into them ? We can try and prevent large numbers of new workers from going into industries that are known to be contracting now. We can guide them into industries that are visibly expanding, but to prophesy the changes in demand and the developments in industrial technique that are going to take place in the next twenty or thirty years is beyond the powers of the expert, much more of the modest members of the local advisory committees. Moreover, it is equally doubtful whether there can be sufficient knowledge of the capacities of the child.

The advice given to the school-leaver is usually based on his school record and on the estimate of his capacities formed by his teacher. But it is impossible for the class teacher, with all his exacting duties, to give to this part of his work the thought and attention it requires if it is to be well done. Nor is there any reason to expect that the teacher has a sufficiently intimate knowledge of different kinds of industrial work as to be able to judge of the special combination of qualities that will make for success in them. Nor has he, again, the chance to acquire any very detailed understanding of his pupils. He may know one boy to be quick and intelligent, another slow and painstaking, a third better at handwork than brainwork, and so on—a rough and ready summing-up of each of the boys under his care. But he has generally too many pupils in his class to be able to do more than this. Moreover, the child of fourteen is not easy to assess. Very often he has not yet struck his true form. If his home background has been narrow it is possible that his special interests have not yet been awakened ; the potentiality is there but the spark has not yet caught alight. The shy and diffident child, who is afraid of expressing interests or of betraying knowledge different from his fellows, may be classed as quiet and ordinary by those in authority, who cannot devote to one pupil the time that would be necessary to draw him out and win his confidence. But even the average boy with no exceptional gifts or characteristics has not had the chance, by his fourteenth birthday, either to become conscious himself or to make others aware of much more than his superficial qualities. They are possibilities rather than actualities ; and the shape they finally take depends on the stimulus of the following few years.[1]

Despite these difficulties, much could undoubtedly be done to improve the present methods by which the new entrants find their way into industry, but this, by itself, would do little to solve the problem of making the most economical use of the country's labour power. The rate of industrial change has increased so greatly that it is not enough to rely on the flow of new recruits into the industrial army to change the occupational pattern. The majority of those entering modern industry cannot expect to be employed in the same type of work throughout the fifty years of their wage-earning life, and it is to the greater versatility and increased mobility of adults that we must look if full use is to be made of our growing knowledge so as to enable general standards of living to be raised.

[1] Gertrude Williams, " A Study in the Industrial Career of Secondary School Boys ", *Sociological Review*, Oct. 1938.

CHAPTER II

THE INCREASE IN RIGIDITY

I

SYNOPSIS OF CHAPTER

1. Many factors have helped to increase labour mobility—the decreased importance of skill, improvements in education and communications and the establishment of an organised labour market—yet on balance mobility has decreased.

2. The last war accelerated developments which were manifesting themselves earlier and also introduced further causes of maladjustment. While it thus made flexibility more essential it also postponed adjustment.

3. Adjustment to the new situation was delayed partly through ignorance of the problem but principally on account of institutional changes.

4. Collective control of wage rates by Trade Unions and statutory bodies slows down movements in wages and consequently hinders wage differentials from attracting labour from one occupational channel to another. The rigidity in wage rates has been materially increased by the establishment of unemployment insurance.

5. The decrease in labour mobility is not an isolated phenomenon. The growth of combines and cartels, the imposition of tariffs and exchange controls, and the attempt to develop national autarky are signs of the same movement.

6. The immobility of workers has been increased by other factors—the housing shortage, psychological difficulties, and changes in political philosophy and social values.

DURING the last twenty-five years the mobility of labour has decreased both absolutely and relatively. The need for rapid adjustment to changes in demand and technique has grown more insistent, but the response has grown more sluggish. At first sight this seems a surprising statement, because it appears that the general trend should have been towards a much greater mobility both between trades and from place to place. And even though, in fact, elasticity has decreased on balance, there are yet many factors in modern life which have exercised an influence in the opposite direction. For one thing, industries are technologically no longer so distinct from one another. As the field for skilled work has narrowed in manufacturing industry, the boundary lines have become less marked. It is reckoned that nowadays less than one young person in seven is apprenticed to a trade and only a slightly larger proportion have some kind of definite learnership. At the same time the wider educational facilities that are now offered to all sections of the community not only widen the choice of employment open to the new entrants but increase their versatility and adaptability. But probably the outstanding factor in the increase of fluidity has been the rapid increase in communications. The network of bus routes, the establishment of a quick and frequent electric train service and the good surfacing of roads which enable cyclists to get about quickly and cheaply have enormously extended the radius within which work can be sought without the necessity of changing one's home. But they have done more than this, for by increasing personal mobility they have altered people's attitude to change. At the beginning of this century the life of the average country-man was bounded by his own village. To step out of it was a great adventure to be undertaken only under the spur of severe provocation. Nowadays, he and his wife think nothing of jumping on to a bus and travelling several miles to visit the cinema and shops in the neighbouring town ; and his children go to and from school or work by motor-bicycle or push-bike. The town worker with a low wage was as much tied to his own few streets as the agricultural labourer to his village. Now, with buses and trams and electric trains to serve him, he no longer looks upon another part of the town as " foreign parts " to be entered with bewilderment and apprehension. Familiarity with travel to neighbouring places makes it easier for him to con-template the possibility of getting employment elsewhere than in his own immediate locality. He has a chance to see signs of other kinds of lives and occupations than his own and to find out more of the trades which might offer him a more agreeable or better paid employment.

During the last quarter of a century there has been a big development in the organisation of more formal channels of information to reinforce his own observation. Until just before the first World War, there was no means whereby people might obtain authoritative information about vacancies in their own or other districts. The labour market was still organised in a very sketchy and haphazard way. The Trade Unions catering for the more highly skilled workers had generally some means of getting to know where there were jobs suitable to their members. Some had properly constituted Labour Bureaux to which employers notified vacancies, and even where there was no such formal arrangement, branch meetings were a very good opportunity for hearing of firms that were taking on men. But Trade Unions had no reliable knowledge of the requirements for labour in any other trade than their own. And while they had some influence in increasing mobility within the trade, they had none in getting their members into other occupations where they might be better employed. Rather the contrary. There were also certain philan-thropic bodies, founded to befriend such particularly helpless sections of the population as discharged prisoners and young domestic servants, which had registration schemes to help in placing their clientèle. The Unemployed Workman Act of 1905 had empowered local Distress Committees to maintain employ-ment registers, but only in London was the opportunity taken to establish registers which were unconnected with relief. And this was all. For the rest, workpeople had to depend on gossip and hearsay, or sometimes on newspaper advertisements, or most often, on a weary tramping from place to place calling at those firms where a notice was displayed " Hands Wanted ". In an age when organised markets were being developed for all sorts of commodities less valuable than human labour, it is remarkable how slow was the appreciation that occupational distribution could only be economic if men had some means of knowing where workers were wanted. It was not until after the passing of the Labour Exchange Act in 1909 that there came into being a nation-wide, interlocking system by which workers could learn (at least in theory) of jobs in all trades and in all parts of the country. The qualification in parenthesis is important. For in peace-time there has never existed any compulsion on an employer to notify the Employment Exchange of a vacancy and he can fill it in any way that seems good to him. The Exchanges have to collect their data as best they can and their ability to persuade employers to keep them informed of their needs depends on the success they have had in supplying the right type of labour when it was demanded. In the early days, this success was not spectacular ; partly because the Exchanges had not yet learned their job. The officials had no intimate detailed knowledge of the nature of the various types of work carried on in the locality and sent workers who were wildly unsuitable. A parsimonious Government must also bear part of the blame in refusing to supply the funds for an adequate staff and premises. But also a good deal of their early failure was due to the fact that the system was established after a period of bad trade during which many schemes for relief of the unemployed had been tried and the workers, in common with a good many others, were under the misapprehension that the Labour Exchanges (as they were then called) were intended solely for the registration of unskilled labour suitable for employment on relief works. Skilled and semi-skilled workers deliberately kept aloof, and it was not until compulsory unemployment insurance was introduced that it became the normal and regular practice for a worker to register at the Exchange when unemployed. But while the insurance system enabled the exchanges to gain very full knowledge of the labour available, it overwhelmed them with an immense amount of clerical and administrative work and prevented them from concentrating on their main task of acting as placing agencies.

(Then, during the war, a further overwhelming task was put on their shoulders in the mobilisation of men and women for the Forces and for war industry, and their particular work was again postponed.) This drawback was even greater in the years following 1920 when unemployment was so severe that the administration of insurance was far and away the matter of outstanding interest in domestic politics, and the real purpose for which the exchanges had been set up, that of acting as a clearing house for employers and workers, receded into the background.

Yet these additional duties had also their credit side. As the *Report of the Enquiry into the Work of the Employment Exchanges* [1] pointed out in 1920, " The Exchanges were an essential part of the machinery required for the utilisation of the national resources for the purpose of the war ; had they not existed it would have been necessary to improvise some less adequate machinery for the purpose." They had the job of deciding which men should be enrolled in the Forces and which were of greater value in their civilian employment ; they registered and transferred thousands of workpeople under special schemes ; they steered more than a million additional women into war work and arranged for their accommodation near to their work. When demobilisation required the machinery to be set in reverse the exchanges arranged for the reabsorption of men and women into civilian life and into industries producing goods for peace-time consumption. So that by the time that unemployment insurance problems took the centre of the stage millions of men and women had come to look upon the exchanges as a normal and important factor in the labour market, a place to which it was natural to turn for information and through whose agency knowledge of jobs in other trades and places might be obtained. And similarly the experience gained by exchange officials during the war and the couple of years immediately following, gave them a much clearer and more detailed picture of the working of the industrial world than they would have been likely to get in many more years of struggling peace-time development. Unfortunately there have been no similar circumstances to bring the employers of necessity into closer touch with the exchanges and, until the present war, there was no compulsion to notify vacancies. Even so, however, many large employers voluntarily entered into agreements with their local exchanges to engage all their labour through them and to exhibit notices to this effect on their factory gates. And even where no such agreement was made, employers in certain localities have made this their practice. So that there were some areas in which 70–80% of the placings were made through the exchanges. But this was not common. As a whole the exchanges

[1] *Report*, Cmd.1054/1920.

did nearly half the job-finding for boys and girls over 16, 33% for women and 20% for men, with an average of only 22% for all.[1] This means that despite many years of compulsory notification of unemployment (in order to claim benefits) the vast majority of workers did not get reabsorbed into employment through official guidance but by the same methods they had used before the exchanges were established.

There were, however, two further ways in which the exchanges have helped to increase mobility. Firstly, they have the power to advance fares to a workman who, through their agency, has found work in another locality. In some cases, the employer undertakes to repay this advance but more often the debt is incurred by the workman himself and the employer is asked to deduct an amount weekly from his wages. The remarkably small number of bad debts arising from this practice is evidence that the majority of those placed in other areas retain their jobs for a reasonable time. Secondly, since 1925 a great deal of care and effort has been put into organising training to fit the unemployed for further employment. Training Centres of two types have been set up. The first, the Government Training Centres, were intended for those who were fitted to learn a skilled trade. The course, which lasted for five or six months, was designed primarily for the building and certain metal trades, and the men who completed training were practically guaranteed jobs. The second, ·the Instructional Centres, were much more numerous and catered for men of the labourer type. The course lasted only twelve weeks and was intended primarily as an agency for physical and moral rehabilitation. The aim was, through good food, a regular routine and simple work, to bring men back into a state of health and efficiency and to accustom them to the use of tools and the normal discipline of industrial life. Both kinds of centre, however, suffered from a lack of recruits for a variety of reasons. Many of the men who would have been good enough material for the Training Centres had moved on their own initiative if they were single. The married men were mostly unwilling to contemplate removal to another area for the reasons discussed earlier. The unskilled men whom it was hoped to attract into the Instructional Centres had often deteriorated through prolonged unemployment. Many of the younger among them had grown to manhood during the severe industrial depression that followed the collapse of 1920 and had never had an opportunity to adapt themselves to regular work or to learn the self-discipline that is necessary to retain a job. They were bitter and resentful against a society that seemed to have

[1] *Report of Royal Commission on Unemployment Insurance*, Evidence of Mr. Eady, Q. 3822.

no place for them and suspicious of any scheme which, in their minds, seemed to savour of the " Slave Camp ". As most of the work that was suitable for the courses, such as clearing sites for forest planting and Land Settlement schemes, was inevitably carried on in rather remote places, they were afraid of committing themselves to such a perilous adventure. Few of them had any first-hand knowledge of the conditions under which they would be expected to work and live. As most of them had been unemployed throughout their early manhood they had not even the few extra coppers to spend on bus fares around their own homes and had seen little else than the streets of their own neighbourhood. To jump voluntarily from this to a communal life in a remote camp or centre, which their imagination painted as existing under rigorous prison discipline, was more than they could make up their minds to. So that neither type of training touched more than a very small number of the population. They are interesting experiments in improving mobility rather than a contribution to it. They were certainly not enough to counter the hardening of the arteries which affected the body economic in the period between the two wars.

II

The greater need for elasticity in the economic system was not a consequence of the last war ; the development which made this necessary began to be apparent earlier. But the war acted as a forcing house and accelerated the growth of tendencies that would probably have taken many more years to mature if the peace-time pace had been retained. In one way, perhaps, the war may be said to have been directly responsible. During the years of actual fighting and the following period of exchange chaos, much of the old economic world was destroyed and a new world can never be rebuilt on an old pattern. Materials, methods, ideas, attitudes, all had changed to some degree throughout the war, and when people thought that they were simply restoring the old world they found that they had, in fact, created something new, with its own problems that did not respond to pre-war solutions. Part of the difficulty of meeting this situation was due to the inability, perhaps even the unwillingness, of those concerned to recognise that the world as they had known it had gone for ever. The World War of 1914–18 was the first cataclysmic experience to which people had been subjected and it was natural that they should think of the pre-war era, by contrast, as " normal " and should take it for granted that they would revert to the familiar life when the strains and stresses of war were over. But, of course, the world of 1914 was not normal in the sense of being the point to which the world would inevitably return after the oscillation set up by war. It was merely one arbitrary moment in a constantly shifting series of economic and social relationships. For those who had eyes to see it was already clear that fundamental alterations were taking place and that, even had there been no war, the twentieth-century world would be a very different place from its predecessor.

The outstanding characteristics of the nineteenth century struck the imagination so forcibly and persisted for so long as to appear to most people as natural phenomena whose continued existence they assumed to be part of the eternal order of things. They were, on the contrary, the result of a number of factors which were essentially temporary. Even had international relationships continued to preserve the peace, the twentieth century would inevitably have been a period of serious readjustment to changing circumstances. The war made this process more difficult not only by speeding up the rate of change but by preventing, at the same time, the gradual and piecemeal adjustment that would probably have taken place in peace-time.

Nineteenth-century economy was founded on coal and iron and Great Britain with her rich, easily-worked mineral deposits got off to a flying start in the industrial race. Her geographical position and her long experience in sending trading ventures over the seas, her political stability and comparatively elastic social organisation, all contributed to enable her to take advantage of this fact, so that by the 'eighties she was still the only true "industry State". In international trade she stood supreme. Her manufactures were welcomed all over the world and valued for their cheapness and good quality. No other country could compete either in the cheapness or the variety of the goods offered or in the network of agencies and financial institutions through which one market after another received the benefits of British industrial specialisation. As steamships linked the world together and railways opened up interiors, more and more remote communities became potential consumers of British goods. Nor was it only in this sense that the world was expanding. The population at home increased fourfold during the century and this meant more mouths to be filled and more bodies to be clothed. As this country concentrated more and more exclusively on large-scale manufacture and supplied a rich and expanding market for the food and raw materials of other parts of the world, higher standards of living all round still further added to the demand for British goods. Before this time, most communities both at home and overseas, had been accustomed to a very restricted consumption, and higher standards of living, therefore, showed themselves in a demand for immensely increased quantities of cheap, mass-produced goods—just the things that Britain was organised to offer. The time had not yet come when, sheer basic needs being met, improved standards allowed for individual choice in methods of consumption. For the time, cheapness and quantity were the dominating requirements. Cheap clothes and household utensils and all the mechanical equipment on which modern economy depends were the apparently insatiable demands of the nineteenth-century world.

Already by the turn of the century profound changes were making themselves felt. Britain was still the most important trading and industrial country, but the distance between her and her competitors was narrowing and it was fairly certain that a time was approaching when her rivals would draw level with her. In fact, some of those circumstances which had helped to give her her position of supremacy now contributed to drag her back in the race. Britain had been the great experimenter and innovator ; she had built up her great industries by trial and error and each stage in this development left behind a legacy of obsolete institutions and methods. Other countries learned from her experience and could establish their industries on a clearer and more efficiently organised foundation. The Lancashire cotton industry, for instance, would never have been split up into its traditional sections if it had first come into existence in the 'eighties, though that type of organisation had enabled it admirably to meet the problems thrown up when it was pushing its feelers out into unknown markets half a century earlier. British producers could, of course, have changed to meet the times, but their long predominance made them unwilling to do so, or to think it necessary. That markets should be eager for their goods and that coal should be the great source of power seemed to them matters of belief about which it was unnecessary to argue. Yet already by the end of the nineteenth century the electrical age was superseding that of coal, though it was in Germany and America, rather than in England, that experiments in long-distance transmission of power were being made. And it was electricity which did more than anything else to change the pattern of industrial specialisation.

Coal and iron are heavy and bulky articles, difficult and expensive to transport, so that as long as steam is the power used in manufacture it is cheaper to bring raw materials and labour to the coalfields and transport the finished product from there to its market. But when electricity takes the place of steam industry can establish itself more or less where it likes and many countries which had been dependent on British goods eagerly seized the opportunity to set up their own manufacturing industries, with electric power generated from their own water supplies. Changes in industrial technique aided them in this endeavour, for the increase in the scale of the production unit had two important results. By permitting each process to be specialised and standardised it enabled large manufacturing plants to be staffed by a labour force which had had little or no previous experience or training in industry; and it made it possible to produce the machines themselves on mass production lines. Britain's pre-eminence in the nineteenth-century world was due as much to the skill of her mechanics and industrial workers as to her supplies of coal and iron. Other countries, with less experience in this field, had found it difficult to make use of machines imported from this country unless they could also import the British workmen whose skill and knowledge could be relied on to keep the machines in order and repair them when they broke down. But the twentieth-century mass-produced machinery requires no such careful and skilled attention. With a stock of numbered spare parts in reserve most firms can depend on being able to repair day-to-day breakdowns without calling in any expert help, and this has allowed agricultural countries that formerly relied on British goods to establish thriving industries to meet the demands of their home markets.

At the same time as the outlet for British manufactures was contracting through the increased competition of other countries, it was narrowed by the slackening in the rate of growth of population. During the preceding century an unprecedented increase in numbers had been the consequence of the maintenance of a high birth-rate, while improved sanitation, better midwifery and medical knowledge were lowering mortality rates. This flood of population offered a seemingly insatiable market for the products of industries catering for basic needs. But during the last seventy years the serious decline in fertility has introduced profound changes into the nature of demand. For some time this was not easy to spot because the reduction in mortality more than kept pace with the decline in fertility, so that despite a lowered birth rate the number of births each year went up on account of the larger number of childbearing women in the population. Since 1909, however, this has no longer been the case and the number of births each year has been falling rapidly. The consequences of this simultaneous reduction in mortality and fertility rates are to be seen in the changing age-composition of the population, and these profound alterations in the social make-up of the community have exercised far-reaching influences on demands. At the beginning of this century 32·5% of the population was below 15 years of age and 6·2% above 65. At the present the comparable figures are 20·6% and 12% and stability has not yet been reached. In 1901 there were more than five children for every person of pensionable age, but as the proportion of children has gone down the typical family or social unit has changed its shape. Instead of a household consisting of mother, father and a number of young, dependent children it is now much more likely to be composed of several adults with only one or two young children. In each group there are now more earning members (the proportion of the population in the earning ages has risen from 61·3% in 1901 to 67·5% in 1941). The emphasis of wants has altered in consequence. The needs of adults have come to play a proportionately more important part than those of children (rubber hot-water bottles and bath chairs are bought instead of glass feeding bottles and perambulators). Moreover, with fewer children to support out of higher wages, families have needed to spend less on the basic necessities of food and shelter and have had a larger part of their incomes in which individual choice can play a part—furniture, radio, bicycles, clothes, etc.[1]

The shifting in the social pattern is by no means confined to this country. It is a phenomenon common to all white communities. In some countries it started later than in others, but it is significant that in those communities where its first appearance was delayed the subsequent rate of progress has been much quicker.

> While it took France over seventy years to experience a drop in her birth-rate from 30 to 20, while this process lasted about forty years in Sweden and Switzerland, and about thirty years in England and Denmark, in the last twelve years (from 1924 to 1936) the birth-rate has fallen in Bulgaria from 40 to 26, in Poland from 35 to 26, in Czechoslovakia from 26 to 17. While in 1922 and 1923 the birth-rate of Central and Southern Europe was still at least as high as in Western and Northern Europe in 1881–5, it had dropped by 1935–6 to the level held by Western and Northern Europe in 1911.[2]

The general effect of all these factors would have been to increase the need for adaptability in industry even if the developments had taken place in a world of peaceful international relationships. The war complicated the situation by speeding up the rate of change and by introducing further new difficulties of its own. For ten years pre-war trading relations were broken, for

[1] It should be noted that this situation is rapidly disappearing. According to present estimates (see White Paper on " Current Trends of Population in Great Britain ") 1941 will be the peak year in so far as the proportion of the community of working ages is concerned. From then it will decline as the proportion of pensionable age groups increases and the emphasis will be more on bath chairs and less on bicycles.

[2] " The International Decline in Fertility ", by R. R. Kuczynski in *Political Arithmetic*, edited by L. Hogben, p. 53.

although the war itself lasted only four and a half years, the financial chaos which succeeded was almost as effective a bar to international trade as had been open hostilities. And it was not until 1924 that the foreign exchanges were stabilised. Many of the countries which had been struggling to industrialise themselves had practically a decade of freedom from British competition in which to dig themselves into their home markets. Others had sought and found other sources of supply and saw no reason to change back again when Britain was once more ready to serve them. It was, too, only to be expected that the war would stimulate nationalist sentiment and one of the easiest and most usual ways for this to express itself is by the erection of tariff barriers, and the inculcation of the view that it is unpatriotic to buy from the foreigner. The insecurity of peace lent support to this belief. Even those who, fundamentally, were convinced of the value of free trade were uneasy at the prospect of being cut off again from essential supplies of food and raw materials or of commodities which played an important part in their internal economy and were anxious to encourage the home production at least of those things which they held to be key products. Had it not been for the changes in industrial technique this position could not, perhaps, have been long maintained. But the war was a forcing house here as in other respects. The whole inventive genius of all the industrial nations had been concentrated on the problem of overcoming the chronic shortage of men and materials. Skilled jobs were broken down into their component processes so that they could be undertaken by quickly trained women and youths and there was continual experiment in new methods to enable those with little or no industrial skill to be employed. These new methods affected more than the industries which were directly connected with munitions and the rapid elimination of the skilled element removed one of the principal advantages enjoyed by the older industrial countries and made it easier for the newly industrialised communities to hold on to the position they had gained for themselves during the war.

All these changes bore with particular severity on this country because of the unusually large part played by international trade in her economy. Before the last war, one in every three persons engaged in industry was employed on goods for export. When the war was over many of the markets for these exports were lost and owing to the fact that trade had been either cut off completely or seriously dislocated for a decade, it took some time for the country to realise that the loss was permanent. An additional complexity was introduced by the fact that war needs had drawn millions of men and women into occupations whose value decreased or ceased entirely when the war came to an end. Some of these workers, a minority, had entered employment for patriotic reasons and were eager to get back to their normal lives. Men who had postponed their retirement or had already left work had been recalled, and married women who in peace-time found caring for home and children a full-time occupation were only too ready to give up their industrial work. But the majority of those in the swollen war industries were not in this position. The men in the Forces were impatient to be demobilised and get back to their pre-war jobs. A pledge had been given that the women who had been taken on to replace men should not be retained when the men were once more available, and that Trade Union pre-war agreements governing the demarcation of work should again be enforced. But this was not as simple as it had seemed. Methods and machines had changed so rapidly during the war that it was not possible to restore men to jobs that no longer existed or to types of work that were obsolete. In addition, many industries were swollen out of all proportion to peace-time needs—in particular, the engineering trades, shipbuilding, mining, cotton and agriculture.

When the war ended, therefore, many different kinds of adjustment had to be made at the same time. There was, firstly, the change-over from war production to civilian goods. There were, secondly, the changes in technique. Thirdly, as shipping was released and imports were again more freely available, many industries that had expanded when they had no foreign competition to fear were forced to shrink to their former size. Fourthly, the dislocation of foreign exchanges introduced a gambling element into commerce and upset any attempt at rational calculation of future needs of production for certain markets. And fifthly, in addition to all these there were the effects of the pent-up accumulation of changes in trading relations which the war years had hidden.

III

The degree of the maldistribution of labour which faced the post-war world was consequently unprecedented. Unfortunately adjustment was long delayed and never completely accomplished. This was partly because the fundamental nature of the changes that had taken place was not realised for many years. Until the very end of the 'twenties most people believed that they were simply being tossed about in the wash of the war; they did not realise they were being swept along a new current. For a decade, therefore, attempts at adaptation were half-hearted and temporary in character. As there was no real appreciation of the profound and far-reaching changes that had taken place there was no stimulus to the formation of a coherent policy. Most people were simply anxious to weather the storm so that they would still be afloat when the post-war hurricane had blown itself out and everything returned to " normal ". It was, no doubt, as illogical to think of the chance situation which had happened to be in existence in 1914 as normal as it was to assume that a world which had been through such experiences could take up life again just where it had left it before the war. But it is, perhaps, intelligible that a community which had suddenly been forced to face the rigours and sorrows of war should long for a return to a life which, by contrast, seemed so safe and peaceful. It thought it could rid itself of the effects of the war as easily as a dog which shakes itself vigorously after swimming the stream across its path and then runs on in the same direction. The wage-earning population shared this general unwillingness or inability to recognise that the world had profoundly changed and that, no matter how long they waited, the old industrial pattern would never return ; and they, consequently, dug themselves in to wait.

There was a further factor which played an equally important part in delaying adjustment. The institutional nature of the industrial system has undergone considerable modification during the present century in the course of which it has lost a good deal of the flexibility and elasticity it formerly possessed. The most outstanding change in this respect is the growth of collective regulation of wages and conditions of employment. During the second half of the nineteenth century the Trade Union movement had become strongly entrenched in the highly skilled industries, but it was not until the last decade that it began to touch the unskilled and semi-skilled workers. When it did, the development was very rapid and within the short period between the turn of the century and the beginning of the World War, the total membership had jumped from under two million to over four. Industrial discontent, coupled with labour shortage and soaring prices, combined to give a further impetus during the war years and by 1920 the membership was nearly eight and a half millions. It was not to be expected that this high level would be maintained. Many of those included in this huge total were workers who had been drawn into the expanded engineering trades and had joined the strong unions already established there, but their membership had not lasted long enough for it to have become a matter of course with them to join or to found a Trade Union in the employment into which they were later absorbed. This would have been so even if the transition from war to peace had been made without any severe jolt to the regularity of employment. But the serious and wide-spread unemployment of the early 'twenties led to a rapid exodus from the unions and by 1925 the number had dropped to five and a half millions around which figure it has become more or less stabilised. It is true that during the worst depths of the depression in the early 'thirties this figure was reduced by a million, but this was probably due in large part to the fact that many workers were compelled to fall out of membership by their inability to pay subscriptions during very prolonged unemployment, and as the unemployment figures fell, the Trade Union membership figures rose again.

Trade Union organisation was not, however, spread evenly over the whole industrial field. Most of the new industries which were established or which greatly expanded after the last war—electrical engineering, radio and car manufacture, and the host of light industries making consumption goods—settled in areas away from the principal coalfields ; areas which were rural or semi-rural in character and in which there was no tradition of workers' organisation. Most of the employees were engaged in semi-skilled processes which were not sharply differentiated from one another so that it was not practicable to try to collect all those capable of doing the work into a union and, further, the preponderance of women and juveniles made spontaneous organisation particularly difficult. The bulk of Trade Union membership, therefore, was concentrated in the older heavy industries and in textiles ; that is, in the industries which, because of losses in the export market or because of changes in technique and demand were finding it necessary to contract. It is no matter for wonder that the men in these industries should use all the power given by their collective organisation to resist changes which would bring their world tumbling in ruins about their heads.

There is probably no other industrial change which causes such resentment as the substitution of a machine technique for the work of a craftsman with hand tools. This is not surprising. A reduction in wages is disliked and is generally bitterly opposed ; yet at the same time there is the recognition that it need be only a temporary setback and that wage rates can be pushed up again when the occasion offers. But a change in technique is permanent and means the loss for ever of all the accumulated skill and experience that the worker has acquired in his job. The child of working-class parents has surmounted many obstacles in becoming a skilled worker and has had to make many sacrifices in his early years. If he thought it worth while it was because he looked on it as an investment for the future. He believed that with a craft at his finger-tips he could face the future with some equanimity and with the assurance that his work would always command a fair price. Any attempt, therefore,. to replace his skill by a machine is a direct threat to the whole fabric of his life and he naturally seeks for ways to protect himself. He argues that, even if new methods are introduced, he has a prior claim over other workers in doing the particular job and that his long and intimate knowledge of the material and the product mark him out as the most suitable person for it even though the same degree of manipulative skill is no longer called for. The employer, on the other hand, sees no reason why he should spend a great deal of capital on expensive plant which could be worked by quickly trained operatives if he is to continue to employ skilled men at craft wages. There is here no possible point at which the diverging interests could be reconciled. It is of little use for the armchair economist to point out that the lowered cost of the more easily produced articles will raise the standard of living of the purchaser and will increase his demand for both this and for other goods previously beyond his pocket. This, though true, is no consolation to the skilled worker whose skill is no longer in demand and who is not trained to make the other articles on which consumers will spend their incomes. And even while recognising that his efforts to stop the new methods are likely to be as effective as the commands of King Canute, one can hardly blame him for using all the power he possesses to postpone their adoption as long as possible.

The same fear of being ousted from the position he has struggled so hard to reach lies at the bottom of other Trade Union policies, in particular, two which have a bearing on labour mobility—the restriction of entry to a trade and the demarcation of trade boundaries. Neither of these is quite simple in motive. The control of the intake of apprentices is probably concerned less with the wish to keep numbers down than with the effort to prevent half-trained juveniles from being employed as cheap labour to be dismissed when they are of an age to demand an adult wage. And anyway so few industries still require a regular apprenticeship that such restrictions, whatever their intention, could not influence more than a narrow field. For the most part, young workers are taken on in the lowest-grade jobs and gradually work up to better ones as their knowledge and experience grow. It is rather by defining the frontiers of the work that properly " belongs " to a particular type of worker that the attempt at restriction is made. In carrying out this policy the Trade Unions are, of course, influenced by as wide a variety of considerations as any professional association which refuses to allow an individual to practise unless he can prove that he has taken the requisite training to give him the necessary competence.

The desire that the work should be well done by men who know how to do it and the wish to preserve the dignity of the calling undoubtedly play their part. But the dominant consideration is the fear that the unqualified practitioner will undercut the recognised rates of pay. The strong craft structure of the older Trade Unions has proved something of an anachronism in a world in which a host of slightly separated machine operations has blurred the outlines of trades. There are many jobs which could be equally well undertaken by the members of several crafts and each tries to prevent the invasion by the others of what it considers its territory. The Trade Unions, themselves, have come to realise this problem and have tried to meet it by a greater degree of amalgamation between the associations catering for allied trades so that men may move from one type of job to another without passing over guarded trade frontiers. But this amalgamation has been slow and difficult. Trade Unions, like other associations of men, are proud of their past and jealous of their peculiar traditions. They dislike losing themselves in a wider community and hold with tenacity to their individual identity. The Union badge may call up as strong an emotional response as the old school tie.

There is another branch of Trade Union activity which, valuable in itself, also acts as an obstacle to labour mobility. Most of the older unions came into existence at a time when Poor Relief was the only statutory provision for workers who, for one reason or another, were not able to earn, and they built up important friendly benefit funds, which they retained even after the social insurance schemes were established. Some insured their members against sickness, some against short terms of unemployment, some against old age or funeral costs. The member's claim to receive these benefits depends naturally on the number and regularity of his payments, and a man who gives up his membership because of moving to another industry loses the security he has paid for. Even if he joins another union organising the employees of the industry into which he is absorbed, some considerable time must elapse before he can qualify for as much as he has forfeited. Such a consideration might not be enough to prevent a man leaving an industry which he knew definitely held no further prospects for him. But when he has no such certitude it is quite certainly enough to put a brake on his eagerness to search for new fields of work and to convince him that prudence dictates that he remain where he is in hopes of the old trade picking up.

The inability to determine the future course and needs of industry led also to the wide extension of a policy which had long been employed in a narrower way, that is, the organisation of short-time working. It had for many years been the practice in the coalfields to spread the incidence of a temporary reduction in demand over the whole of the personnel. Instead of dismissing a certain proportion of the workers, the entire labour force worked fewer shifts per week. While there was no other industry in which this practice was as thoroughly organised as in coal-mining there were many others in which it was resorted to to meet special emergencies. The cotton industry, for example, made use of it when the sudden reduction in the supplies of raw material might otherwise have necessitated the closing down of some of the mills.[1] And in many other industries, engineering, boot and shoe, pottery, glass, etc., individual employers practised this device to avoid dismissing their workmen.[2]

Before the war short time was essentially an emergency measure designed to meet a very temporary situation ; it had great value in keeping together a body of workmen who could normally expect to be working at full pressure again in a short time. But when this same policy came to be used on a very extensive scale to meet the problems of the depression of the 'twenties its effects were very different in value. Had the depression been due simply to the violent dislocation caused by the war there would have been much to be said for it, though it would still have had the disadvantage of placing the main financial burden for the maintenance of the unemployed on their fellow-workers. But it was already most strongly established and most widely used in just those industries—coal-mining and cotton—in which the changes were not only the most profound but were likely to be permanent. The organised short-time policy had the effect in these industries of tethering to them a much larger labour force than could ever hope to be fully employed again in the calculable future. It is unlikely that short time would have managed to exist as long as it did as an organised policy had it not been for the emergency developments in unemployment insurance. The original plan of the scheme had been designed to exclude the possibility that it might be used to subsidise casual labour. The insistence on a minimum waiting period before benefit could be received had this, among other ends, in view. But those who planned unemployment insurance had never dreamed that they would have to tackle the thousand and one problems involved in chronic mass unemployment and the original scheme had to be twisted and made to serve the urgent needs of the moment. In consequence it early became legal to claim benefit if the necessary " waiting days " were not, in fact, consecutive but occurred within a period of several weeks. This enabled

---

[1] H. Clay, *Problems of Industrial Relations*, p. 137.
[2] W. H. Beveridge, *Unemployment*, p. 221, note (2).

workers and employers to agree on methods of organised short-time working whereby large bodies of persons spent half the week in production earning wages and half in idleness for which they received an appropriate proportion of unemployment benefit. The two sums combined were not, it is true, as much as full-time wages would have been, but they were not far below it and this arrangement acted as a very strong inducement to the workers concerned to stay where they were rather than seek for work elsewhere.

IV

It has been pointed out earlier that in a price economy the principal motor power in distributing labour is to be found in the relative movements of wages. Fluctuations in wages are the sluice-gates which control the flow of workers into the channels where they are needed, and if anything happens to clog the mechanism stagnant pools will form instead of a regular flow. The institutional changes to which reference has been made have had just this effect. Since the last war collective control of wages has become the rule instead of the exception. No responsible body of employers would now attempt to alter wage rates without first carrying on careful negotiations with the representatives of their organised workpeople and this practice covers the majority of the large industries. Although there are many industries in which the workers have remained unorganised so that there is no representative association with which the employers could normally negotiate, statutory forms of collective bargaining—i.e. Trade Boards—have been developed to perform a similar function to that of the Trade Unions and Employers' Associations. Trade Boards were originally set up by an Act of 1909 as a revolutionary experiment to cope with the exceptionally low wages that were prevalent in a group of " sweated " industries. Much as they differed from each other in many respects these industries had certain characteristics in common. In all of them a considerable proportion of the workers were women and a great deal of the work was done in the workers' own homes or in small domestic workshops. To such workers the protection to be obtained from Trade Union action was denied. Women have always found it more difficult than men to organise, mainly because of the temporary nature of their wage-earning occupation. But for women, working in their own homes, isolated from one another, with heavy domestic obligations and receiving wages that barely served to keep body and soul together, the obstacles were insurmountable. After twenty years of arguing about the evils of the situation, the Government finally decided to take a hand in wage determination and the Trade Boards were set up for this purpose. The Trade Board for a regulated industry is composed of representatives of the employers and workers in the trade with a number of appointed persons to hold the balance and to ensure that a decision is arrived at within a reasonable time. The wage rates agreed by a Trade Board have the force of law and sanctions are imposed on those who pay less than the agreed amount. This method of protecting the sweated worker proved so effective and so free of the dire results that had been prophesied for it that there arose an insistent demand for its extension to other classes of worker than those for whom it had been designed. In many factory industries the workers, both men and women, were finding it almost as difficult to organise themselves as had the women outworkers of the sweated trades and the Trade Board method seemed well planned to protect their interests. Enthusiasm for the democratic principle was a potent influence in this respect. The heightened sense of national unity and social responsibility which is the outcome of a nationally supported war expressed itself in a determination to build a better world when the war was over. The contrast between the comradeship and shared vicissitudes of the trenches and the group hostilities of ordinary industrial life was too obvious to be missed. Much was said of the need for a new outlook in industry and, in particular, that the worker should be recognised as a partner in industry rather than as a subordinate under the despotic control of the management. An elaborate scheme of joint representative councils was worked out, but it was realised that this could not be attempted in any industry which had not already spontaneously developed separate representative bodies for employers and workpeople. And it was as much with the object of creating the machinery through which unorganised workers might have some say in controlling their working conditions as with the idea of preventing too rapid and too catastrophic falls in wages after the war that the Trade Board system was extended. By the Act of 1918 the Minister of Labour was empowered to set up a Trade Board in any industry in which (a) the wages were exceptionally low or (b) the workers were so unorganised as to be unable to negotiate wage rates with their employers, and by 1922 there were Trade Boards in existence covering a million and a half workers. A similar organisation was set up in agriculture by the Agricultural Wages (Regulation) Act of 1924, and just before the war the Road Haulage industry was brought under the same kind of control.

This legislative machinery was not designed to enforce minimum wage rates in the sense of a basic income related to needs. What it has done has been to establish statutory collective bargaining in those fields in which the appropriate negotiating bodies have not been sufficiently developed spontaneously. In general their agreements are conditioned by exactly the same forces as those that are reached by the voluntary negotiation of Trade Unions and Employers' Associations ; that is, by the state of trade, the demand and supply of various types of labour, willingness or unwillingness to risk serious friction and the general enveloping body of associated ideas of what is " right and proper ", or " fair " or " reasonable ", what people have a " right to expect " and so on. No Wages Board, any more than a Trade Union, can compel an employer to pay a worker a wage that is higher than he believes him to be worth. The employer always has the final word because he can cut down his employment. But what such bodies can do is to fight a delaying action.

This wide extension in collective bargaining, both statutory and voluntary, has coincided with a growing sensitiveness of the social conscience. From the beginning of the century there had been a sense of uneasiness over the low standards of living of large sections of the population, particularly of the unskilled labourers. The war, with its acute shortage of labour of all types, gave an opportunity for the wages of these groups to be raised, particularly as the legal prohibition of strikes by the Munitions of War Acts forced the Government to take a decisive part in determining wage rates. The Committee on Production which became the State arbiter in wage disputes standardised the rise in the pay of low-grade labour more quickly than would have been the case if decisions had been left entirely to unregulated group action, the more so as the rise so often took the form of a flat rate cost-of-living bonus which affected the lower wages more than the higher. So that by the end of the war there was a well-established and widely held view of what wages " ought to be " and the members of Trade Boards and Trade Union negotiating committees had certain standards of wages in their minds to which they felt the rates of different groups of workers ought rightly to conform. Sufficient importance is not usually given to the influence of habit and custom in settling rates of pay. Neither side comes to the bargain with a completely detached and open mind but is aware of the place in the social hierarchy that has been filled by the particular type of worker whose remuneration is under consideration. So that it is much more likely that the new agreement will be composed of variations on an already existing set of wage rates, however out of date the industrial situation to which they originally bore reference. In the cotton industry, for example, wage agreements are made as percentage changes in lists dating from 1860, and in sections of the dock industry " the rates for work done with the aid of elaborate derricks and gantries are being calculated on a basis that relates to hand work and bare poles ".[1] The mediæval conception of the "just price" still exerts a potent, though generally unrecognised, influence on the minds of those whose job it is to consider wage rates. The Janus character of wages causes many complexities which are the more serious because their origin is not understood. From one point of view the wage is merely one price among others whose function it is to regulate the supply and appropriate distribution of different types of labour. From the other it is the basis of social life, the method by which a citizen fulfils his social obligations to himself and his family, and the social reward for work properly done. Levels of wages to which people have become used take on an almost sacramental character. To most workers it seems " natural " that a skilled man should get a higher wage than an unskilled, something so self-evident that no argument is necessary to justify it or to explain it.

> Skilled and unskilled [says Mr. J. W. F. Rowe in analysing Trade Union policies] were accustomed to a certain differential between their wage rates and provided this differential was maintained, both were satisfied. Any infringement led to immediate action, particularly, of course, by the skilled man in defence of his own interests. . . . The differentials were fixed almost rigidly by custom and their origin is in some cases lost in the mists of antiquity. Professor Bowley has shown that the building labourer's rate in London was two-thirds of the bricklayer's rate throughout the nineteenth century and probably away back into the Middle Ages. For many years before 1914, threepence had become the customary differential in all large centres and this continued up to 1914 and even throughout the war and immediate post-war period, despite the doubling of the actual money rates. Before the war in many districts a plumber always got a halfpenny or a penny more than the bricklayers and carpenters.[2]

No amount of proof that changes in technique had reduced the importance of his skill would convince a worker that his relative value had altered, though he might eventually have to bow to the pressure of circumstances. Such pressure was, in fact, exerted in the years following the last war. The catastrophic depression which affected certain industries so profoundly and for so long made it impossible for the workers to preserve the

---

[1] Prof. J. Seebohm Rowntree and others, *Are Trade Unions Obstructive ?*, p. 334.
[2] J. W. F. Rowe, *Wages in Practice and Theory*, p. 154.

wages to which by comparison, grade by grade, with other workers they considered themselves entitled. But the strength of their conviction of what was " right " and " natural " backed by collective bargaining power delayed the fall in wages and made it less precipitous than it would otherwise have been.

Evidence of the power to resist wage changes can be seen in an analysis of the movement of wages.

	Money Wages (1929 = 100)	Real Wages (1929 = 100)	Unemployment, Percentage Insured	Employment Index, i.e. Numbers in Work (1929 = 100)
1927 .	102	100	9·7	98
1928 .	100	99	10·8	98
1929 .	100	100	10·4	100
1930 .	100	104	16·0	96
1932 .	96	110	22·1	92
1936 .	100	111	13·2	107

It will be seen from this table [1] that during the years 1929 to 1932, when Britain was experiencing the worst depression in her history, real wages rose by 10% despite an unemployment rate of 22·1% and although, with a population half a million larger, in 1932 only 92 people were employed for every 100 at work in 1929. But these are averages which show a general situation and which bear witness to the increased power of wage-earners as a whole to resist reductions during trade depression. To see the effect of this resistance on labour mobility one must examine the position in the shrinking industries over a longer period. Between 1922 and 1935 average yearly earnings in coal-mining fell from £125 2s. to £118 8s.,[2] a drop of 5·5%. During the same period the cost of living fell from 176 to 143, a fall of 19%. The numbers employed in the coal-mines fell from 1,162,754 to 779,502,[3] but at the later date there were 981,450 insurance books recorded as belonging to coal-miners,[4] which means that over 200,000 were unemployed and the yearly average of unemployed was 19·5%.[5] In the shipbuilding industry the lowest rate of unemployment recorded during 1935 was 37·7%.[6] Yet the weekly wages of shipwrights had risen to 60s. from 52s. 4d. in 1922 and of labourers to 41s from 39s. 1d.[7] In general engineering the weekly rate of fitters and turners rose from 56s. 1d. (1922) to

[1] Quoted in G. D. H. Cole, Short History of British Working Class Movement, p. 232.
[2] Abstract of Labour Statistics, Cmd. 5556/1937, p. 112.
[3] Ibid., p. 36. [4] Ibid., p. 18. [5] Ibid., p. 60. [6] Ibid., p. 60.
[7] Ibid., p. 82.

60s. 9d. (1935)[1] though the average rate of unemployment in 1935 was 13%.[2]

Now according to orthodox wage theory the situation shown in these three industries should not have arisen or should, at least, have been quickly self-liquidating. The pressure resulting from such large bodies of chronically unemployed should have forced down wage rates which, in its turn, should have caused an exodus from the industries affected into more favourable channels of employment. In fact, however, wage rates were maintained together with a large body of workers, technically attached to the industry but actually unemployed. The chief explanation of this lack of reaction to the lessened demand for the products of these industries is to be found in the effects of unemployment insurance.

Before the advent of unemployment insurance a far-seeing Trade Union negotiator had to weigh very carefully the balance of advantage in pursuing a certain wage policy. Experience taught him that if he pressed wage increases or resisted reductions to the point at which a considerable number of his members were left without jobs, there would be danger of a break away from the union. Many unions paid out-of-work benefit to their members in the hope of preventing this dry rot, but none could afford to pay more than a small weekly sum for a definitely limited period. Even so, any serious amount of unemployment constituted a dangerous drain on their funds and was likely to weaken the reserves on which they relied for their bargaining strength. For the sake of preserving the union, therefore, the negotiator was compelled to agree to rates of pay that would not force too large a number out of work. But the establishment of a compulsory system of insurance strengthened their hands immensely. At first the amount of benefit provided was intended to be nothing more than an additional help to the individual's own resources during a temporary emergency. But the mass unemployment which began in 1920 and which remained as a characteristic of the export industries throughout the whole of the inter-war period soon changed this and made it imperative to provide maintenance for the unemployed worker and his family on a scale which, though low, was enough to cover the bare necessaries of life. This created an entirely new situation in wage bargaining whether through Trade Unions or through statutory Wages Boards. Reductions could be strenuously resisted because unemployment maintenance offered a cushion to soften the fall of those pushed out of work. There was little fear that workers would break away from the unions and undercut agreed rates of pay however long their unemployment lasted.

---

[1] Ibid., p. 82.   [2] Ibid., p. 60.

There has, consequently, arisen a degree of inflexibility in wage rates which is an entirely novel phenomenon.

There is much to be said in favour of this policy of keeping up wages even at the expense of unemployment. There is a good deal of evidence to show that the reduction in wages which suggests itself as the first and most obvious course to employers faced by falling demand for their products is not in the long run the most effective way of dealing with the situation. It enables costs to be cut quickly and on a wholesale scale but its very simplicity postpones the much more difficult task of over-hauling the business to eliminate wasteful methods and tighten up organisation. Experience has shown how effective a spur to progress high wages can be, and there is little doubt that the resistance to wage cuts forces managements to do some hard thinking that otherwise they would be only too ready to evade.

There is as much to be said for this policy from the social point of view. A general fall in wages which is serious enough to squeeze excess personnel out of an industry brings with it a widespread fall in the standard of living with all its attendant miseries. It is, on the whole, the younger, unmarried men who are the most mobile, while the family men have many obstacles to surmount before taking the decisive step of searching for a different kind of job. And to allow such a drastic fall in wages as to bring about an appreciable exodus means to plunge thousands of families into poverty. In a time such as that between the wars, with its exceptional amount of dislocation, those responsible for wage negotiation were probably pursuing the wisest policy in putting all their strength into maintaining wages. To enable any considerable number more to get work the drop in rates would have had to be extremely pronounced and it is doubtful whether it would have been worth while for the whole labour force of the depressed industries to have been plunged into abject poverty in order to have 90% instead of 85% in jobs. It is better that the smaller number should have been employed at a wage on which it is possible to rear one's family even if this entailed that the remainder required to be maintained from some other source. But if this decision is reached it is necessary to face the consequent maldistribution of labour and to appreciate that some other mechanism must be devised to take the place of wage changes in getting workers to where they are wanted.

v

This decrease in flexibility in the response of labour to changing needs in industry is merely one aspect of a general trend towards rigidity in the economic world. In the same way that collective control of wage rates slows down the speed at which adaptation is made to changing circumstances in the labour market, so too collective control of prices of goods prevents changing tastes and techniques from exerting their full influence on the pattern of production. Nothing is more significant of this change than the revolution in opinion with regard to monopoly organisation. As late as 1919 the Committee on Trusts was debating the methods that could usefully be employed to curb the growing power of trade associations, but less than a decade later those industries which persisted in retaining their individualist structure were being condemned as anti-social. When markets were generally expanding and the typical unit of production was comparatively small, supplies could be rapidly adjusted to fluctuating demands without too severe a strain. If a temporary set-back took place some firms were unable to weather the storm and gave up. The others overhauled their methods and reduced their costs, and, with smaller supplies and lowered prices, they were able to make the necessary adjustments. But at the same time that rising standards of living have increased the instability of demand (since new comforts and amenities which have not had time to become part of conventional habitual expenditure are subject to the vagaries of individual choice) the increased scale of business enterprise has made the productive system less flexible. A large firm with heavy overheads is prepared to sell for a long time at almost any price which tops running expenses sufficiently to contribute even a little to supplementary costs. Its temptation is to produce an excessive amount so that by selling at a loss in this way it may keep its place in the market. In this aim it is aided by the many firms and organisations which are joined with it in the network of economic relationships. All those who provide it with raw materials and machinery, who undertake its subsidiary processes or who have invested capital in it feel themselves bound to try and keep it solvent in the hope of salvaging what they have already risked. If the fall in demand were merely temporary this would be an admirable way of spreading emergency losses and keeping afloat until the storm is over. When the cause is a permanent change in demand it has the effect of postponing the necessary adjustment of productive capacity to purchasers' requirements.

In order to get over this difficulty a policy of orderly marketing and rationalisation was much canvassed during the post-war years, and this cannot be achieved without some form of corporate control. By amalgamation among competing firms output can be cut down so that prices can be kept at a remunerative level and costs of production can be reduced by the elimination of redundant designs. The advantages to be gained are so great during a period of rapidly contracting markets that the Government took a hand in compelling dilatory industries to reorganise on this basis. But while these processes of cartellisation and integration may facilitate the adjustment of an industry to new circumstances when this change is suddenly called for, it introduces an element into the structure of industry which makes it less generally adaptable to dynamic conditions. At its best such corporate organisation should enable production to be concentrated in the most efficient units and the most economical techniques, thus releasing surplus capacity for other uses. But in consequence of the limitations of human nature the monopoly power which it entails is more often used to keep up prices than to maintain the ceaseless examination of methods which economy demands. Uneconomical firms remain in existence under the cloak of the amalgamation, and new experimental methods which might involve big capital changes in productive processes are prevented from getting a footing. Men whose managerial ability has been trained in a particular industry are as unwilling as skilled manual workers to recognise permanent changes in public demand which reduce the value of their accumulated experience, and are more ready to use the authority that amalgamation gives to resist change than to adjust themselves to it.

Similar efforts to maintain one's place in the sun in a narrowing world are seen in the raising of tariff barriers and the attempts at national autarky which have been so marked a feature of the inter-war period. The old idea of " keeping trade in the family " is one that dies hard. To the majority of people it is still extremely difficult to remember that we buy goods in order to get what we want and not to do a favour to the seller. It would be interesting to know how far this is associated with childhood memories of tradesmen " soliciting custom " or of the old adage that " the customer is always right " or whether, as is more probable, it is due to the fact that as sellers, whether of our services or goods, we are specialists, but as buyers we have (in peace-time) an endless variety of choice. Whatever the origin, the fact remains that most people think that by buying they confer an act of patronage on the seller rather than that they are simply pursuing their own interest. In general, therefore, minds are receptive to the idea that we should confine our purchases to those on whom we wish to confer special privileges, either by imposing tariffs on goods from foreign countries or by admitting the products only of those countries which are prepared to make equally large purchases of the things we produce ourselves. These efforts to create self-sufficient economic units by the rigid control of international trade have been motivated in the Fascist countries more by political than by economic considerations. But even in countries such as this where freedom of enterprise and trade still remains the fundamental principle of the economic system the severe dislocation caused by the changed direction of world trade has led to a policy which, through State control of markets, aims at substituting a narrower, though stable condition for the highly flexible multilateral trade of the end of the last century.

VI

The loss of elasticity in the labour market is, then, no exceptional phenomenon but is part of a widely diffused tendency to protect the interests of particular sections against the insecurity of a dynamic world. But in the case of labour the problem has been exaggerated by the influence of other conditions. It has already been pointed out that mobility is hindered by the natural reluctance of the worker to uproot himself from his familiar ground and replant himself and his family in unfamiliar territory. The acute housing shortage of the inter-war years added a further obstacle to movement. During the period of good employment many working-class families had bought their homes or were in process of doing so by mortgage. As long as they remained where they were, they had at least a roof over their heads and insurance benefits provided them with their basic needs. The home represented their savings and they realised that if they left and tried to sell or rent it there would be little chance of getting anything like the amount it had cost them. The same circumstances which were driving them to leave the district spoiled the market for working-class homes. Even when, as in the majority of cases, the house was rented on a weekly tenancy, the workers recognised that they had poor prospects of getting a home at the same rent in the new area. In their home districts their rents were probably still controlled by the war-time Rent Restriction Acts, while even if they were lucky enough to get a house in the new area it would be at a decontrolled rent and, in an expanding locality, the rents are usually high. But there was very little chance that they would be fortunate enough to get a house at all since neither municipal nor private enterprise was finding it possible to cope with the shortage. To a middle-class family with some knowledge of the world and with some savings in reserve such a matter would not prove an insuperable obstacle. Probably the family would be left behind while the breadwinner went out to prospect and make the best arrangements for their removal. But a wage-earner who had been out of work long enough to contemplate removing was more shackled.

Afraid of being homeless or forced to take expensive lodgings, he often enough decided it was better to bear the ills he knew than to fly to others that he knew not of.

The psychological atmosphere of the last twenty-five years has also played its part. Before the last war the State impinged very slightly on the economic life of the average man. He took for granted the conditions in the factory and was hardly aware of Factory and Public Health Acts. Labour Exchanges had been set up, but they were hardly used by any but the unskilled and not very much by them. Health and Unemployment Insurance had only just begun and had had little time to affect men's minds. Old Age Pensions were still only for those below a certain income level and were remote from the ordinary worker. But the war changed all this. It was the Government which decided which men should stay in civilian jobs and which should go to the war. The Government decided what should be produced, fixed prices and settled rations. The Government became the principal employer and, through separation allowances, pensions and out-of-work donations, was recognised in millions of households as the general paymaster. The Government, through the Committee on Production, settled industrial disputes and fixed wages. From being a shadowy force in the background, the State took the front of the stage as the authority responsible for every detail of life. When the unprecedented changes of the post-war world began to be evident, men felt themselves to be helpless victims of uncontrollable and incomprehensible forces and it is not to be wondered at that they looked to the State to restore to them their familiar world. It was felt that those who had lost their livelihood through war dislocation had as much right to compensation from public funds as those who became physically incapacitated through war injuries. The State was responsible and therefore the State should either maintain them or restore to them the jobs by which they might maintain themselves. " Work or Maintenance " was one of the most popular slogans of the day. A pamphlet issued by the Trades Union Congress argued that there was no difference between the unemployed from civilian jobs and the soldier who remains idle when there are no hostilities. Both are being held in reserve for future needs and just as the soldier receives his pay when he is not fighting so should the unemployed member of the industrial army be maintained by the State until work is found for him. There was here, of course, a confusion of thought. The soldier is under orders and is compelled to go wherever he is sent by his superior officers and to undertake whatever duties are required of him. Men of the same rank in different arms do not receive different rates in order to induce more to join one regiment and less to be attached to others. But the civilian wage-earner is not under orders of this sort and wages are not solely a reward for services rendered but also an indication of where more workers are required. For the most part the workers passionately maintained their right to refuse to do work other than that to which they were accustomed. " Work or Maintenance " was understood by most to mean the right to receive an adequate allowance until it was possible to carry on with the same sort of work as they had been doing before they were unemployed.

Stated as crudely as this the attitude seems to have little justification and to betoken a peculiarly narrow and selfish outlook. But there was, in fact, a good deal more to it than that. Looking back over the last quarter of a century we can now see that there were already in the early 'twenties unmistakable signs that the post-war world was something vastly different from the one that entered the war. But at the time only a very tiny and disregarded minority appreciated the significance of these signs. As late as 1927 the Blanesburgh Committee on Unemployment Insurance was taking as the basis for its recommendations the assumption that in the next year or so the volume of unemployment would fall to its " normal " proportion. Coal and cotton, engineering and shipbuilding had been the foundation of Britain's economic prosperity and there seemed no reason to believe that they would not be so in the future and offer as good a livelihood as in the past, once the turbulence of war upsets had been got over. It was not until the end of that decade that the extent and importance of the changed emphasis in the relation of industries began to be understood by those in authority, and it is not to be wondered at that the workers concerned should expect that there would eventually be as much employment for them in their own industries as there always had been.

To a worker who has spent his whole life in an industry the thought that his particular work is no longer required is at first beyond comprehension and, when believed, is indescribably bitter. A good deal of unimaginative nonsense is talked about the effect of large-scale production in reducing the individual worker to a cog in a machine in which he feels no interest. Nothing is further from the truth. Particularly in those cases in which the worker has been associated with the same firm for many years his sense of " belonging " to it and his pride in its achievement and standing are very real and important ingredients in his life. Even if the job that he individually does is lacking in variety and scope, a very large part of his interest is bound up with the gossip and contacts of the " shop ". He feels, though without putting the feeling into words, that he has a recognised place in the world and that he fits into an understandable social background. Without that recognition and support he has the awful loneliness and isolation of the individual cut off from the society whose idiom he speaks and in which he is understood and appreciated. Even when he is unemployed he still belongs to that community, particularly if a large number of his fellows were also out of work, and one reason he clings to the belief that he will be reabsorbed is that he does not then have to face the bleakness of being thrust out of his world. To leave not only his home but also the industry whose work has given meaning to his life and to try a new job in which he is an outsider, as unfamiliar with the trade jargon as with the mechanical processes, requires very real courage. If he has enough coming in each week to provide the necessaries, it is natural that he should either continue to hoodwink himself into the belief that the luck will soon turn and he will get his old work back again, or that he should angrily throw the responsibility on the Government to restore his old job to him.

The psychological atmosphere of the inter-war years has been particularly unfavourable to the growth of individual initiative and courageous experiment. Society put " Safety First " as its objective in both international and domestic affairs. Everything conspired to glorify the old safe way of doing things and to deprecate the untried and experimental. The unemployed maintenance allowances, whether insurance benefit or assistance, were absolutely certain, even if the standard of living they provided was lower than what the recipient was used to. They represented safety in contrast with the unknown dangers of a new industry in a different locality. It is small matter for surprise if workmen, to whom the consequences of insecurity are a matter of bitter experience rather than of speculation, should take on the general protective colouring of the period. This does not mean, it must be stressed, that workers had learned to prefer maintenance to a job. All the evidence collected in sample enquiries of the administration of Unemployment Insurance and by detached individual investigators goes to prove the contrary. During the long depression, there was always a much larger number of applicants available for every job that was going than could possibly hope to be taken on. To be in work is a source of great psychological satisfaction; it restores one to one's place in the world and justifies one's existence. This is not primarily because the worker again has money in his pocket, though this naturally plays a part in a world that is so dominated by money values; but it derives more from the generally subconscious and unexpressed shame at being " not wanted " in the community in which he had before taken his share as a matter of course and of right. But it does mean that they were less ready to contemplate change and less willing to face the fact that they had been thrust out permanently from their customary community.

In one way the admirable institutions which developed in areas where there was chronic mass unemployment contributed to this shirking of reality. The Occupational Centres and Unemployed Clubs which grew up to provide for the months, or even years, of enforced idleness came to offer a " substitute " life and community to the worker who had no longer any real hope of being reabsorbed into his industry. In sharing the club activities, in helping to build the club accommodation and equipment, in the part he played as club committee member or section secretary, in knowing its gossip and jargon, he got back that sense of " belonging " to a community. Many thousands of men who had bravely gone to other districts to take on new jobs drifted back again after a very short time because they could not stand the loneliness and knew that in their own towns and clubs they had a recognised and secure place. Of those moved under the official Industrial Transference scheme 27% of the adults were known to have returned home.[1]

Men bring to a period of unemployment the attitudes and scales of values that they have developed before when they were workers. The generation which grew up before the last war and which was faced with the changed post-war world had had little opportunity for choice or initiative in work. There was a clear line of demarcation between managerial authority and wage-earner. The management gave orders, the worker was expected to obey without asking the reason why. The scope for individual judgment and decision was bounded by the possibilities of the actual operation on which he was employed. And the narrowness of life on a small income does not offer opportunities for the cultivation of judgment, initiative and choice in those facets of life that are not governed by the workshop. Rising standards of living resulting from cheap mass production showed themselves in a higher level of conventional expenditure. Standards of consumption which come to be conventional to a group in society do not of themselves offer much scope for individual choice. The comforts and amenities enjoyed by the majority of the wage-earning population were available to them because they were cheap and their cheapness depended on their standardised production. But while both home life and work had offered such narrow alternatives as to give little scope for initiative and experiment, yet the workers of this generation shared

---

[1] A. D. K. Owen, " Consequences of Industrial Transference ", *Sociological Review*, Oct. 1937, p. 338.

with the rest of the community the belief in individual responsibility and the obligations of family life, and the conviction that wherever possible you should look after your own troubles and not expect others to bear them for you. The greater part played by the State after the war, both in controlling economic activities and in supporting those who were unable to take care of themselves, may have modified, but they did not eradicate, these fundamental convictions. They were passionately eager for work so as to regain their independence and self-respect; but nothing in their previous experience had developed such initiative as to lead them to choose to make a profound change in their way of living unless they were forced to do so by outside authority.

There was, in this respect, a considerable difference in the general attitude of the generation that grew up after the last war. They were reared in a different social·tradition. The boy who reached working age in the twenties had spent all his life in an industrial world in which the individual seemed to count for nothing and the State or Big Business for everything. He had had no opportunity to acquire the pride in working and of belonging to a particular industry or firm that the older man got. He had grown up in a family dependent on money that came from Insurance benefit or Assistance or Poor Relief rather than earnings. To him there seemed nothing exceptional in this dependence. He was used to it himself and, as thousands of his mates in the district were in the same position, there was no reason for him to question it. During the whole of his most impressionable years he had had hammered into his consciousness the thought that no matter how skilled or independent you may be, the chance of a job was something over which you had no control. Skilled man and loafer equally queued up at the Exchange. What sense was there in pretending that anything that a man did could have any influence in getting him work? It was all the responsibility of the people in authority. " They " ought to do something about it. There had been nothing in their experience of life to suggest that they owed any obligation to the community on which they threw the whole responsibility for maintaining them. To a certain extent this willingness to throw the burden of their lives on to an impersonal " they " was the result of the sense of frustration and impotence consequent from living in a world that offered no outlet for their energies and no use for their capacities. It is part of the normal development of youth to plan the great things they mean to accomplish and the shining rôle they mean to play in the world. But the young people growing up in the years between the two wars were met on all sides by insurmountable barriers. They were filled with baffled resentment at a world which did not want them. Wherever they looked the individual seemed to be an insignificant and disregarded plaything of incalculable and uncontrollable forces. Lacking both the independence and the belief in individual responsibility of their fathers, with no reason to feel a sense of obligation to a community that refused them a place and without any foundation on which to build a hope for the future, it is not surprising that they showed little incentive or initiative in the search for work. But while they cannot be blamed for this attitude to life, it must be accepted as an additional contribution to the factors making for occupational maldistribution.

CHAPTER III

EXPERIMENTS IN INCREASING MOBILITY

I

SYNOPSIS OF CHAPTER

1. The emergence of chronic mass unemployment necessitated fundamental changes in the system of unemployment insurance.

2. The provision of unemployment maintenance for unlimited periods brought into the forefront the problem of persuading workers to transfer from industries and localities where they were redundant. No solution was found for this problem and many thousands settled down to a routine of maintained unemployment.

3. A great deal of migration, both organised and unorganised, did take place between the wars, but it fell far short of what was necessary.

4. The general result of these institutional changes is to weaken the old incentives to seek remunerative employment without replacing them by new ones.

THE danger of impeding the flow of labour was very present to the minds of the originators of compulsory unemployment insurance and many of the features of the early scheme were designed to overcome it. Insurance was never intended to do more than provide a first line of defence against strictly temporary unemployment. It is of the essence of insurance that the risk against which provision is to be made is calculable, that is, that there are reasons for assuming that the experience of the past will be repeated in the future with only such degrees of variation as will be negligible or as can themselves be foreseen and estimated. Without such an assumption it is impossible to know what premiums are necessary to maintain solvency when claims are made. At the time that the scheme was being put forward, various investigations led to the conclusion that a very large part of the incidence of unemployment was due to recurring factors in the economic world, the effect of which was to institute some sort of pattern of unemployment. Cyclical fluctuations in industrial activity caused a general ebb and flow in the demand for labour over a period of years ; seasonal fluctuations had a similar influence over a shorter period in industries dependent on climatic conditions or certain social customs ; the ups and downs in the fortunes of individual firms led to a constant movement of workers into and out of jobs and so on. Varied as were these in their origins and in the seriousness of their effects, they had one characteristic in common—the men and women whom they threw out of work had a strong chance of being soon reabsorbed into the same sort of jobs as the ones they had lost. Provided there were adequate means of bringing together available jobs and those experienced in doing them, little more was required than some means of preserving health and efficiency during the periods of enforced idleness. It was recognised that the personal factor, though no longer regarded as the main determinant of a man's employment record, might still play some part in his ability to get and retain a job and it was with the idea of getting round this difficulty that those responsible for the scheme believed that it was essential to put limits on exceptionally bad risks, to frame the scheme in such a way that eligibility for benefits could be determined by some simple automatic test, and to give workpeople a direct inducement to reduce the amount of their claims.

Most of the familiar characteristics of the original scheme were designed with these objects in view. The amount of the benefit was small (only 7s. a week) and was intended as an addition to personal resources rather than as an alternative to them. The maximum period during which benefit could be drawn was strictly limited (only fifteen weeks in any one year) and the number of weeks' benefit that could be claimed bore a direct ratio to the number of contributions that had been paid in. The purpose of this last condition was to prevent the frittering away of the funds on those who were perpetually falling into and out of work and to give workers a financial incentive to get back into work quickly so that they might build up a good reserve of untapped contributions against the danger of lengthier spells of unemployment as they grew older. Moreover, the scheme was deliberately restricted to those industries in which organised short time had not been introduced (" unemployed benefit was regarded as an alternative to short time, not as a subsidy in aid of it " [1]), and in which, as a result of Trade Union records, there was considerable knowledge of the periodic incidence of unemployment. It will be seen that unemployment due to casual methods of engaging labour and to lack of personal capacity were purposely excluded, as was also the long-term unemployment due to changes in methods of production and the relative emphasis of consumers' demands.

The exigencies of the post-war situation compelled modifications to be introduced which gradually changed the whole nature of the insurance scheme and which led, step by step, to the abandonment of those checks on immobility which the founders of the scheme had been at such pains to establish. Immediate necessity made these modifications imperative but

[1] Sir William Beveridge, quoted in *Report of Royal Commission on Unemployment Insurance*, Cmd. 3872/1937, p. 12.

they, in their turn, led to a profound change in public opinion both as to the objects to which a statutory scheme should be directed and the method of attaining them. In the earlier period the existence of unemployment due to a decline in an industry or a far-reaching change in method was not unknown, but it was exceptional. The rate at which change took place had, on the whole, made it possible for adjustments in personnel to come about through natural wastage and the absorption of the rising generation into the expanding trades. Where, occasionally, the middle-aged skilled worker was caught in a shrinking industry, the situation was necessarily affected by so many circumstances peculiar to the individual, that it was generally considered to be better to deal with it on its merits rather than as one of a category, and this entailed philanthropic rather than statutory provision. So that when people were found to be out of work for such long or frequent periods as to exhaust their right to benefit, it was justifiable to assume that the dominant factor in their position was some form of personal incapacity rather than a serious decline in the demand for labour.

In the post-war world the recognised causes of unemployment continued to function, though in a very exaggerated form, but they were completely overwhelmed by a novel and unforeseen phenomenon—the emergence of mass long-term unemployment amongst the ordinary able-bodied and experienced skilled and semi-skilled workers. As a result of large-scale movements in the direction of international trade, coupled with profound changes in habits of expenditure and in methods of production, we were faced with the problem of hundreds of thousands of workers who had lived independent, self-respecting, hard-working lives but who, while still in the prime of life, were unable to find any employment for their knowledge and experience in the industry to which they considered themselves to belong. If the early principles of the insurance scheme had been adhered to (as was undoubtedly the intention when, in 1920, the system was extended to cover most of the industrial field) the result would have been to throw out of insurance, and on to Public Assistance, a very large proportion of the unemployed generally and, in particular, the whole of the long-term unemployment due to the wide and deep disturbances in the economic system. Such a policy was open to criticism on many counts. It shocked the social conscience that decent hard-working families who had never before needed help from any outside authority should, through no fault of their own, be compelled to seek the form of assistance to which was attached a serious social stigma. The insurance system had demonstrated the possibility of maintaining the unemployed by an alternative and more dignified method and there seemed no justification for treating one section of the unemployed differently from another section that was equally lacking in responsibility for its condition. Many people felt that the economic dislocation was so much the result of the war that the unemployed ought to be considered as war casualties and dealt with as such. And the effect of leaving thousands of workers who had exhausted their benefit rights to be kept out of Public Assistance funds (which, before 1929, were raised almost entirely locally) caused the breakdown of local finance in badly hit areas and everywhere brought about a wide disparity in local rates with serious social and industrial consequences.

Almost immediately, therefore, after the system was extended to cover the majority of the working population breaches in its defences had to be made. Benefit was paid to those whose statutory rights were exhausted on the plea that they would ordinarily find work within the insured field and so the benefit was merely an anticipation of sums to which their future contributions would entitle them. With the exception of one short period during 1924 this " extended " or " uncovenanted " benefit was, for nearly a decade, not recognised as a statutory right but was granted at the discretion of the Minister of Labour. Discretion was exercised to exclude certain classes, in particular young single workers with no dependants or those with other resources on which to draw, but the main body of the unemployed continued to draw benefit and made little distinction between the statutory benefit and the discretionary allowance. Even the technical distinction was later removed for, following the report of the Blanesburgh Committee, the discretionary element was discontinued and " transitional benefit " (inaccurately so called as it turned out, since it became a permanency) was allowed as a right to all who could prove that they were within the insurable field. The next change was the increase in the amount of the benefit. A small sum may be quite sufficient to bridge the gap between savings and the minimum cost of living for a short time, because expenditure can be cut to the bone and some items of consumption can be postponed for a few weeks. But the longer the period without earning, the more precarious does this bridge become. Savings are soon exhausted and expenses on many necessities (such as mending the family's shoes, replacing worn-out garments, or essential household equipment) cannot be postponed indefinitely. The longer that unemployment persists, the more necessary it becomes for the benefit to be adequate to cover the whole of basic needs, and as soon as this consideration is taken into account, the fact that needs depend on the size of the family leads inevitably to the introduction of dependants' allowances. When the dependants' benefit was first introduced in 1921 it was intended as a temporary measure to meet a special emergency and the fund from which it was paid was kept financially independent of the main Insurance Fund. But the emergency proved not to be temporary and the dependants' allowances were merged into the general scheme and have come to be an integral and much-valued part of the system.

II

The various Governments that introduced these modifications into the insurance scheme did so under the pressure of circumstances and without realising how profoundly they were altering the principles on which the original experiment had been founded. A benefit of a few shillings a week for a strictly limited period is unlikely to add much to the already existing obstacles to labour mobility. A weekly payment calculated to be sufficient to meet basic needs, according to the size of the family, and continuing more or less indefinitely, is a very different thing and has very different effects on men's attitude to the future. This is not to say that the original conception was better than the later developments. It was designed to meet a less formidable problem and, if it had remained unchanged, would have proved totally inadequate to the post-war situation. When men are unemployed, proper maintenance for themselves and their families must be forthcoming for as long as the unemployment lasts. The alternative is a mass of human suffering and degradation whose results, through the effects on the younger members of the family, reach far into the future. But if the provision is made both adequate and permanent it is necessary to devise new incentives for getting people into work which are more appropriate to the changed situation.

There was indeed some realisation of this need and as early as 1924 a condition was imposed on those claiming benefit to prove that they were " genuinely seeking work ". This meant that the lack of any offer of work at an Employment Exchange was not accepted, in itself, as proof of a man's involuntary unemployment (and considering the low proportion of placings made by the Exchanges there is some justification for this attitude) but that, in addition, the claimant had to prove that he was making an effort on his own account. During the period this condition was in force it raised storms of protest and proved impossible to administer. What proof can be offered that a man is " genuinely seeking work " ? Judgment on such a matter requires a careful analysis of the applicant's mind and a nice assessment of effort in relation to circumstances that is quite beyond the competence of the exchange official and would, indeed, baffle the trained psychologist. Moreover, it is putting too great a strain on human nature to expect that the man who has been out of work for months, or even years, who knows from conversation and from newspapers that unemployment is general and severe over many parts of the country, and who sees the long line of unemployed waiting whenever he goes to sign on at the Exchange, should start out each day with undiminished hope and vigour to ask for work from firms that he knows are turning off the workers they already have. Where shall he go and what shall he do ?

This condition was eventually removed (in 1929) and benefit was refused only if (a) the claimant refused to accept or failed to apply for a suitable situation notified to him by the Exchange, or (b) the claimant, without good cause, refused to carry out written instructions given him by the Exchange with a view to assist him to find suitable employment.

The whole importance of this disqualification rests on the interpretation of the word " suitable " and, in general, the interpretation has been narrow, i.e. suitable employment has been the kind of work to which the applicant has been accustomed or so closely allied to it that he could, in fact, undertake it without further training. Such a condition for the receipt of benefit turns this more into a test of character. It may be a method of distinguishing between the " deserving " and the " unworthy ", but it does nothing to overcome the hardening of the arteries in the economic system. This fact was recognised by the Royal Commission on Unemployment Insurance and was one of the reasons for their recommendation that there should be two separate methods for providing maintenance for the unemployed —an insurance system for short-term temporary unemployment and an assistance scheme for long-term, when something more is required than willingness to take a suitable job when offered one.

It is part of our conception [it reported] that the Unemployed Assistance Committee should not regard itself as a mere assessment and paying Committee, but that it should actively concern itself with the position of applicants under its jurisdiction.. The Committee should have the right to require recipients of assistance to accept such occupation and training as it thinks desirable . . . the devising and use of schemes of occupation and training are an integral part of the functions of the Unemployment Assistance Committee and an aspect of its duty to which in the interests of unemployed workers and of the community as a whole we desire that it should give the most earnest consideration.[1]

Consequent on this recommendation the Act [2] setting up the

[1] *Report of the Royal Commission on Unemployment Insurance*, 4185/1932, para. 548.
[2] *Unemployment Assistance Act*, 1934.

Unemployment Assistance Board included amongst its functions
" the assistance of persons to whom the Act applies who are in
need of work, and the promotion of their welfare, and, in particular, the making of provision for their improvement and re-estab-
lishment of the conditions of such persons, with a view to their
being in all respects fit for entry into, or return to, regular employment " and empowered the Board to provide training courses
for those under its care. The Board decided, however, not
to make use of its powers to set up training facilities of its own
and arranged to take advantage of the Government Training
Centres and Instructional Centres that had already been set up
by the Ministry of Labour some years earlier. The Board had
only a few years to pursue this policy before the outbreak of
war changed the whole labour situation, but the history of its
efforts is extremely instructive.

It must be remembered that the period between the passing
of the Unemployment Act and the beginning of the war were
years of industrial recovery with considerable expansion of certain
industries, in particular the engineering and allied trades, on
account of the rearmament programme. This affected the
Government Training Centres, the volume and type of whose
training is geared to the capacity of industry to absorb the trainees.
In the last full year before the war between 11,000 and 12,000
men entered the Training Centres, of whom just about half were
Unemployment Assistance Board applicants (i.e. whose unemployment had been so prolonged that they had exhausted their right
to insurance benefit) and the large majority (86% of trainees)
got jobs on the completion of their training.   Most of the Board's
applicants were, however, not suitable for the Government Training Centres and strenuous efforts were made to persuade them
to enter one of the Instructional Centres whose aim is not so
much the teaching of skill as physical and mental reconditioning.
Of the 195,000 men eligible for the Centres (i.e. between the ages
of 18 and 45) only 23,000 (of whom 88% were long-term unemployed) actually entered during the year and less than 3,000
men secured jobs on completion of the course.   Enquiry into
the subsequent history of trainees showed that a further similar
number had found employment within six months of leaving
the Centre and it is probable that the treatment they had undergone had helped both to renew their hope and to increase their
employability. But the Board felt bound to admit that there
was little indication that the men who had been through the
Centres were appreciably more successful in obtaining work
than those who had remained outside. This was, in fact, one of
the most serious deterrents to recruiting and represents both
an explanation and a justification of the unwillingness of the

men to submit to an ordeal that was feared and disliked for other reasons. Nevertheless it had to be admitted that there were a considerable number of men who had settled down to a life of allowances and who needed to be shaken out of their apathy if they were ever again to be fit for a life of independence. The prolonged unemployment among younger men at a time of general prosperity was particularly disquieting.[1] A statistical analysis of applicants under 30 years of age made on a sample basis in October 1938, showed that 75·4% had had less than a year's employment during the preceding three years and 58% had had either no employment at all or less than six months' during that period. Very many of these were the industrial casualties of the period of neglect during the twenties. They had been pushed into blind-alley jobs during which they had acquired neither skill nor industrial training. When they were sacked at 17 or 18 years of age in favour of a new batch of school-leavers they could find no market for themselves in a world of severe depression and, having drifted hopelessly from one unskilled job to another, they had settled down apathetically to the narrow, but safe, life that was possible to them on the weekly sum they drew from the Board. Some of these could be considered to fall within the category of " capable of work " (a necessary condition of the Board's applicants) only by straining the words. Through defects of teeth, or eyes, or hearing, or through chronic ill-health, they had little chance of getting employment on other than compassionate grounds unless the demand for labour was so acute as to necessitate the lowering of the standard normally demanded by employers. But there were also very many, especially in the Special Areas where unemployment had been extensive over a long period, whose situation could only be accounted for by psychological factors. Sometimes it was a marked unwillingness to leave the district which was the trouble. Sometimes it was a lack of personal self-control—jobs thrown up through some personal friction in the works. Sometimes it was unwillingness to think any job " suitable " unless all the conditions appertaining to it conformed to the high standard the applicant had set up for himself. More often it was the hopeless apathy bred by the unemployment itself which was the root cause. Most of these men were not " work-shy " or " shirkers " in any right sense of the word. They would have taken a local job of a familiar sort if it had been offered to them. But they had, outwardly at least, resigned themselves to their fate and were not ready to do anything that required an effort. They were not " dodging the column " in any active sense ; they were just not doing anything about it. The regularity of their allowance

[1] *Report of the Unemployment Assistance Board for 1938*, Cmd. 6021/1939, p. 45.

enabled life to be lived in an established and monotonous routine, which still further lessened the sense of individual responsibility and initiative and made any effort to break away from it increasingly difficult. Such men could not be considered as eligible for employment without a course of training and reconditioning. But the psychological inertia which made the training essential prevented them from *choosing* to undergo it or from allowing themselves to be persuaded to try it. Only by making the allowance strictly conditional on training might the vicious circle have been broken and this the Board had no right to do.[1]

Some years before this enquiry was made the Government had tried to take special steps to encourage the transfer of workers from those areas where large bodies of unemployed were stranded with no alternative local openings to replace their declining industries. The Industrial Transference Board had been set up in 1928 to deal primarily with the surplus of coal-miners. It confined its activities at first to young, single men who, because they were without family obligations, could be considered as generally mobile, but later it tried to encourage the movement of married men by financial assistance towards the cost of household removal. Openings for these men were hoped for from three causes. Firstly, as many new industries were expanding in the Home Counties and the South-East, opportunities for the employment of men of good physique and with a high previous employment record could be anticipated. Secondly, the Mining Industry Act of 1926 had given the Ministry of Labour power to make Regulations giving preference in employment in mines to those who had been so employed before the coal strike of that year. The aim of this Act was to ensure that the new coalfields in South Yorkshire and Kent should be manned by the unemployed coal-miners of South Wales and Durham rather than that new entrants should be drawn into the industry while there were large numbers out of work in other localities. Owing to the conservatism of the coal industry and its hatred of outside control the Minister had not made use of this power, but the Mining Association had given a voluntary undertaking that no new entrants over 18 years of age would be accepted unless a vacancy had been notified to the Employment Exchange for fourteen days and no suitable applicant had offered himself. The age proviso was put in to prevent a too serious distortion of the age composition of the labour force in the industry by limiting it entirely to those already employed in it.

[1] Sect. 40 of the Unemployment Assistance Act empowered the Minister to make allowances conditional on attendance at a work centre in cases of " special difficulty " : But the refusal of a job which would not have been considered " suitable employment " (see p. 65) under the regulations for Unemployment Insurance benefit did not constitute an applicant a case of " special difficulty "

In the third place, grants were made to local authorities to enable them to put in hand public works that would otherwise have been postponed to a later date on condition that a proportion of the men used were drawn from the unemployed in the depressed areas.

The transference policy had only a very moderate success. In its first and most successful year 32,000 were moved. After this, the numbers fell; only 8,000 were transferred in 1933 though there was some slight recovery in the following years. The most serious cause of this failure was the profound and widespread depression that swept the economic world from 1929 to 1932 and which resulted for a time in the colossal total of 3 million amongst the unemployed workers. It was exceedingly difficult to find jobs for transferred workers when the situation was bad everywhere and, moreover, the workers in the better-off areas resented the introduction of outside labour and feared that it would make their own prospects more precarious. It had been realised that the special subsidies made by the Unemployment Grants Committee to the local authorities who engaged labour from depressed areas would give only temporary employment to those transferred, but it had been hoped that by the time the work was completed the transferred worker would feel at home in the new district and would get absorbed in the expanding industries of that region. The severe depression killed this hope and thousands of men whose initial job was finished drifted back to their own homes where they could, at least, be unemployed in a community to which they felt they belonged.

III

Emphasis had been laid on the difficulties of mobility because they created so serious a problem and one for which a solution has not yet been found. But it must not be imagined that the number of workers who changed their jobs and their locality was confined to those who came under official supervision. This is far from the truth. Very extensive migrations took place during the inter-war period by people moving on their own initiative to jobs of their own choice and finding. There is evidence of this in the extraordinary change in the distribution of the industrial population between north and south and between the different industry groups into which the insured population is classified for statistical purposes. In the years between 1923 and 1938 the insured population (modified to take account of the statutory changes in the definition of " insurable ") grew by 24·1%.[1] But whereas the increase in the South-eastern Division was 57·2% and in the London Division was 41·1%, in Wales it was only 3% and in the Northern Division, 5%. The

[1] *Ministry of Labour Gazette*, Nov. 1938, p. 422.

London and South-eastern Divisions, which cover roughly an area lying to the east of a line drawn from the Wash to Portsmouth, included in 1938 28·9% of the insured population compared with 24·7% in 1923. The southern half of Britain, i.e. the Southern and Midland Divisions, had only 45·7% of the insured workers in 1923, but in 1938 they included 51·1%. These figures illustrate the general move to the south where the new expanding industries have mostly been established and most of this movement has gone on without any official direction. The same migration is shown in the figures of workers attached to the various industry groups. Between 1923 and 1939 the number of workers classified as belonging to the coal-mining industry fell by 30·5%, those in shipbuilding by 32·4% in cotton by 32·5%, while those in electrical engineering rose by 105·5%, in motor-car construction by 142·2%, in silk and rayon by 104·6%, in the transport and distributive trades by 49·2%, in public works contracting by 196·4%, and in miscellaneous personal services (entertainments, laundries, clubs and hotels, etc.) by 86·6%.[1] These are very big changes over sixteen years. Yet despite this great shift of the population in search of work the problem has not been solved. In 1939, at a time of very good trade, there were still 12·3% out of work in mining, 10·4% in shipbuilding, 9·1% in cotton, as compared with 2·7% in electrical engineering, 5·2% in motor-car construction, 3·5% in artificial silk manufacture with similar negligible figures for other expanding occupations. The conclusion to be drawn from all these figures is that the forces operating to redistribute labour in accordance with the requirements of industry function, even if slowly, to a considerable degree, but that they are not sufficiently powerful to accomplish the task.

The figures given here show overall movements, but the more interesting line of enquiry is into the details which make up the totals. Who moves into what? Are the big increases in the personnel of the electrical engineering industry, for example, drawn out of the contracting mining group, or where do they come from? and into which occupations do the miners go? Unfortunately, no comprehensive information exists to enable us to answer these questions, but from a number of separate investigations which have been made into particular groups, we can get some indications of what the answers would probably be.[2]

[1] *Ministry of Labour Gazette*, Jan. 1940, pp. 26–7.
[2] *Studies in Mobility of Labour*, Oxford Economic Papers, Part I, May, 1939; Part II, Sept. 1940.
Studies in Mobility of Labour, by H. Makower, T. Marshall and H. W. Robinson, Oct. 1938.
"Labour Mobility in the South Wales and Monmouthshire Coal-Mining Industry, 1920–30", by Brinley Thomas, *Economic Journal*, June, 1931.

The only way of tracing the direction and extent of labour movement is by examining the unemployment insurance books lodged at an Employment Exchange and seeing how many are of " foreign " origin, i.e. were originally issued by an Exchange in another district. This laborious examination has been carried out by a number of investigators in different areas and as their results are remarkably similar it is reasonable to suppose that they would prove fairly general if a more extensive enquiry were possible. The general impression is that the long-period variations in relative unemployment lead to corresponding variations in percentage migration, but there is no direct correlation over so short a period as a year. This means that there is always a considerable time lag between the stimulus to movement and the response ; and the enquiries show that the time lag is very much more pronounced during general trade depression than when markets are brisk. Migration sank to an extremely low pitch, for example, during the catastrophic depression of 1930–2 and recovered from 1934 onwards. It appears that movement was twice as active before the slump of 1931 as after, although the need for migration was so much greater in the later period. This is what one would expect. There seems no point in moving when one knows from reports that men are being turned off in all industries and in all parts of the country. The time lag shows great variations in respect of the distances moved. As a generalisation it is true to say that there is very much more readiness to move to a place that is fairly near to one's former home than to a less familiar area. It proved much easier, that is to say, for people within reach of Oxford to make up their minds to migrate into that growing industrial centre than for out-of-work miners and steel-workers in South Wales to transfer to the Home Counties. The serious and significant fact that emerges from these enquiries is not only that " it is found that the magnitude of the response of migration to incentive to move is small " [1] but that the response is least where the need is greatest. It is the chronically unemployed who are the least mobile, though it is just these who must make up their minds to change their homes if they are to be reabsorbed into employment. Jewkes and Campion, who investigated mobility in the cotton industry in 1928, showed that although the industry had never, since 1921, worked to more than 80% capacity the number of insured workers attached to the industry had not been reduced. Moreover, the depression

" Mobility of Labour in the Cotton Industry ", by J. Jewkes and H. Campion, *Economic Journal*, March, 1928.
" Movement of Labour into S.E. England, 1920–32 ", by Brinley Thomas, *Economica*, May, 1934.
" Influx of Labour into London and S.E. 1920–36, by Brinley Thomas, *Economica*, May, 1937.
[1] *Studies in Mobility of Labour*, Part I, Oxford Economic Papers, May, 1939.

was highly localised; some towns were badly off but others were hardly affected. Yet movement from the depressed to the prosperous sections was very slight. In the majority of Employment Exchanges the proportion of workers from other districts was less than 5% and in some as low as 1%. As an average, insurance books which had originated from another Exchange were 3·1% for men and 2·3% for women. Even where movement could be traced it seemed to have no connection with trade developments. There was not, for example, the transfer one might have expected from the badly hit coarse spinning sections to the areas where fine spinning and weaving were still prosperous, and it must be concluded that what mobility there was owed its origin to purely personal considerations. The authors concluded that immobility was probably due to a combination of factors—the high proportion of women workers, particularly married women who, for obvious reasons, are less mobile than workers in general, the close personal relationship which still exists between employers and workers in an industry in which the majority of firms began as family businesses with strong local ties, and the general practice of short-time working organised in such a way as to enable benefit to be drawn for half each week. In the coal-mining industry of South Wales there was considerably more movement than in cotton, both from the less prosperous to the more prosperous areas within the district and outside to other occupations. But here too there was a general "stickiness". The coal-mining industry is the only one in which a study has been made of the direction taken by those leaving their old jobs and shows that, apart from some slight absorption into other forms of mining, and into brick and tile making, the biggest move was into building and public works contracting. In view of what was said above of the special encouragement given to local authorities on condition they employed a proportion of unemployed miners this type of transfer is not very important. Most of it was definitely temporary and very many drifted back to their old homes when the job in which they were working was completed.

IV

Certain general conclusions emerge from all this. The provision of maintenance during unemployment has reduced the urgency of the need for finding new employment and has thereby clogged the economic mechanism through which changing wage levels affected the occupational and geographical redistribution of labour. This result has been achieved not by inducing deliberate malingering since the efficiency of the administration is such that the "column dodgers" can be detected and frustrated, but by weakening the incentive which up to now has been the prime motive for initiative and effort. The foundation of our present socio-economic organisation is individual freedom of choice. It is true that to many the freedom seems illusory, since the alternatives open to them differ only in their degree of disagreeableness. We are bounded both by circumstances and the limitations of our personal qualities. I cannot choose to play the piano like Schnabel nor to write like Shakespeare. And though I might perhaps have the capacity to make a competent lawyer or skilled engineer, I cannot enter these occupations unless my parents were both able and willing to allow me to take the necessary training. To some, these shackles on choice are more obvious than the freedom. The son of the dock labourer has not the same wide field from which to choose as the son of the skilled artisan, and he again has less than the son of the professional man. But the dock labourer's son is not compelled to follow his father to the docks. He could go to sea or do semi-skilled factory work or work on the land or join the Army. No authority determines the work we do, and within the limits of circumstance and capacity we make our own choice.

The corollary of freedom of choice is individual responsibility. Having made our bed we must lie on it. It was for this reason that the Victorians insisted on the importance of " deterrence " and " ineligibility " as characteristics of Poor Relief. What sufficient inducement could there be for men and women to cultivate the social virtues of thrift, independence, careful judgment and industriousness if the idle and inefficient were able to live as pleasantly and comfortably as the toilers ? But if you could attach to State maintenance a feeling of social inferiority, so profound that it cast its shadow not only on the person concerned but on all the members of his family however distantly related to him, you had the most powerful incentive to strain every nerve and to take any action, however distasteful in itself, to retain independence and ability to pay one's way.

Such a rigorous policy could be maintained only as long as there were no doubts as to the close correlation between individual effort and economic rewards. This confidence was beginning to be shaken towards the end of last century and was completely shattered by the results of the last war. It was this change in belief which acted as the sharpest spur in the effort to find some method of providing for the unemployed outside the Poor Law. The break-up of the Poor Law has been propounded as the most essential social reform for many different reasons. Some have demanded it on the grounds that Public Assistance, with its uniform method for dealing with situations of widely varying origins, is essentially non-constructive and undiscriminating ; by dealing with results rather than causes it does nothing to prevent the continuance of the distress it relieves. Others have insisted that by its method it penalises thrift and destroys just those virtues it is designed to encourage. But there is no doubt that the most important reason for the welcome given by the mass of the population to the superseding schemes of the last thirty or forty years has been that they have provided a bulwark against destitution which does not carry with it the social stigma of pauperism. Even after the actuarial framework of unemployment insurance had become quite shadowy there were strong reasons for retaining its form because the recipients of benefit felt that they could accept it without any loss of self-respect or personal dignity.

To the detached observer, Public Assistance is now simply one of a large body of social services serving different needs ; but to a large section of the community it is still something to be shunned as distinct in character and separate in nature from other services. The fear and hatred it inspires are no longer as great as they were and vary in intensity in different parts of the country. In those areas where unemployment was extensive and prolonged in the decade before transitional benefit and the establishment of the Unemployment Assistance Board allowed the chronically unemployed to be kept entirely out of national funds, so large a body of the working population was in receipt of Poor Relief that the sense of social inferiority was lost in that of common misfortune. But in districts that did not suffer so greatly and for so long the distinction has remained.

As so often happens with changes in public opinion the tendency has been to swing to the opposite extreme. As strongly as the Victorian insisted on the duty of self-help and independence, the present generation has tended to concentrate on the rights of the individual to maintenance. The powerlessness of the individual in the face of gigantic, uncontrollable economic forces has so dominated the scene since the last war that the whole emphasis has been laid on the right of the individual to protection from society rather than on his duty to contribute towards it. This view was first given official expression in the Minority Report of the Royal Commission on Unemployment Insurance which took as its starting point the right of the citizen to work or maintenance. The onus of providing both was thrown on to the State. The Majority Commissioners were unwilling to go as far as this, and by instituting the Unemployment Assistance Board with its Means Test and its power to organise training schemes gave expression to their belief that more is required than adequate maintenance in dealing with long-term unemployment. But the tide of events has been against the attitude of the majority. The largest proportion of the applicants to the Board have been able to qualify for allowances, particularly since the Government laid down precisely the narrow range of resources that might be taken into account, and the training schemes have made little impression on their employability. In these circumstances the distinction between insurance benefit and unemployment allowance becomes little more than academic and hardly justifies the retention of two separate systems of administration and finance. The unreal nature of the distinction has been recognised in Sir William Beveridge's Report in which the general trend of unemployment maintenance reaches its logical conclusion.

Just as the Victorians stressed self-help without bothering to measure the immense suffering involved in the elevation of this stern doctrine into an absolute rule of conduct, so the present generation has demanded its civic rights without appreciating the repercussions in the wider economic field. The general effect of inter-war developments in unemployment maintenance has been to remove one set of incentives to work without replacing it by another. As so often in modern life, the individual has had forced upon him two patterns of behaviour which are in conflict with one another. The nineteenth-century philosophy had its crudities, but it was consistent; it hung together. It tried to relate work and reward. If you had the wit to see what the rest of your fellows wanted, if you produced it better or more cheaply than your competitors, and if you worked hard, kept your needs moderate and saved for the future, you would prosper. You might then enjoy the solid satisfaction of knowing that at one and the same time you provided for your own wants, you fulfilled your social obligations to your family and you contributed to the progress and welfare of the community. But the coin has two sides. If you count the size of the income as the measure of the citizen's contribution to society you must attach moral censure to those who, by their penury, show that they have failed to do what society expects of them. The nineteenth century believed that " the poor i' th' loomp is bad ". It was a Christian duty to be charitable to the unfortunate, but it was an even more insistent duty to attempt to strengthen their moral fibre, to help them to stand on their own feet and to take on their own shoulders the burden of their own responsibilities. Whether one agrees with them or not, there is here a coherent set of moral principles to act as a guiding light whatever the circumstances.

Nowadays, however, we have no such uniformity. We uphold one set of principles for one part of life and another, and conflicting, set for another part. In the workaday world, your income and your standard of living depend on your own efforts, on your quickness in seizing new opportunities, on your discipline and industriousness, your skill and training. The need to give value for money is something which cannot be ignored. If your employer does not think you worth the wage he pays you, you will not be employed. But once you have lost your work your income becomes a right, a claim on society, paid by some impersonal authority with which you have nothing to do and towards which you have no reciprocal obligation. No longer does your income depend on any effort of your own. It does not bear any relation to your skill as a workman nor to your value as a citizen. It falls as the manna from heaven on the just and the unjust alike. The only test that you have to pass is that you are willing to take suitable work if it is offered you.

It has been a matter of surprise to some and of congratulation to others that the provision of maintenance for the unemployed has so little fostered voluntary idleness amongst the mass of the working population. Every investigation, both official and private, made during the twenty inter-war years has produced evidence of the strenuous and heroic efforts made by unemployed workers to try and get jobs even when the wage was very little more than the sums they were already receiving in benefit or allowances. The mere rumour that men were being taken on by a firm a few miles away was enough to bring hundreds of applicants from every side. And many tragic stories tell of the silent and bitter misery endured by men who felt they had forfeited both the respect of their children and the equal comradeship of their fellow-workers by their involuntary idleness. But this should be no cause for surprise. Psychologists tell us that the attitudes to life formed in early childhood never completely cease to influence our conduct. The working population that was adult between the two wars acquired its moral colouring during the end of last century when it was considered shameful to have to ask for charity or public help. And, despite the revolution in social relationships of which the twentieth-century social services are both the effect and the cause, these early patterns of behaviour have profoundly influenced their response to the challenge of the new world. Men and women who had been bred in a spirit of independence and whose self-respect was inextricably bound up with the place in industrial society that their own efforts won for them, could not find happiness in a world where their skill and experience and strength had no market value, even though their material needs were provided for.

The really significant feature, however, is the very real difference between the generations in this respect. The young men who should have been the backbone of the working population in the 'thirties had passed the greater part of their impressionable childhood and adolescence in unusual economic circumstances. During the war years their fathers had been in the Forces and the family income was paid by the State. And when their fathers later returned to a changed and disorganised world, the State still remained the source of income in hundreds of thousands of homes. These young men grew up in a world where it was part of normal experience to draw your income through the Labour Exchange and it was, therefore, a matter which required neither justification nor apology. Few of the deep-seated and unexpressed convictions which direct our' actions are the result of deliberate teaching; they are more generally imbibed as part of the prevailing atmosphere in which we live. It is natural that the child who has grown up in a family in which work and income bore no perceptible relationship to one another should take it for granted that the receipt of income carried with it no reciprocal obligation. To the mature generation, the emphasis laid by the new philosophy on the *right* of the individual to social help in meeting undeserved misfortune was a necessary corrective to the sterner beliefs in which they had been reared and enabled them to maintain their dignity and self-respect in a time when they were the helpless victims of forces beyond their control. But to the young, particularly in those regions where unemployment was wholesale and chronic, who had never been subject to industrial discipline and who had had no opportunity to acquire habits of industry nor to develop a sense of personal responsibility, this emphasis led to a lack of balance. Although it is in general to the younger members of the community that society must look for greater adaptability and for willingness to learn new methods and strike out in new areas, it has proved just here, amongst the younger generation, that there has been less than average readiness to adjust to changed conditions. Denied the opportunity to enter skilled industries and later unwilling to submit themselves to training, the most that they could hope for was an unskilled or semi-skilled job. The wages offered for such work were often only a few shillings more than the unemployment allowances which they could draw without working. Moreover, they knew by experience that the wages might be irregular while the allowances were certain and unvarying. Lacking the incentives for regaining the independence of work that played so large a part in their fathers' lives, they could calculate that the extra shillings they would receive as wage-earners would hardly compensate for the physical wear and tear of work and refuse to make any effort to get themselves out of the ranks of the dependent.

For much of the flexibility that the economic system still showed during the inter-war period we were drawing dividends from the past. With every succeeding decade a larger proportion of the working community will be drawn from the generations in which the old incentives to work have been weakened or completely discredited. It is not that those who are secure invariably prefer idleness to work. There is too much evidence to the contrary for this to be believed. The vast majority of people are happier when they have a definite and regular job to occupy their time and stimulate their interest. Thousands of people have found life fuller during this war than they have ever done before because they are devoting every spare minute to acting as wardens and fire-guards and carrying on the multifarious communal activities that the war has made necessary. But it is worth noting that it was not until they had started doing these things from a sense of public duty that they discovered the happiness to be gained from them. Before the war there was no lack of valuable social work waiting to be done—in clubs and institutes, in infant welfare centres and community halls, in adult education organisations and municipal government—and going undone for lack of willing helpers. But it was not until the inducement was sufficiently strong to make men and women willing to do the work, even though they disliked the prospect and believed it to be a sacrifice, that they found by experience that the gain in interest and in sense of community was greater than the effort and time involved. And even so, enough have remained deaf to the call of public duty to make it necessary to introduce a measure of compulsion in certain cases.

But there is a more important aspect than this. The main question is not whether any large number of people deliberately choose idleness to work that pleases them. It is rather whether they choose idleness to work that doesn't please them but nevertheless has got to be done. There is here no wish to draw an unreal distinction between work that is creative and interesting and work that is monotonous and repetitive. Such distinctions are always arbitrary and rarely have any relation to experience. A job that seems enjoyable and absorbing to one person is wearisome to another. One person welcomes change and responsibility—another hates and dreads it. A piece of work that seems to have no inherent attractions may prove agreeable because of the happy companionship of fellow-workers associated with it, while another, at first sight more interesting, may lose in comparison because it is done in solitude. Most jobs have their wearisome moments and practically every job demands a certain amount of discipline. The work that needs doing may not be where one wants to live or may be of a type that one is not used to. Under the old regime fear of the consequences of unemployment proved a hard taskmaster and a stern disciplinarian.

But to the extent to which unemployment maintenance is forthcoming from public funds this fear is removed and work and income cease to bear any direct and recognisable relationship to one another. It is of no value to argue that the majority of people prefer to be occupied when as a matter of experience we know that many thousands of men have been compelled to be idle over long periods and have not, in fact, chosen voluntarily to fit themselves for any occupation. This is no matter for pointing an accusing finger. The fault lies not so much in the individuals, who were the unhappy and frustrated victims of circumstance. The chronically unemployed were bitter and ashamed of their position even while they refused to undergo the training, that might possibly have enabled them to change it. But perhaps the most acute feeling of all was their resentment at their lack of social status. They were alternately badgered and cajoled, but they were never given any valid reason for altering their behaviour. They felt unwanted in a community which seemed to have no use for them. Why should they feel any sense of obligation to a society which offered so little outlet for their loyalty and enthusiasm ? If blame is to be apportioned it lies rather with society which had not troubled to integrate its social values. It has needed the war to awaken men to the idea that citizenship has its obligations as well as its rights.

CHAPTER IV

LABOUR CONTROL IN WAR-TIME

I

Synopsis of Chapter

1. The proper utilisation of labour power in war-time depends on war strategy and the course of events. It is, therefore, not possible to establish a lasting scale of priorities, but flexibility is the prime essential.

2. The Schedule of Reserved Occupations prepared before the war broke out was intended to provide this flexibility.

3. When general labour shortage began to be evident steps had to be taken to ration scarce categories of worker and to mobilise woman-power.

4. Orders have been made to prevent the unnecessary movement of workers. The most comprehensive of these is the Essential Work Order which has brought into prominence many problems of industrial discipline.

5. Machinery has had to be devised to determine priorities in the use of labour.

6. Dock labour has been completely decasualised and special arrangements made for the coal-mining industry; these throw into relief some of the problems involved in labour control.

7. Concentration of Industry and Limitation of Supplies have reduced the demand for labour for non-essential purposes.

8. Provision has been made for training workers for new jobs, but this has been both dilatory and inadequate.

9. Welfare arrangements have been made for transferred workers.

10. Assessment of the effectiveness of war-time labour controls can only be tentative as sufficient material for judgment is not yet available to the public. But dependence on voluntary transfer of labour is shown conclusively to be inadequate when speed is needed. Mistakes have been made in training and there has been lack of co-ordination and foresight; the administration has not been sufficiently flexible. Yet, on the whole, a remarkable feat of labour mobilisation has been accomplished.

THE need to mobilise all the labour resources of the country for the war has provided an opportunity for a full-dress experiment in planned labour distribution. The problem to be solved is not the same as that of occupational distribution in peace-time; but the two have sufficient features in common for war-time experience to offer a valuable guide to possible peace-time practice. The objectives of a war-time labour policy can be fairly simply stated. The general aim is to achieve such an allocation of resources between the Forces and industry as will give the most effective striking power while at the same time enabling essential civilian requirements to be met. An increase in the number of fighting men will not be of much use unless adequate arrangements are made for their provisioning and transport and for their equipment with the different types of arms they need. The problem is not primarily a numerical one. Neither the men in the Forces nor the workers in industry can be regarded as undifferentiated units, capable of being moved about at will to fill any vacancy. They differ in age, physique, capacity and industrial experience. The problem is not, even, simply that of choosing the best man for a particular job, but of deciding whether, despite the fact that he may be the best person for that task, he may not be of even greater value in something entirely different. War-time labour needs are definitely lopsided. There is a very strong premium on strong, healthy young men. The main body of the fighting services must necessarily be drawn principally from this section of the population but also the industries on which their equipment mainly depends, engineering, mining, transport and metal working, are just those which in ordinary times have a preponderantly male personnel. There would not be much sense in drafting the workers in these industries into the Forces unless their places could rapidly be filled by workers from other occupations—older men, boys and women—who are not needed in the Services. The extent to which this is possible and the speed at which it can be done depend on the degree of skill required in the jobs they are asked to undertake. Much oan be done to facilitate the use of "green labour". Skilled jobs can be broken down into their component processes and workers trained to perform one process solely. New types of machine can be employed which require less knowledge and experience in the operator, and inventive genius can be focused on the simplification of techniques. But this takes time to accomplish and, however much may be done in this respect, there still remain many jobs in which the necessary knowledge, manipulative dexterity and trained precise observation can be acquired only by long years of practice. There are some men, then, who, however useful they might be in the Armed Forces, are irreplaceable in industry and must be retained because they are key men. There are others who must remain as civilians while new methods are being tried out and new workers trained to take over their work. How long this takes will depend on the speed of invention, the rate of production of the new tools and the time taken to find and train the new workers. It is not possible, therefore, to determine at the outset a scale of priorities and keep to it. Flexibility is the prime essential. The great problem is to keep things moving in step ; to take care that men are not recruited into the Forces more quickly than the equipment for their training and arming becomes available, that the replacement workers are not mobilised before adequate facilities for their training and employment can be arranged and that the Armed Forces are not starved of skilled men in order to pile up armaments that there are not enough trained soldiers to use.

The need for flexibility becomes more apparent when one realises how closely labour requirements are geared to war strategy. It is not merely the all-over relationship of military to civilian numbers that will be affected by changes in policy, but also the relative numbers needed in the various industrial groups. If the War Cabinet decide to concentrate on a campaign of persistent heavy bombing the appropriate industrial pattern is entirely different from what it would have been if bombing were discredited and greater emphasis was put on land and sea fighting. A different kind of armament must be produced in the factories and workshops, employing machines of a different design and workers of different capacity, and a quite different number and type of fighting personnel is needed. Again, the amount and type of labour required in English industry depends on the agreements made with the United States of America as to the allocation of function between them. If the U.S.A. agrees to concentrate on providing certain kinds of munitions, industrial workers in Britain are released either for other types of production or for military duties. When the United Nations decided to invade North Africa preparations had to be made months before to get ready the right kind of arms, clothing, food and transport that are suitable for a desert campaign. If at that time the decision had been taken instead to invade Europe, the demands made on industry would have been different in their relative emphasis.

War strategy itself must be prepared to make necessary adjustments to the course of the war. Whatever agreements Britain and U.S.A. may come to with regard to their respective contributions in men and munitions must obviously depend on their success or failure in meeting the submarine danger. It would be unwise for Britain to rely on America to produce vital munitions if the products of American engineering workshops went to the bottom of the sea instead of reaching their destination. Again, England may find at one point of the war that she is doing more to further her own cause by building tanks and aeroplanes for Russia than by equipping her own army with artillery. Or such an unforeseeable and incalculable event as the fall of France, by completely cutting off certain sources of materials and by rendering certain shipping routes too dangerous, made necessary a fundamental replanning of British production. Before the Lease-Lend Agreement was negotiated, the manufacture of those goods which, unimportant in themselves as they might be for direct war purposes, could be exported and so provide dollar exchange was an essential part of war production, but it ceased to be so when the American produce available to us was no longer restricted by our accumulation of dollars.

If it were not for this perpetual shifting of values the problem of labour mobilisation would be very much simpler. But it is not possible to draw up a scale of priorities that will hold good for more than a very short period. The term " essential " proves to be relative to the moment. As civilian standards are cut down to release more and more labour and materials for war production, many things which were considered necessities in the first year of the war come later to be looked on as amenities that can be quite happily given up for the duration. At one time all available labour is wanted for the manufacture of shells, at another for tanks, at another for aircraft. Building labour plays an important part in the early years in putting up the new factories, preparing new aerodromes, etc. As these are completed it is engineering personnel that is wanted and the builders are then available for the Forces. Then such a development in the war as that which brought a part of the American Army to this country necessitates postponing the calling up of builders until the airfields and other accommodation for the American troops have been provided. There is no need to stress further this point of the impossibility of seeing more than a very short time ahead, but it must be kept constantly in mind in considering the machinery of labour mobilisation.

This constant movement in priorities, which is inextricably bound up with the conduct of the war, puts flexibility as the first essential of any system for labour control. It is necessary for somebody to be in a position to survey the whole field to decide where, at any moment, labour can be most effectively used and to discover the sources from which that labour can be withdrawn with least loss and dislocation to other branches of production. The labour supply of a country is not, however, a fixed and inalterable amount. Even though the size of the population is comparatively stable over a short period, the quality and quantity of the labour power can be very materially expanded. Skill and efficiency can be increased by training and more workers can be drawn into the productive field from groups not previously industrially occupied. In addition, a considerable increase in productivity can be achieved if the people who make up the labour force understand and sympathise with the demands made on them.

II

The experience gained during the war of 1914–18 had made us appreciate the importance of an orderly allocation of labour between the Forces and industry. When the last war broke out few of those in control seem to have realised that battles cannot be won without a properly organised industrial front, and in the early years of the war thousands of skilled and key industrial workers were not only permitted, but encouraged, to volunteer for military duties. The consequent loss in essential war production led to frenzied experiments in selection resulting, in 1917, in a Schedule of Protected Occupations whereby men employed in listed occupations necessary for the war were classified according to age and medical category. As increasing numbers of men were needed for the Forces, withdrawals from civilian work could be made in an orderly fashion, taking into account the situation of the trade at the time and the likelihood of being able to find substitutes to carry on the work.

The administrative experience thus gained was put to use when, in 1938, it began to be obvious that active preparations for war had to be made and already in January, 1939 a Schedule of Reserved Occupations was drawn up. When war started the Schedule was extended to cover a wider range of occupations and it has since been amended from time to time, but the general principles on which it is founded remain the same. The Schedule is drawn up on an occupational basis with an age reservation attached to each occupation. As a general rule the age of reserva-. tion indicates the relative importance of the occupation and is altered as the situation demands. This means that those occupations which are not in the first priority retain their older men but release the younger ones for the Forces, whereas the more essential trades retain a larger proportion of their younger personnel. In some cases men are allowed to volunteer, or may be called up, provided they are to be enrolled in the Services in their trade capacity, but not for General Service. In other cases two ages are associated with an occupation, the lower one indicating the age of reservation for calling up or volunteering for General Service and the higher for service in the trade capacity. In a few very highly important employments, such as certain types of mining or agriculture, there has been at times a complete ban on withdrawal for military duties.

It is obvious that a very considerable degree of flexibility can be introduced into this system by careful alteration of the ages of reservation. As more workers are trained to take their places in these occupations, bulk withdrawals of the younger men can be made. But it may happen that while a particular occupation is, in general, of great importance there may be individuals whose actual work cannot be considered as essential as the service they could give in another capacity. On the other hand, there may be individual men carrying on work of especial importance, even though they fall within a category which, as a whole, is not rated as essential. Two ways have been found for meeting this difficulty. In the first place, any of the Military Service Departments may apply for the waiver of the operation of the Schedule in the case of a man whose qualifications are such that he would be of particular value to the Service concerned. And secondly, it is open to an employer to ask for the deferment of the calling up of an individual on the grounds that the job he is doing is of vital importance and that it is not possible for it to be done by a substitute. The classification is, therefore, on both an occupational and individual basis and is intended to ensure that the rather rough and ready selection by age and trade shall be refined by a more careful scrutiny and evaluation of individual capacity.

III

For a considerable time after the outbreak of war there was no general scarcity of labour. In fact, it was exactly the opposite —it seemed difficult to take up the existing slack. An increase in the number of unemployed might have been expected as an immediate result of the declaration of war because productive and trading activities are dislocated by shock and apprehension. But the numbers on the registers continued to increase until February, 1940, when no less than 10·3% of insured workers were unemployed. From that point each month showed a decline in those out of work until by the end of that year the great majority of those on the registers were only technically unemployed, i.e., they were moving from one job to another and were recorded as out of work for a short period because the two jobs did not completely dovetail. The figures given in the *Ministry of Labour Gazette* in December of that year showed that 43% of those on the register had been unemployed for less than two weeks, 53% for less than four weeks and that only the small total of 54,000, of whom 75% were over 50 years of age, had been out of work for more than a year. By that time, therefore, the " hard core " of unemployment had been liquidated and general scarcity was beginning to make itself felt. The length of time taken for this *dénouement* to be reached is to be accounted for partly, by the fact that there were a million and a quarter persons out of work when the war started and partly, by the slow pace at which war production got into its stride. Although a programme of rearmament had been planned more than a year before the war began, there had been little sense of urgency to quicken the movement from plan to practice and probably the " phoney war " did its bit to keep the pace slow even after the war had started. New plants had to be erected and machine tools to be produced before the mass demands for quickly trained labour could be made effective. In these circumstances little direct organisation of transference was required in the early days of the war.

The Government had provided itself with powers, should such control prove necessary, by passing the Control of Employment Act immediately the war broke out. This gave authority to the Minister of Labour and National Service to collect the fullest information as to the movements of those types of labour which might be scarce in relation to war demands and enabled him to exercise some influence on the use of skilled labour by prohibiting certain employers from advertising for, or engaging, specified kinds of workman without permission. The Act in itself conferred only general powers and these could not be made effective unless the Minister issued an Order, before which he was bound to have close consultation with representatives of the employers and workers concerned ·and report their recommendations to the House. In fact, however, no use was made of the Act except that in April of the following year an Order was issued which prohibited employers in the building and civil engineering contracting industries from advertising for carpenters, joiners and bricklayers.

Both the careful terms of the Act and the unwillingness to make use even of the slight powers conferred by it illustrate the reluctance on the part of the Government to interfere with normal peace-time industrial procedure. The Schedule of Reserved Occupations exerted an indirect influence since there was an inducement to those who preferred civilian to military service to transfer from less essential to more essential work in order to come within the reserved groups. Similarly Regulations issued in 1940 disqualified for insurance benefit an unemployed worker who refused to take work of national importance, provided it was paid at standard rates, merely because it was outside his usual occupation or because he had been accustomed to higher wages in his own former trade. But apart from this, reliance was mainly placed on persuasion and appeal on the one hand and on movements in wages on the other. The first of these proved totally inadequate to effect its purpose ; the second was disorderly and created further problems of its own.

Employers were urged to release skilled workers for work that was more vital to the war effort and workers were asked to notify their Trade Unions or the Employment Exchange if they considered that their skill might be put to better use in some other occupation of greater national importance. But no amount of eloquence on the part of members of the Government and no amount of cajolery and exhortation over the radio could have any appreciable effect in such a matter. Every employer naturally thought that his work was important ; even if it was not directly connected with munitions he could argue that it was an essential contribution to civilian needs or was valuable in helping to maintain our export markets. His knowledge of other types of production was necessarily limited and he had no means of finding out how the various industries cogged into one another in the economic machine. It was, therefore, impossible for him to estimate the relative importance of different enterprises and know whether the Government's admonitions were addressed to him or not. The worker was equally unreceptive and for equally good reasons. After such a couple of decades as England had just passed through, the holding down of a decent job at reasonable rates of pay was considered enough of an achievement by almost any worker. They had never before been asked to consider their work from the point of view of its importance in the life of the nation. It was not any lack of patriotism on the part of the workers, but simply the effect of the industrial experience of a life-time, that it never entered the minds of most of those who listened to the exhortations of the radio that the appeal to transfer their skill to more essential jobs was really directed to them, and was urging them to take the initiative in giving up regular, decently paid work in order to offer themselves for other employment. Few of them indeed were even aware that their skill could easily be made applicable to war production.

But if verbal persuasion had little effect in inducing workers to transfer to other jobs, competition in wage rates undoubtedly had more success. Whether it achieved the desired object of drawing the workers into work in which they could be of the greatest use in waging the war is more open to question. Firms outdid one another in competitive bidding for engineering personnel. The papers carried advertisements offering bonuses and specially attractive conditions of work in addition to normal payment. Some firms even sent out labour scouts in the evenings to persuade skilled men to leave their present jobs for others. The Select Committee on National Expenditure in commenting on these practices pointed out that advertisement does not increase the available personnel and that an offer of high pay is no guarantee that the worker enticed away is being used to greater advantage by the firm to which he has been persuaded to go. The results of such movement might, in fact, be definitely uneconomic. For example, the poaching of one highly skilled man in the machine tool industry, one of the serious bottlenecks in aircraft production, might easily throw out of work a very large number of men while the seduced worker was performing less important work at a higher wage elsewhere. As long as employers had the chance of getting skilled workers by these methods they were not prepared to give adequate attention to dilution measures nor to bother to make arrangements for the training of new workers. Although the Select Committee was at this time unanimously in favour of using voluntary methods whenever possible they came to the conclusion that " Control of inducement would be preferable to the control of labour, but it may be that a measure of both may be necessary ".

The Emergency Powers (Defence) Act which came into force in May, 1940, gave the Minister of Labour and National Service power to deal with this situation, by conferring on him the authority to make Defence Regulations, requiring everybody to place themselves, their services and their property at the disposal of His Majesty.[1] Regulation 58A issued under the Act on the same day granted the Minister the control and use of all labour by giving him power to direct any person to do any job specified, to require people to register themselves and give information about themselves, and employers to keep and produce records of their labour. The various Orders which have subsequently been issued to control and direct labour have been made under this Regulation which has, in practice, superseded the Control of Employment Act of the previous year.

The first of these Orders, the Undertakings (Restriction on Engagement) Order, was designed to prevent the enticement of workers in the building and engineering industries by controlling placements. No employer in these industries might henceforth engage, nor a worker seek work, except through an Employment Exchange and advertisement and unregulated transfer became illegal acts. At later dates similar restrictions were placed on the engagement of workers in the shipbuilding and electrical equipment industries. At the same time as the first Order was issued a Labour Supply Board was set up under the chairmanship of the Ministry with local Committees composed of local officials together with men with practical experience in industry. Inspectors of Labour Supply were appointed to visit firms and see that skilled labour was used to the best advantage. They were instructed to keep compulsion as a last resort and to try to advise managers to reorganise so as to economise skilled labour.

The effect of this new machinery was not merely to stop the poaching of workers but practically to stop transfer altogether. The Minister had so impressed upon his officers his preference for voluntary co-operative effort that they were rarely prepared to use their full powers and the Select Committee found itself

[1] *Ministry of Labour Gazette*, June, 1940, p. 156.

bound to urge that there should be more speed and less delicacy, in dealing with matters which were becoming so urgent. By the end of 1940 the problem was no longer confined to the more highly skilled workers; there was a general shortage of labour which bid fair to become more acute as more and more of the newly erected war plants swung into full production. Slowly and rather reluctantly it was beginning to be recognised that the task with which we were faced was something bigger than that of rationing a few specially scarce categories of workers between employers; the problem that had to be tackled was that of planning the whole labour supply of the country so that every available person was used in the most economical way on the most urgent jobs.

By the beginning of 1941 the main features of this problem were beginning to emerge. (1) We needed to survey our total labour resources so as to know what was available. (2) Some scheme for establishing priorities in the use of labour had to be worked out so as to ensure that what was available was put to the best use. (3) As most of the plants which required large staff had, for security reasons, been sited in areas that were remote from centres of population and could not, therefore, draw on local labour supplies, means must be found for selecting those classes of workers who could be moved to where they were needed with least dislocation to existing industries and with least personal hardship. (4) If workers were to be moved from their homes to work in distant areas, provision must be made for their lodging, welfare and social recreation. (5) Labour resources must be extended by tapping unused reserves in sections of the community which are not normally engaged in industrial work. (6) Training facilities must be devised and increased so as to fit the new workers for the jobs they are required to undertake.

In solving these problems a comprehensive set of controls has been brought into existence but, while the period since the beginning of 1941 has seen a continuous growth in Government power, the policy has remained one of persuasion rather than compulsion. In a speech to the Works Management Association towards the end of 1940 Mr. Bevin, the Minister of Labour and National Service, laid great stress on this aspect of his labour control and insisted on the importance of retaining the democratic habit of basing our actions on policies which have been the subject of full discussion with those principally concerned.

It is true [he said] that Parliament gave to the Government very elaborate and comprehensive powers, but we have worked in the main on this voluntary basis and industry as a whole has responded.

D

. . . Our enemies rely on compulsion, the Gestapo, threats of the Concentration Camp, fear ; we work on the old basis of confidence and freedom.[1]

By the establishment of a series of Controls, the Government has provided itself with sanctions to be held in reserve, but for the most part, the principal effort has been to persuade the workers to choose the job for which he or she is wanted and to give every opportunity to the individual to explain any special circumstances which he believes ought to be taken into account in deciding what can be expected of him.   As more and more of the country's labour power has been mobilised and as labour shortages have become increasingly acute, a greater degree of compulsion and a narrower range of choice have been imposed. But this development has been both gradual and slow.

An essential prerequisite for the transfer of workers is the fullest and most comprehensive information of the resources available for allocation.   For men of military age this was obtainable from the necessary registration of age classes under the Armed Forces Act, but there was no knowledge of the numbers and types of women available nor of men over military age. Provision for this was made by the Registration for Employment Order issued in March, 1941, and by a series of registrations based partly on age classes and partly on occupational groups, extensive data of labour reserves have been accumulated.   The obligation to register and to give the necessary information on the day appointed for one's age or occupational class is statutory, but the decision as to whether the registrant should be transferred or not, and if so, to what work he should be sent, depends on a number of considerations which have to be weighed against one another.   These considerations fall into two categories : (a) those relative to the nature of the work done, and (b) those relating to the personal circumstances of the individual.   The second group of considerations has come to be of increasing importance as the stringency of the labour situation has made it necessary to depend more and more on woman-power.   The obstacles to mobility to which reference has been made in earlier chapters can be overcome to a marked extent in war-time so far as men are concerned.   Men enlisted in the Forces are at the disposal of authority and can be sent anywhere at any time, so that those who are retained in civilian occupations as an alternative to military duties cannot be allowed to put personal predilections before national service.   Exceptional circumstances are taken into account by the Military Service (Hardship) Committees but, on the whole, men can be looked upon as generally transferable.   But

[1] *Ministry of Labour Gazette*, Oct. 1940, p. 260.

the rôle of women in social life sharply differentiates them from men in that respect. It is the women who have to look after the home, prepare the meals and care for the children. A woman may be able to combine these household responsibilities with one kind of job, carried on near to her home or which allows her to get to the shops on her way to or from work, while another job, a little farther away or not so well arranged as to hours, might be beyond her powers. Such matters are highly individual. One or two general principles may be laid down, such as that a woman who has the care of her young children cannot be expected to take on full-time industrial work, but for the most part the decision as to whether she is available for employment and, if so, with what qualifying conditions, must depend on a careful balancing of many factors peculiar to the individual. For this reason great stress has been laid on the personal interview as part of the procedure under the Registration for Employment Order. The woman whose registration documents show her to be either unoccupied or unemployed (the technical difference is that the unoccupied worker does not normally seek work for pay whereas the unemployed one does but, at the moment, has not got it) or is engaged on work that is not rated as vital for the war effort, is called to an interview at which she is given an opportunity to discuss her household responsibilities. The main purpose of the interview is to establish two points : (1) whether it is reasonable to expect her to undertake full-time industrial work or not, and (2) whether she is " mobile ", i.e. whether she can be expected to take up work in another locality or must be employed within reasonable daily travelling distance of her own home. If the worker and the interviewing officer (who is always a woman) fail to agree, the matter is referred to the Woman's Panel of the Local Advisory Committee attached to the Employment Exchange. The Woman's Panel, which is intended to represent a cross section of the local community, is likely to know and understand the registrant's problems, many of which may draw their particular colour from the peculiarities of local industry, housing and transport with which an official, who is not usually a local person, may not be familiar. The aim is to get a definition of what can reasonably be expected of a woman which commends itself to the good sense and fairness of the general public. When these questions have been satisfactorily settled, the woman's name is put on the appropriate National Work Register as available for work in the locality, or as mobile.

From what has been said it has been indicated that a woman who is already engaged on vital war work is not usually summoned for interview, but there may have to be exceptions to

this rule. This is a matter which has caused much bewilderment to the public and a good deal of heartburning to the individuals primarily concerned. Many of the factories producing
essential munitions have deliberately been sited in remote country
districts where they are less likely to suffer interruption from
enemy action. All the labour they need must be brought to them
from elsewhere. It may, therefore, be necessary to transfer to
them the women from more populous regions who have been
classed as " mobile " even though they are already doing exactly
the same sort of work as the jobs to which they are to be moved,
because in a centre of population there are many local women,
with household responsibilities, who can step into the vacancies
thus created but who could not reasonably be expected to move
from their homes.

To facilitate this movement the areas of the country have
been classified according to their labour situation : those in
which the supply of women is inadequate to the demand and
which must import women workers, those in which the local
supply of women virtually balances the demand, and those in
which the supply of immobile women is enough to meet local
demands and which have a surplus of mobile women who can
be transferred to other areas.

When women were first registered for transfer to war work they
were offered a wide choice of occupation. There were so many
new branches of production coming into existence at once, and
such huge numbers of workers to be placed, that a high degree
of individual selection was quite practicable. But it was also
part of a deliberate policy to go very slowly along such a new
and untried path as the industrial conscription of women. The
Government recognised that this involved much more than the
fitting of so many industrial machines into their appropriate
niches. There were many old prejudices and traditions to be
overcome or modified as well as many justifiable fears to be laid.
It was surprising to find how large a proportion of young women
had never slept away from their homes or had never been separated,
for even a short time, from their families. Many parents were
extremely apprehensive that their daughters would be forced to
be in close contact, both at work and in their lodgings, with
people of coarser social manners or with offensive habits and
vocabulary. If women had been ruthlessly compelled into particular jobs the social discontent aroused might have had a serious
effect both on war output and on general morale. But as time
has gone on the choice of work has been more and more narrowly
restricted. The need to economise labour has proved so overriding a consideration that available resources have had to be
concentrated at the particular point indicated by the war needs

of the moment. But also people have quickly got used to the idea of compulsion. Most, it is true, dislike it, particularly when it involves moving to a locality far from home, but experience has toned down some of the lurid pictures that anticipation painted.

If a worker does not agree to undertake the work offered to her she may be " directed " to it by a National Service Officer to whom the Minister of Labour has delegated his powers under Regulation· 58A. She may appeal against this decision to a local Appeals Board—a tri-partite body composed of a Chairman (usually a lawyer) and one representative each of employers and workers who may advise, but cannot compel, the National Service Officer to change his decision. The Appeals Board is not allowed to offer judgments on the relative importance of the worker's present job and the one to which she has been directed —that is a matter for the Employment Exchange which alone has the relevant knowledge on which to decide. Its business is to consider the matter from the point of view of the personal circumstances of the worker, who may claim that the job to which she is being sent may involve her in exceptional hardship. If the decision is against the worker, there is no further right of appeal, and if she refuses to transfer she may be prosecuted and, subject to conviction, fined, or imprisoned or both.

The mobilisation of woman power for industry has been further affected by the passing of the National Service (2) Act in December, 1941. Before that date women could be enrolled only as volunteers in the three women's auxiliary services, the W.R.N.S., the A.T.S. and the W.A.A.F., and although much propaganda was directed towards persuading women to enter these services the response was inadequate. Women, called for interview under the Registration for Employment Order, were invariably given the choice of volunteering for the Services as an alternative to industrial employment, but comparatively few availed themselves of the opportunity. The difficulty was not felt equally by all three Services—the W.R.N.S., for example, which is much smaller than the other two, has generally had a waiting list of applicants and has been able to be fairly selective in its choice, but every service has experienced serious scarcity in certain categories of worker. As long as the supply of women was so small, manpower in the Forces was necessarily used for all sorts of non-combatant jobs and it was with the the object of releasing as many men as possible for fighting service that it was decided to apply military conscription to women. The women affected by the Act become equally liable with men for compulsory service with the Armed Forces, with the exception that they cannot be compelled to undertake duties which involve the use of lethal weapons ; but once again, the special rôle of the woman in the family has been recognised by confining liability to single, widowed and divorced women who have no children of their own living with them. By Royal Proclamation the provisions of the Act have been applied to women between the ages of 19 and 30 but, in fact, only the age-classes from 19–23 inclusive have been called up. The experience gained from dealing with these groups shows that the marriage rate rises very steeply wth every year of the 'twenties. Moreover, as a result of two years of propaganda, patriotic feeling and selection through the Registration for Employment Order, a very large proportion of young women had already entered war work from which it would be uneconomical to withdraw them. It is not worth while the man-power involved to comb through the dossiers of several millions of people for the sake of the few thousands of single or widowed women, who alone are liable under the Act, if, in addition, there is a strong probability that they are already employed in the types of work which are as essential to the war effort as the military duties to which they would be called.

By no means all those in the younger age groups have been compelled to enter the Services. The application of military conscription to women has been a bold and revolutionary step, without precedent in any country. It was necessary to move cautiously in order to mitigate as far as possible the fears and distress of the young women and of their parents. The conditions in certain sections of the Women's Services had been the subject of serious adverse criticism, part of it undoubtedly well founded, but much of it the result of ignorance, fostered and spread by a sensation-loving Press. Whether justified or not, however, it had the effect of exaggerating the apprehensions that would anyway have been felt by a population confronted for the first time with so stupendous a change. If the early administration of the Act had been harsh or unimaginative the resentment aroused might have lowered public confidence and reduced the general willingness to make sacrifices. But there was a further reason for a cautious policy in that those in control were themselves moving forward in the dark. While there was accurate information regarding the numbers of liable women in the various age classes, there was none of how many were still available for military duties. Conscripted women share with men the right to claim exemption on grounds of conscience and to ask for postponement of calling up (which, if granted, may be continually renewed) on account of the exceptional hardship that would be involved in their transference to the Forces. It was quite impossible to estimate in advance how many women would be affected. While there were reasons for believing that their claims of conscience were unlikely to differ appreciably from those made by men, it was fairly certain that their domestic obligations would entitle them to special consideration on grounds of hardship. But what proportion would be so affected could not possibly be foretold. And similarly there was no means of knowing beforehand what proportion of them had got into employment which would rank as reserved occupations and would therefore not be available for transfer. The numbers required for the Services, while much larger than they could obtain through voluntary enrolment, were still strictly limited, both by the accommodation and training facilities as well as by the number of jobs that women could be expected to undertake. If the women available in the younger age classes proved to be more than the Services needed it would be necessary to make an arbitrary selection which would undoubtedly cause needless suffering by putting many round pegs into square holes. The sensible thing was to allow people to classify themselves according to their own wishes. Accordingly, women called up to military service have, as a matter of administrative practice, been allowed to express an option for the form of national service—military or industrial—that they prefer to undertake.

Although, therefore, the statutory liability to service in the Forces remains, and it is expressly stated that no guarantee is given to allocate a woman to the type of service for which she has expressed a preference, in practice no woman has actually been compelled to enter the Armed Forces if she has " opted " for industry. But the fact that women called up under the Act are technically military conscripts has made possible their industrial allocation on rather stricter terms and with less individual range of choice than those drafted into industry under the Registration for Employment Order. Moreover, they are automatically served with a written " direction " in order to make it quite clear that they are conscripted and there is no right of appeal against this direction to a local Appeals Board ; it must be obeyed. This is not as harsh as it may appear. In common with those who have opted for military service, they have already had an opportunity of making an application to the Military Service (Hardship) Committee. By the time they reach the stage of " direction " they have been judged " mobile " and consequently are available for transfer anywhere.

The options expressed by women conscripts have shown a remarkable steadiness in pattern. Usually about one-third opt for the Services, one-third for industrial work and the remainder express no preference at all. At first sight it may seem strange that so large a proportion of young women are indifferent to the kind of work they will be called upon to do, but it is generally found that the preponderant majority of " non-optants " are already doing vital war work and realise that it would be unlikely that they would be withdrawn from it.

The choice of alternatives offered to women conscripts has rendered this large body a particularly flexible instrument of labour policy, a point of special importance when it is remembered that these age classes contain by far the largest proportion of " mobile " women workers. While always retaining the basic freedom offered to the woman, it has enabled the administration to direct the flow of labour along the channels where it was most needed by applying and releasing pressure at special points. For example, the non-optants who are in less urgent war work may at one time be enrolled in the Services, at another in the particular sections of the munitions trades where extra personnel are most urgently required. When the labour shortage has been exceptionally severe in certain fields, as, for example, in the Nursing Services, further recruits have been gained by allowing women to change their original option provided they wished to enrol in this work. At other times, when large numbers were urgently demanded in the Forces, women in reserved occupations have been allowed to volunteer even though they were doing work from which they would not ordinarily be withdrawn. This variation in administrative practice not only regulates the supply of labour into the various employments but has the added advantage of using a process of self-selection to get workers into the jobs where they most wish to be.

IV

The machinery for the control of labour described so far is concerned with only one side of the problem. It provides for the mobilisation of all available personnel, for its classification into groups according to its availability and suitability, and for its direction into various occupations enjoying a high priority. But little is achieved if the stream coming out by the exit gate is as large as the flow directed into the entrance. In ordinary times there is no reason why workers should not be entirely free to leave their employment if they see an opportunity to better themselves ; and similarly there is no objection to an employer dismissing a worker if he finds him redundant, inefficient or indisciplined. But with the war-time need to ration resources in short supply this freedom neutralises the attempt to ensure the economical use of labour. Until 1941, however, no restrictions were placed upon a worker's freedom to leave his employment at will nor upon an employer's freedom to dismiss, and much of the carefully allocated labour was wasted. The Essential Work (General Provisions) Order issued in March of that year attempted to stop up this leakage. The Order applies only to " scheduled undertakings " and before placing any firm on this register, the Minister must be satisfied not only that the firm is engaged on essential work but that the conditions of employment are such as not to prejudice the interests of the workers unduly by this restriction on their liberty. The terms and general conditions offered by the firm must be at least as favourable as those agreed by collective negotiation, training for workers must be provided if necessary and there must be satisfactory provision for welfare, both inside and outside the factory. The welfare inside the factory is, of course, the direct responsibility of the firm. Outside welfare, which includes suitable housing, travelling and feeding facilities, need not be provided by the firm, but unless these amenities do, in fact, exist the firm cannot be scheduled. The Order prohibits a scheduled firm from dismissing any member of the staff (including managerial) from its employment and any worker from leaving his job without the written permission of the National Service Officer. The worker is guaranteed a minimum wage, even if temporarily unemployed, provided he is available for, and capable of work and is " willing to perform any service outside his usual occupation which in the circumstances he can reasonably be asked to perform during any period when work is not available for him in his usual occupation in the undertaking ". As with direction under Regulation 58A, appeals against the decision of the National Service Officer may be made to the Local Appeals Board which may recommend, but cannot compel, a change of verdict.

The Essential Work Order has helped to focus attention on the seriousness of the problem of discipline that emerges when the shortage of labour is acute. The majority of workers are decent, self-respecting persons, whose sense of fitness makes them efficient and industrious workers without any need for disciplinary measures. It would be as absurd to suggest that most workers do a good job of work because they are afraid of getting the sack or a reduction in pay if they slack as to say that the majority of law-abiding citizens refrain from stealing their neighbours' property because they are afraid of being spotted by the police. This is particularly true at the present time when strong patriotic fervour acts as a further spur to effort. But just as between the territories of the shiningly honest and the positive thief there is a No-Man's-Land peopled by weaker brethren, who sometimes allow themselves to fall below accepted standards of honesty if they think there is a fair chance of concealment, so too there are workers who, while generally doing a fair day's work, are inclined to dodge work when possible or to allow themselves time off for frivolous reasons. In ordinary times many of these are kept in the straight path by fear of unemployment, but this fear is removed at present, especially in firms under the Essential Work Order. The employer can get the permission of the National Service Officer to dismiss a man who is persistently late or absent, but this is a very slight deterrent to a worker who knows that he will be snapped up again at once. In more serious cases the firm can appeal for the man to be served with a " direction " and prosecuted if he fails to carry it out adequately, but the procedure is extremely slow and cumbersome. In part, this is deliberate and is in line with the policy of the Ministry of Labour to keep compulsion in reserve to be used only as a last resort. An amendment that was introduced after a few months' experience of the Order permits the employer to suspend the worker for three days without pay as a disciplinary measure, and the worker is allowed to appeal if he thinks he has been unfairly treated. But while this has some effect on the casual offender, it has no influence on the persistent. An important cause of absenteeism (which will be discussed more fully later) has been the ability of workers employed at high piece rates to make much larger weekly incomes than they have been accustomed to, at a time when there is very little on which to spend. The majority have not slowed down on this' account, partly because of genuine patriotism and partly because they welcome the opportunity to put by for the future. But there are a good many who are not affected by either of these considerations and who persistently stay away from work when they have earned the amount they want for their immediate needs and pleasures. A short suspension of work without pay is no punishment to this group.

The Essential Work Order is, within its own boundaries, the most comprehensive of all the labour controls since it covers everybody within the scheduled undertaking irrespective of age and sex. It does not matter whether the employee got into the job by direction or persuasion or by his own volition, nor does it matter if he or she is above the age of registration ; once employed by a scheduled firm he loses his freedom to leave. But although the scheduling, which began rather slowly, now covers over eight million people there are still large sections of industry which do not come either under the Order nor within the occupations covered by the Restriction on Engagement Order. As far as men are concerned the control is fairly complete. Their liability to military service is held over because they are in reserved occupations or because a special claim for deferment has been made in respect of them, and as soon as they leave the job their liability is once again in force. With women, however, there were for a time many loopholes. At the moment of registration a woman might be doing a job from which she could not be withdrawn. Unless it happened to be a scheduled firm there was nothing to prevent her from giving in her notice and finding herself another job in less essential work at higher pay or nearer to her own home. The Employment of Women (Control of Engagement) Order came into force in February, 1942, to prevent this waste. Women between certain ages (at present, 18 and 41) are not permitted to take employment except through the Employment Exchange, and employers are prohibited from advertising for or engaging women, who come within the scope of the Order, except through the official agency. It is the responsibility of the employer to see that any worker he engages directly is not covered by the Order, which means that she must be outside the age limits, or have children of her own under 14 living with her, or be in certain employments. The position created by the Order is, therefore, that a woman employed by a firm which is not scheduled under the Essential Work Order is free to leave if 'she wishes, but she and her employer are bound to notify the facts to the Employment Exchange [1] and as she cannot get another job except through the Exchange there is less danger of her drifting off to less important work. What is more difficult for the Order to check is the practice of leaving work and fading back into the domestic background, thus evading the compulsion to do war work altogether. In theory there is a check on this since the Exchange has particulars of the woman's registration and can periodically go through the registers and verify that she is actually performing the work there given as her occupation. In practice this is impossible, in view of the immense amount of clerical and administrative work entailed in keeping track of so many millions of people.

The Employment Exchanges are well qualified to guide into employment workers whose industrial qualifications and experience make them suitable for classification in one or other of the recognised occupational groupings. But they have neither the necessary knowledge nor staff to place those whose qualifications are of a more professional nature. Some of these may belong to types of employment such as teachers, hospital almoners, house property managers, etc., which have their own professional associations equipped to act as employment bureaux. Others may have qualifications which are more individual and for whom no such body can cater. Women in either of these categories may be given a permit to find work through their own efforts or through one of a list of approved agencies. The permit specifies the kind of work that the holder is permitted to do and fixes a time limit within which the job must be obtained.

---

[1] This regulation was later extended to cover all employees, whether under E.W.O. or not.

The Control of Employment Order completed the machinery for the mobilisation of all full-time labour, but the situation in 1942 made it evident that even the most economical use of these resources would not bridge the gap between demand and supply. The only reserve which still remained to be tapped consisted of women whose household responsibilities were sufficiently heavy to exempt them from full-time compulsory work, but who might be prevailed upon to do a certain number of hours per week. The mobilisation of this last reserve followed the familiar course. At first, persuasion and propaganda and consultation with representative organisations to help solve the difficulties; next, exercise of pressure while still retaining the voluntary nature of the decision; finally, the resort to compulsion by means of the Control of Employment (Directed Persons) Order which came into force in May, 1943.[1]

The difficulties in getting a large body of part-time women into industry have been at least as much due to the reluctance of the employers as of the workers. The reorganisation of a firm so as to employ labour for varying periods of time presents many ticklish problems. The shifts are not easy to arrange if consideration is to be given both to the work of the business and to the needs of the workers' households, each of which has its own individual characteristics. There is also danger of a certain amount of resentment on the part of the women who are compelled to work full time when they see their fellow-workers released in time to do their household shopping and cooking. The majority of women, whether with families officially relying on them or not, have to do a considerable amount of domestic work and it is rare for a woman worker to be able to rely, as a male worker can, on having most of this burden lifted from her shoulders. Again, in such businesses as retail distribution, which seems particularly suitable for part-time employment because of the variation throughout the day in the amount of custom, the part-timers are naturally concentrated in the rush hours and this means that the full-timers are left with the rather trying and bothersome work of cleaning up, rearranging stock and preparing for the next day's work when the part-time employees go home. In factory work, there is the difficult task of assigning responsibility for faulty work or bad treatment of tools when more than one worker is employed on the same machine on different days or during different parts of the same day.

[1] This Order gives power to the Minister to direct women between the ages of 18 and 45 into part-time employment up to a maximum of 30 hours a week. Women with children under 14 living with them are exempt and no woman can be directed under the Order to work which is beyond reasonable daily travelling distance. In effect the Order applies the Essential Work Order to part-time work, which up to this time had not been controlled even in scheduled undertakings.

Many firms have, however, managed to overcome all these obstacles by careful planning. The success has probably been greatest with those firms which were accustomed regularly to re-engage their women employees, who had left them on marriage, to help them during their seasonal rush. These women were already familiar with the routine of the firm and could fit easily into place. Even those who had not been re-employed since marriage had experience of the machinery and material to help them. The adjustment of women who have had no previous industrial experience has been a more serious matter but many thousands have rapidly grown accustomed to the work, most of which, of course, has had to be confined to repetition processes which can be easily learned. There are very many women who welcome this opportunity to share in productive work and who enjoy the companionship of the factory as a contrast to the loneliness of their domestic lives. The combination of duties has proved a real stimulus, and it is significant that many factories have found the output of the part-timers to be proportionately higher than that of the full-time workers.

The use of compulsory powers has proved necessary, however, because so many firms have been unwilling to try the experiment of using part-time women or have shirked the hard thinking which is a necessary prerequisite of a successful scheme. They have relied on making good their claim to deferment of withdrawal of their full-time staff. In those frequent cases where the work of the firm was not of the first priority and yet could be considered a necessary contribution to the war effort, the Employment Exchange was at a loss if it could not offer substitutes for the workers it wished to transfer elsewhere. The control of part-time labour enables this difficulty to be overcome. By the offer of an adequate number of part-time workers, dilatory firms can be spurred to undertake the necessary planning which releases the workers needed for more urgent jobs.

V

To concentrate labour in those sections of the industrial field where it is most wanted, the problem has to be attacked simultaneously from two separate sides. In the first place a scale of priorities must be settled for the first call on supplies that are scarce. As has been pointed out earlier, this scale must be the subject of constant revision as the position of various occupations relatively to one another is perpetually changing. A new move in the strategy of war has its repercussions on the types and quantities of armaments required; or the course of the war may cut off certain sources of raw materials or manufactured goods or make others newly available. Sometimes a comparativaly small occupation may rush up the priority scale because shortage of its products is acting as a bottle-neck and holding up output in a much bigger and more important industry. But apart from external causes of this sort, it is obvious that the more labour that is directed into one occupation, the less urgent is it for it to have further supplies, until the point is reached when labour can be of more use if deflected into another industry. The estimate of priority, that is, is concerned primarily with the comparison of the marginal value of additional supplies of labour, a much more difficult matter to assess with any nicety than the relative importance of industries as a whole, and one which it is much more difficult to explain to the public.

During the period when reliance was placed on voluntary incentives to transfer, little was done to determine priority scales and when, later, machinery was set up for the purpose it was not realised that production priority and labour priority were two separate, though related, problems. The Production Executive, a committee composed of the Ministers of the Supply Departments with the Minister of Labour in the chair, determined the priority to be given to different types of munitions and it was assumed that this was adequate guidance for the correct movement of labour. Growing experience gradually showed the danger of making all-embracing correlations of this sort and a new body was established (a sub-committee of the Labour Supply Co-ordinating Committee) to fix labour priorities more accurately. The Sub-committee meets regularly at short intervals and, on the basis of information collected from the regional offices of the Supply Departments and the Minister of Labour, determines the order of priority in the demands of individual firms engaged in war production for labour of different grades. These particulars are circulated to the regions and firms are supplied with labour in the order of urgency indicated. If local labour is inadequate, a report is sent to Headquarters and the deficiency made up by supplies from other regions. In addition to this general routine, orders to fill bottleneck vacancies for key workers may be circulated and are given preference for the time being over all other priorities.

The second line of attack is through variations in the rate and extent of withdrawal. Division into reserved and unreserved industries is all very well as a first rough-and-ready method of drawing a line of demarcation, but it cannot hope to be more than this. Just as when the guidance of workers into jobs is under consideration, it is recognised that an individual firm, even though in an industry which rates low in the scale of priorities, may be engaged on a particular job which entitles it to a first claim on available supplies of labour, so too, when withdrawal is being dealt with the same possibility must be kept in mind. There are two methods employed with the object of getting a greater delicacy of adjustment of supply to demand. In the first place, the various occupations inside the reserved industries are accorded different treatment. For example, there may be an overall reservation of workers engaged in productive processes but not of those employed in ancillary work (clerical, packing, etc.). In the second place, the number of reserved industries has been reduced and greater emphasis placed on the examination of the nature and value of the work done by the individual. For this purpose, there have been set up over forty District Manpower Boards which began their operations early in 1942. Each Board consists of five officials—a Chairman, a Labour Supply Officer, a Military Recruiting Officer, a Deferment Officer and a Woman Power Officer. Its job is to examine the applications made (generally by the employer, occasionally by the worker himself) for the deferment of the withdrawal of an individual employee on the ground that the work he is doing is of vital importance in war production. The Board may grant indefinite deferment or may allow the firm a few months in which to make other arrangements or may allow it to retain the employee until the Exchange is able to provide a substitute.

While the effect of this procedure is undoubtedly to introduce a greater degree of flexibility, the contrast between the work of the Man-power Boards and the operation of the Schedule of Reserved Occupations has not been as marked in practice as at first sight appears likely. Many employers seem to have acted on the policy that it is worth while to ask for deferment of every worker whose withdrawal is threatened, without giving serious consideration to the question as to whether they could, by tightening things up a little here or reorganising there, make shift to manage without him. There is always the chance that the application might be favourably received, and even if it is eventually turned down the period of delay during which the case is awaiting enquiry postpones, for a few months at least, the unpleasant moment when new arrangements have to be made. The number of girls of 20 and 21 who, according to their employers' applications, were performing pivotal work and whose withdrawal would bring disaster to the firm can only lead to the conclusion that the majority of young women have been content to work for remarkably low wages, considering the incalculable value of their work to their employers. There are, of course, many true instances in which, particularly in small firms, the calling up of the male staff has, indeed, left one or two girls as the sole links in the continuity of the firm's administration, and in such cases the loss of the only employees with knowledge of the firm's work and clientèle may lead to a serious slowing down in output. And in other cases, the girls were taken on and trained to replace male staff before the conscription of women was officially contemplated, and the employer finds himself faced with the whole dreary business of commencing again with another batch of green workers. There is no wonder that he should make every effort to keep those on whom he has already spent so much time and patience. But much more often the application has been made by an employer who does not want the bother of substituting new workers for those to whom he has already got used. Yet if their women staff had resigned in peace-time in order to get married, most of these employers would not have dreamed of trying to prevent them from going. They would have taken it as the normal course of events, would most likely have themselves insisted on resignation and would have found themselves in six months or so just as used to and dependent on their new staff as they had been on their old.

It has taken much time for the Man-power Boards to learn to distinguish between serious and more frivolous applications for deferment, partly because of the overwhelming burden of work with which they had to cope in the first few months of their existence and partly because it is only by carrying on for some time that they can accumulate that comprehensive and detailed knowledge of the requirements of firms in different types of industry, on which competent judgment depends. But there has been a second factor which has brought deferment administration close in practice to that of occupational reservation. Over a large part of the field nation-wide agreements have been negotiated directly with the Headquarters of the Ministry of Labour by representative associations of firms in particular occupations, covering all the workers in various age classes or engaged in certain processes. By these " blanket " agreements the deferment of the workers concerned ceases to be granted after individual enquiry of the job actually done, and is granted as automatically on ascertainment of occupation as if the employee were in a reserved trade.

During the first few months of the work of the Man-power Boards the number of deferments granted either for a period or indefinitely rose to alarming proportions. For a long time only about one-fifth of the applications for deferment of women employees were refused. This was particularly serious as the groups being dealt with were composed mainly of the women in the early 'twenties who represent the only considerable mobile labour force in the country, and many attempts were made to persuade the Boards to be more ruthless in their treatment of employers' applications. But as Headquarters urged them with one voice to greater severity and with another announced blanket agreements with employers' associations, the Boards cannot be blamed for their failure to make available a larger supply of labour by their decisions.

VI

In certain industries the peculiarities of their structure and organisation have necessitated some variation of the general labour controls described above. For example, a special Order prohibits employers in the building and civil engineering industry from hoarding their skilled labour by transferring workers from one job to another without giving the Exchange an opportunity to decide whether the new job to which they are to be moved justifies the retention of labour which is exceptionally scarce. The Essential Work Orders applied to the Chemical and Iron and Steel industries have been so framed as to build a ring fence round these employments, the effect of which is to ensure that no workers may be transferred outside the industries unless their services cannot be used within. With regard to shipyard labour District Shipyard Controls, representing the Ministry of Labour and the Admiralty, have been appointed to advise on dilution of skill and general conditions of work. The Essential Work Order for the industry allows the Shipyard Controller to group together several undertakings so that labour may be transferred among them as required. Each Shipyard Control has attached to it a Consultative Committee representing employers and workers which it consults on welfare and on transfer arrangements.

There are, however, two industries—the docks and coal-mining —which have presented such problems of control as to merit a more detailed account.

For the last sixty years the casual methods of engaging labour in the docks have been a matter of active concern to the public and a source of bitter discontent to the docker. The industry is one which, by its nature, finds difficulty in offering regular employment. Its activity is governed almost entirely by influences over which it, itself, can have little control—the general state of trade, the quantity of imports and exports, the tides, the climate, political or industrial disturbances in another country, and so on. While skill is required in the handling of certain commodities, e.g. meat and timber, the greater part of the work can be done by any man of average muscular strength and physical endurance, and there is, consequently, no need for an employer to build up and retain a regular labour force. He can depend usually on getting an adequate supply when he needs it and the only guarantee that a worker in the past has had when taken on was that he would be employed for a four-hour shift. By dint of applying always at the same few stands some men did, in fact, gradually get known to the foremen and were probably given first chance of a job when work was available. But this had the unfortunate, result that it divided the labour force of a port into a large number of unconnected compartments so that not only did it often happen that labour was in demand at one wharf while surplus workers were turned away at another, but as each stand accumulated its own reserve, the total number of men attached to a port was larger than could get full employment even if all the sections were busy at once. The serious under-employment which was the normal characteristic of dock work and the consequent incalculable irregularity in earnings have had disastrous social and economic effects, but the many attempts at decasualisation had but poor success up to the outbreak of the war. In some ports schemes were established to grade the workers and to give the preference in engagement to those in certain groups, with the aim of building up a nucleus of workers who would, in fact, be fairly regularly employed even though they had no guarantee of regularity. In other ports a register of dockers was compiled, and only those whose possession of a tally gave proof that their names appeared on it could be taken on. But none of these experiments succeeded in making any fundamental change in the casual nature of dock employment. They were all up against the same difficulty. There is no possibility of reducing underemployment unless the numbers on the register or in the preference grades are kept down to the total that can reasonably hope to be regularly employed. At the same time recruitment to the industry cannot be completely closed down because, if this were done, there would soon be too large a preponderance of ageing men for the work to be done efficiently. Some additions must be allowed ; the question is how many ? Unless employers have a financial inducement to keep down the total their tendency is to press continually for elasticity with the result that the numbers remain perpetually in excess of general requirements. It has long been recognised that the only way to curb this pressure is to put employers under an obligation to pay a retaining fee to all those on the registers, but this suggestion was invariably met with determined opposition from the employers.

The outbreak of war brought many new problems to the docks. The amount of traffic to be handled could not be estimated in advance with any degree of accuracy. A raid on one port might put part of its machinery out of action and necessitate a sudden divergence of ships elsewhere. Expected cargoes failed to arrive because ships had been sunk or damaged *en route*, or unexpected cargoes reached ports to which they had put in to avoid enemy action. With all these additional incalculable factors it was impossible to foretell from one week to the next how much labour would be required in any port. What was obviously needed was some arrangement whereby labour could be quickly diverted to wherever it was needed.

The steps by which this has been achieved show the now familiar trend from persuasion to compulsion. Early in the war an agreement was reached between the Ministry of Labour and National Service, the National Council of Port Labour Employers and the Transport and General Workers' Union to provide for temporary transfers on a voluntary basis from one port to another. The Union agreed to prepare lists of men who would be willing to move when needed and the actual arrangements were placed in the hands of Port Labour Controllers working through the Employment Exchange machinery. A pledge was given that any man who was transferred beyond a reasonable daily travelling distance would be given free travelling facilities and allowances, a daily subsistence allowance and a guaranteed daily wage for as long as he was retained in the new port, whether he was actually employed or not. Further, no man would be moved unless he would be needed for at least six days.

The scheme proved totally inadequate to the problem. The difficulty of calculating ahead how many might be wanted led to volunteers continually finding themselves at a port where there was nothing for them to do. Such mistakes were inevitable, particularly in the early days of the scheme while the administrative details were being worked out and while the ports were subject to continual bombing. But a few false calls, however justified by circumstances, had a disastrous effect on volunteering. What was required was a large mobile labour force which was under orders to move immediately to wherever it was needed, and this could not be obtained without complete control. Without this control labour was wasted because dockers could not be released for service with the Forces or with other industries unless there was a certainty that the deficiencies of one port could rapidly be made up by reinforcements from another.

Two different procedures have been established for the exercise of this control. In the Merseyside and Clydeside all registered dockers are employed directly by the Minister of War Transport. For all other ports the National Dock Labour Corporation (a body representing the Ministry, employers and employed) has a general supervisory authority and the power to approve schemes submitted to it for the control of labour in each port. Although in one case the administration is in the hands of a Government Department and in the other of a joint representative body, the conditions of employment of the two schemes are pretty much the same. A registered dock worker receives a guaranteed weekly wage, but in return he is bound to report every half-day to do whatever work is reasonably required of him and to be prepared to travel to wherever he may be sent. Failure to carry out the conditions involves loss of pay and disciplinary action. The weekly wage is a minimum and is paid whether he is employed or not; but he may receive more than this sum if the work on which he is engaged carries a higher rate or if he is paid by output. With regard to the ports directly under the control of the Ministry of War Transport the workers are Government employees and no special arrangements are necessary to provide the funds for the guaranteed wage of men not working. In the case of the ports under the Dock Labour Corporation, however, funds must be set aside for this purpose. These are provided in a National Management Fund, underwritten by the Exchequer, to which employers contribute sums in proportion to their gross wages bill. Only registered employers are allowed to engage in port transport work and they are prohibited from engaging any men other than those allocated to them by the Port Labour Manager. They are bound to keep records of the men they employ and to give due notice of their labour requirements on pain of being removed from the register.

Here then, after sixty years of effort, has been at last achieved the complete decasualisation of dock labour. Of the two procedures, that of the National Dock Labour Corporation has the more relevance for peace-time conditions. As the burden of the employers' contributions to the National Management Fund increases with every addition to the quantity of redundant labour attached to the port they have a direct financial inducement to regularise their demand for labour, as far as the nature of the industry permits, and to restrain their desire to add unduly to the register. The workers, for their part, are compelled to make themselves available for work wherever they are needed unless they are to lose their security. By centralising the labour reserve the effects of local fluctuations in dock activity can be cancelled out, but the power to guarantee the security of income of the dock worker depends on the ability of those in control to keep the labour force completely mobile. It is on the degree of flexibility in the use of labour that the success of the scheme depends and by which its applicability to peace conditions must be judged.

The special arrangements in the coal-mining industry have

equally been necessitated by the effect of its historical development on war-time needs.   The long-term decline in the industry
which began in the early 'twenties and which has been one of
the outstanding features of the inter-war period led to a reduction
in total labour requirements.   In the decade or so before the
war a great deal of effort was put into the task of drafting the
redundant labour into other occupations and other localities.
Direct transference was officially organised by the Industrial
Transference Board and by the special grants to local authorities
who used transferred miners in their development schemes.   A
good deal of indirect pressure was exerted in the same direction
through propaganda and through the Employment Exchanges.
Though the exodus of miners was slow, its cumulative effect in
numbers over the whole period was very considerable and, when
the expansion of the munitions industries offered remunerative
employment the rate of transference was much accelerated.
Those who left the industry were drawn more proportionately
from the ranks of the young and vigorous, so that the smaller
labour force which remained contained an unusually high proportion of middle-aged and elderly workers.   In the early part
of the war the need for a strong and efficient supply of workers
in the coal industry was insufficiently realised by those in authority
and the numbers of young men were still further depleted by
their withdrawal for military service.   During the spring of 1940
the occupation of Northern Europe put a sudden stop to the
demand for coal and many pits were closed down, throwing
thousands of miners out of work.   With the urgent need for
workers in the munitions trades these men were rapidly absorbed
into other jobs, often at much higher rates of pay than they had
earned for many years in the pits.   Not until the men had got
established in new work did the authorities realise the seriousness
of the fuel shortage, both for shipping and for the rapidly expanding industries, and the Government then issued an appeal to
miners who had gone into other civilian employment to return
to the pits.   It is no matter for surprise that this appeal met
with little response.   In July, 1941, therefore, a register of
ex-miners was compiled and those who agreed to return to the
mines were guaranteed a secure weekly wage based on the Trade
Union rates for their grade and occupation, even during the times
when work was temporarily not available for them.   The funds
for this guaranteed wage were to be collected by a levy imposed
on coal sold in all districts.   The effect was not encouraging.
By October the Minister of Mines in reply to a question in the
House was bound to admit that although 105,376 had registered
only 25,468 were willing to go back to the pits.[1]   Even of these

[1] *Ministry of Labour Gazette*, Oct. 1941, p. 196.

a large proportion were found to be men who had left because of physical incapacity and many others had got into essential work from which it would be uneconomical to move them. Only 16,000 could actually be moved and of these only 25% were suitable for work underground.

The total effect of these measures was sufficient to prevent a further drop in output during 1941, but they were expedients that could not be repeated. In spite of the fact that the Essential Work Order had been applied to the industry there was a net wastage of 25,000 men per annum and, unless new supplies of labour could be got into the industry, a most serious decline in output could not be avoided. Means for bridging the gap between wastage and recruitment were essential. An enquiry into juvenile entrants showed that since 1934 the rate of entry of young boys had fallen from 30,000 to 14,000 a year and was far short of the natural decline due to old age, death and incapacity. The causes for this falling off are easy enough to understand. For twenty years the industry had shown a record of severe unemployment, low wages and, as far as could be seen, poor future prospects. Young people had been urged to show some initiative by refusing to follow their fathers' footsteps into the pits and by striking out a new line for themselves. The increased communications provided by a network of bus routes in mining localities widened the choice of occupations open to boys and more and more of them had snatched the chances thus held out to them. Only a long-term policy which gave a greater sense of economic security and a firm assurance of a progressive career could hope to reverse this trend.

Since the coal strike of 1926 there had been no national machinery to negotiate wages and with the long depression in coal-mining the wage levels in many districts had fallen far below those obtainable in other occupations employing comparable grades of labour. No amount of persuasion or even compulsion would provide an adequate, efficient and contented labour force as long as this lack of adjustment remained in existence. Efficient wage-negotiating machinery must evidently be reconstituted and a Board of Investigation under the chairmanship of Lord Greene was set up to advise on the matter. The Board recommended that a national minimum wage should be fixed at once for the industry together with a scheme whereby additional bonuses should be paid if attendance at the pits was regular and output in excess of an agreed standard. For the future, an elaborate system for national negotiation of wages and for the settlement of disputes was devised. All these proposals were made after full consultation with the industry and were accepted both by them and by the Government.

The history of the man-power situation in coal-mining is an interesting indication of the problems involved in controlling labour supply, particularly where there is a need to retain against future demands a quantity of labour which at the moment is in excess of what the industry can usefully employ, and where the industry is carried on at private risk.   Even had the Government realised early enough, as in fact they did not, that the movement of miners into the Forces and into munition industries would later have serious repercussions on fuel supplies they would have been hard put to it to prevent it at a time when the actual demand for coal was slack.   If they had compelled the coal industry to retain a large body of redundant miners they would have been under the necessity of paying a guaranteed wage, out of public funds, to all those for whom there was no work.   It is probable that this would have proved the most economical policy in the long run.   But it would have been very difficult to convince the public of this at a time of general labour stringency and when others were being compelled to leave their own good jobs for more essential war work.   Only a very courageous Minister would be prepared to risk his political standing by backing such a far-sighted policy.

VII

In addition to the forms of control described above for the mobilisation and transference of labour there have been two other types of Government action which have been partly directed towards the same end.   Both of them were designed to curtail the production of civilian goods to the minimum requirements of the community.   The Limitation of Supplies Order prohibits the production of some goods altogether and strictly rations the manufacture of many more by the reduction in the supplies of raw materials.   Such a measure, however, does not of itself increase labour resources for more essential production.   There is no certainty that the workers turned off from industries compelled to lower their output are of the type (i.e. are " mobile " or of an age to be capable of retraining) that can be absorbed into munitions and, indeed, the first results of the Limitation of Supplies were to add to the numbers of unemployed elderly workers.   Many of the younger ones, too, simply drifted off to other occupations that were not always more important than the ones from which they had come.   Nor was it economical to keep the same number of firms as before, each working to half capacity.   Such a system added to proportionate overhead charges, wasted a great deal of factory space and equipment and immobilised an unnecessarily large number of supervisory and managerial staff. Economy dictated that the smaller production should be concentrated in a few units so as to release the remainder for other purposes.

With this object in view, those industries in which there is substantial surplus capacity, as a consequence of Limitation of Supplies or Raw Materials Controls, are subject to a scheme whereby the production of the whole output of the trade is concentrated in a number of " nucleus " firms. The industries are first given an opportunity to work out a scheme for themselves but if, after a certain time, no agreement has been reached, the Board of Trade imposes the reorganisation which is thought to be necessary. In both cases, however, the scheme is worked out in consultation with the Ministry of Labour so as to ensure that the labour problems are not unduly complicated. It is obviously sensible that the firms which continue in production should be mainly in areas where the munitions demand for labour is not so intense and where there is likely to be an adequate supply of local and " immobile " labour to be utilised. On the other hand, if the firms which are closed down release their workers into an area with a large absorptive capacity, the problem of industrial retraining is not complicated by the further necessity for geographical transference. When a firm is listed as " nucleus " an estimate is made of the number of workers it needs to maintain its production and this " permitted labour force " is given a fair degree of protection by the Employment Exchange. This does not mean that its employees would not be called up for military duties and vital war production ; but it does mean that the firm would be given ample time to find substitutes for its younger mobile personnel, while the workers in a non-nucleus firm are considered available for immediate transference. In many instances, the non-mobile workers of non-nucleus firms or those who are too old to be good material for retraining are transferred to nucleus firms to provide the substitutes which allow the release of their younger employees. By this means the labour force that is retained in the concentrated industry is not only very much smaller than was originally employed but consists more of those workers who are less generally useful for direct war service.

VIII

A large part of the responsibility for the effectiveness of any labour policy rests on the adequacy of the arrangements for training and retraining workers. When war broke out the only official provision for training adults was that offered to unemployed workers in the Government Training Centres and

Instructional Centres. For a small number of juveniles vocational training was provided in Junior Technical, Commercial and Art Schools, in which selected pupils remained, generally, until they were sixteen. Although the curriculum of these schools is kept as wide as possible, it has a practical flavour and is designed to teach the fundamental subjects which are useful to a number of skilled trades. In addition to this full-time instruction many local education authorities offered part-time courses in Evening Institutes, attendance at which was voluntary. While many of the courses were cultural, the majority were intended to help the adolescent in his chosen occupation. None of this touched more than a tiny minority, and, for the most part, any training which workers in industry received, either as new entrants to wage-earning or as adults transferring from one trade to another, was got " on the job ". In those trades which demanded a considerable amount of skill and knowledge, the training might take the form of a definite apprenticeship or of a more informal learnership. But the amount of highly skilled work has been diminishing rapidly for some time and the majority of operations could be learned in periods varying from a few days to a few weeks. Between the repetition jobs at one end of the scale and the highly skilled crafts at the other, there is a very large intermediate range which can only be done adequately by those with accumulated experience of handling the particular kind of material or tools, or by those with capacity to take responsibility in organising other workers. Vacancies in these jobs have generally been filled by up-grading workers from the lower semi-skilled operations. The chosen worker gradually builds up his knowledge and learns by varied practical experience to deal with the different jobs, tools and situations with which he may be called upon to cope.

The rate of expansion of the war industries has been conditioned mainly by the speed with which workers could be found to take on this intermediate range of jobs. The highly skilled worker takes years to produce. There is no time during a war to train men to be accomplished craftsmen. All that can be done is to ration as carefully as possible those that are already in existence and to take care that they are not used for any task that does not require their high qualifications. To a certain extent the skilled jobs can be broken down into their component processes and the fully qualified man employed to do only those parts of it that require his trained observation or manipulative dexterity. The remainder is done by workers with much less knowledge and skill who confine themselves to a narrower range of operations. If they have the aptitude for the work (which includes both technical and personal qualities) these workers require only a few months' formal training and gain the rest of their skill in actual work in the factory. Provided facilities are forthcoming for the preliminary training, it is up to employers to be on the look-out for likely men and women and to give them full opportunities to gain the necessary practical experience while they are on the job.   Unless the rate of expansion is to be slowed down, there must be a constant stream of upgraded workers to be tried out for the more responsible tasks.   The main body of workers in mass production are engaged on a single mechanical process which they can quickly learn to do with speed and accuracy and, so long as recruits are available, the quantity of process workers in a factory can be easily increased.   But the work in an enterprise is integrated ; the machines have to be set and maintained ; the work of the sections must be organised and supervised ; certain stages in the manufacture of an article may call for special experience and skill : so that there is no point in adding to the number of process workers unless the size of the skilled and intermediate staff is sufficient to ensure that the more skilled stages will be got through at a pace that keeps the general body of workers fairly fully employed.

At the beginning of the war the importance of training was not fully appreciated. The Government Training Centres had accommodation for 8,700 trainees and the Instructional Centres for a further 4,500.   But they were far from full.   The unemployment figures remained fairly high during the first half-year of the war and it was assumed that there was little need to increase training facilities until this slack had been taken up.   But this assumption was wrong for two reasons.   Firstly, training takes time.   The Government Training Centre course lasted usually about six months, so that even if men had begun their training at once it would have been some time before they were available for work and it was the estimated needs of the future, rather than the demand for labour of the moment, that should have been the guiding consideration.   It was quite certain that, provided the war went on, these needs would be much greater after the first year. When a production programme has to be rapidly expanded, the initial demands are for labour for clearing sites and for building factories and communications.   But as soon as the factories are complete the demand swings over for personnel to staff them, and this demand could not be met unless workers were being trained to work the machines at the same time as the buildings in which they were to work were going up.

Secondly, the unemployment figures did not represent correctly the slack that could be easily taken up for war production.   Only a small proportion of the unemployed had any skill or valuable experience that was of immediate use, since most of those with such qualities had already been absorbed during the recovery in the engineering trades consequent on the rearmament programme. The men who were still unemployed were mostly semi-skilled workers and, however urgent the demand for increased production, they could not be employed until a sufficient body of men was available to undertake the more responsible jobs.

Another difficulty which delayed the training programme was the need to balance the claims of the Production Departments for an immediate increase in output with the demands of the Training Centres for machine tools and for skilled men to act as instructors. To take men and tools from the immediate job was undoubtedly to increase the risk of the moment, yet not to do so was to prevent the later expansion of industry which might prove even more fatal. It was not until the late summer of 1940 that the training problem began to be grappled with seriously. The number of Centres was increased and the conditions of eligibility for admission were altered. Instead of being restricted to the unemployed, workers of both sexes in the non-essential industries were urged to take training to fit themselves for vital war work. There was, however, very little response to this appeal and it is not to be wondered at. While training allowance was no longer based on unemployment benefit, the amount a trainee received, which varied with his circumstances, was still considerably below what he could hope to earn in an ordinary semi-skilled job, and it was too much to expect that workers should voluntarily submit to a serious reduction in income. To overcome this difficulty the whole conception of training was altered early in 1941. Adult trainees are now considered to be working under a contract of service just as if they were employed in a works ; and their pay, which is subject in the usual way to contributions for social insurance, corresponds roughly to the wage earned by a new entrant into the engineering industry. Monthly tests are held and the trainee who passes successfully draws higher pay, corresponding to the promotions open to an engineering operative. Despite the changes in the conditions, however, there has been a great dearth of applicants for the Training Centres and by far the majority of workers in war industry have been trained by employers " on the job ". Unfortunately many employers have been unwilling to set aside the necessary space, tools and men to ensure an adequate supply of qualified workers. To some extent this is due to shortsightedness, but even more to the uncertainty they have been in as to the quantity and nature of future Government demands. They were, quite naturally, unwilling to incur the risk of heavy loss in training workers for processes which might later not be so much needed or, even worse, in producing skilled workers who might later be taken from them and handed over to another employer whose products temporarily enjoyed a higher priority. In conformity with its settled policy of relying on voluntary methods, the Government urged, but did not compel, employers to undertake training. For a time a scheme of collaboration between Government and firms was tried. Skilled workers acted as instructors in an eight-weeks' intensive course for new recruits who were not necessarily to be employed by the firm in which they received their training. The firm was compensated for its trouble by a fee to cover the wages of these temporary instructors. The scheme was not successful and the numbers trained were negligible.

In view of the unwillingness of workers to offer themselves for training in Centres and the reluctance of most firms to provide training for workers who might be taken from them, reliance had to be placed on the upgrading of semi-skilled operatives to more responsible jobs. Where the management is alert to spot talent and is ready to be adventurous in its methods, this is probably as good a way as any of filling vacancies. Unfortunately, however, there has been a scarcity of these managerial qualities. There is no branch of skilled work in which the labour shortage has been more acute than that of management. The enormous expansion of the war industries has put a great strain on the managerial staffs and spread out very thinly those with initiative, judgment and vision. Their lack of adaptability to changing circumstances is well illustrated in the common attitude to the main body of women workers. At an early stage in the war it became obvious that women would be required for more than the quickly learned repetition processes and that many of them would have to be trained to fill the vacancies in the intermediate range of skill and responsibility. But, on the whole, managements have been too accustomed to think of women as confined to the lowest-scale work to be ready to pick them out for upgrading to the extent that war production demanded. Perhaps, too, there has been some fear of the effect on men's future employment if a large number of women were trained to be competent to do jobs that in the past have been the monopoly of men.

IX

Mention was made in an earlier chapter of the effect on mobility exercised by the added costs incurred when a worker finds a job in a locality distant from his home. War has added very materially to this problem and the element of compulsion in the distribution of labour has made it necessary for the Government to accept new financial obligations in connection with transferred workers. When a man is free to choose whether he will accept a job or not, he can be expected to take into account the travelling expenses, costs of removal or of lodgings and so on, in which he may be involved. Either the wages and working conditions must be sufficiently attractive to compensate him or the employer must be prepared to pay a part, or all, of the cost as an added bait to get the vacancies filled. At the outbreak of war it was assumed that the usual practice would continue, and the only responsibility taken by the Government was in the payment of travelling expenses of particularly scarce categories of workers, e.g. dock workers, whose mobility it was essential to speed up. With the tightening of labour controls, however, the Government has been compelled to play a very much bigger part. Workers have been, at first, persuaded, and, later, compelled to leave their homes for work in another district. Sometimes the change of job has meant a decrease in earnings, in any case, there has been the additional expenses of travelling and lodgings. Sometimes this extra expense is temporary, and the worker can soon be joined by his family and resume ordinary family life ; but in many cases they have had to maintain their own homes as well, either because of the difficulty of finding adequate housing accommodation for the whole family or because some members of the family were still at work in the home town. It was neither just nor politic that workers should have to meet these charges out of their wages. When movement was voluntary these costs acted as a severe deterrent to transference ; when it became compulsory, such a heavy burden would have been in the nature of a tax of very unequal incidence. A good many allowances are, therefore, now paid to cover the extra expenses resulting from transference ; travelling expenses, lodging allowances, settling-in grants, housing removal grants and continuing liability allowances where the worker still has to meet obligations in respect of rates, taxes and mortgages in his home district. None of these allowances is conditional on need since their aim is to compensate the worker for losses incurred in doing as the Government has directed.

The Government, however, has had to take a wider view of its responsibilities than simply compensation for financial loss. If authority is used to prevent workers from leaving their employment or to compel them to accept jobs which they might not have taken of their own free will, care must be exercised that the working conditions in the employing firm are fair and reasonable. A good deal of discontent was expressed by workers in the early days of control over the inadequacy of the housing and feeding arrangements with the result that welfare, both inside and outside the factory, has now been accepted as a Government responsibility. Inside the factory, the need for trained personnel staff has been urged and Government courses to train likely persons for these jobs have been instituted. Firms of a certain size may be compelled to maintain a properly run canteen, open to inspection by Government officials, and the factory inspectorate may demand that doctors and nurses should be available where they are likely to be required. The Ministry of Labour takes charge of transit arrangements, sees that transferred workers are met at their destination, provides lodgings where necessary and helps to bring the new worker into contact with recreational and leisure time activities of the new community of which he must, at least temporarily, form a part. When workers are transferred to a district where there is already a settled population their need both for housing accommodation and recreation can best be met from existing facilities ; but this is not always possible. Many of the biggest munition factories have had to be set up in remote areas and, in these circumstances, the Government has had to provide both hostels and opportunities for social intercourse for the workers.

X

The task of estimating the effectiveness of war-time labour controls is made difficult by two factors. The first is the lack of perspective which is inevitable in the attempt to get a detached view when we are living in the centre of a constantly shifting landscape. The second, and much more important one, is that, for security reasons, there are no statistics available of the movements of labour. For the time being we are bound to rely on general impressions. Not until the war is over shall we be able to collect the evidence on which alone accurate judgment can be based.

There are, nevertheless, certain matters on which we can judge with some confidence and some of these are particularly relevant to the general problem of occupational distribution in a dynamic world. The fact which emerges with startling clearness is the failure of the voluntary method to effect rapid changes in the occupational pattern. In every section of the industrial field the response to the appeal to workers to transfer to the trades in which their services were more needed has been so inadequate that it has been necessary to use authoritarian measures to select and direct the required personnel. This has not been due to any lack of patriotism on the part of labour nor to any unwillingness to make sacrifices for the common cause. Far from it. Throughout the war the majority of the community have shown a greater eagerness to shoulder burdens than the authorities have been to ask them to do so. The failure of the voluntary method derives from causes that are much more complex than either individual selfishness or lack of interest in the outcome of the war. It comes from the same type of psychological factor as was discussed in an earlier chapter in connection with the tendency of unemployed workers to "stay put" during very prolonged periods of industrial depression. Our economic organisation has conditioned men and women to think of jobs in terms of pay. All work that brings in the same income is equally valuable. They have never before been asked to consider the work they do for a living as part of a great co-operative enterprise. in which each worker makes his contribution to the general welfare. That a man should take pride in doing a good job of work was not uncommon ; and both law and public opinion expected him to provide for the necessities of his family. But it has never before been his concern to consider whether the work by which he earned his living and provided for his dependants was worth doing at all. He could assume that the very fact that an employer was prepared to pay him was proof that the work he did was worth while. He was not called upon to make judgments of value. He was not expected to decide the relative worthwhileness of the job in comparison with other kinds of work. Anybody who had got a satisfactory job—satisfactory that is from the point of view of pay and conditions of work—was temporarily out of the labour market. If another occupation was in need of more labour it could get it from the ranks of the unemployed or by taking in those whose work was badly paid or irregular. But the men who were already settled in good jobs were not concerned in the matter. The constant appeals made during the first months of the war by Cabinet Ministers, by radio and by newspaper advertisements, urging skilled workers to transfer to more essential war work, fell on deaf ears, not because the workers appealed to were selfish and unpatriotic, but because it never for a moment entered their heads that they were the audience to whom the appeals were addressed. They listened with academic interest and went to their own work the next morning without realising that they were in any way personally involved in the affair.

Gradually, of course, with repeated adjuration and explanation, their attitude changed and they began to understand that for the first time in their lives they were being asked to estimate the social value of their work, instead of simply its monetary remuneration ; but they were still at a loss as to how to act. To every man his own work seems important. For one thing, he knows so much more about it than he does of anything else. The more highly skilled a job is, the greater extent to which the worker's identity has become bound up in it. If it were not that to the shoemaker " there's nothing like leather " there would be little satisfaction in work or pride in craft. So that again, he thinks the appeal is not directed to him since he is already engaged on work of importance. He doesn't know where his work comes in the scale of national urgency. He has only to look around him to see that all sorts of luxury trades seem to be briskly at work and his common sense tells him that a considerable amount of ordinary production must inevitably continue to satisfy essential civilian needs. He has not the necessary information on which to judge whether his own particular job is important to go on with or not. Without any clear guide to his individual position he naturally inclines to take the view that is most favourable to himself.

Besides, he does not know much of the processes in other trades and cannot judge whether his skill could readily be adapted to them. It may be, for example, that the skill of a qualified printer may be just the type that could be quickly adapted for certain skilled tasks in armaments, but the printer has no means of knowing this. He has probably never been inside a munitions works in his life and he has the haziest idea of the actual/processes. His natural reluctance to move is bolstered up by his ignorance of whether, in fact, he is the sort of man who would be of any use. If he voluntarily gives in his notice he loses his chance of promotion in his own firm and he may find himself doing less skilled work in the munitions factory.

To some extent, it is true, such arguments are a rationalisation of a decision that has already been reached by other routes ; but they have a good deal of cogency. Only those who are in charge of the national policy can really know which are the essential trades. It is useless to expect the ordinary citizen with his very limited vision and inaccurate knowledge to estimate the degrees of importance in the national scheme of various occupations. There has, fortunately, been very little of the " white feather " nonsense in this war. The public has rightly argued that, in view of conscription, the fact that a man is not in uniform must mean that the Government thinks he is better employed in some civilian form of national service. The same thing holds in industry. Early in the war the Government was given complete power over all persons and property and much publicity was given to this seemingly drastic step in national policy. It took a long time for the Government to decide to make use of this power, but employees could sensibly put forward the plea that they would be willing to do more essential work when they were told what to do and where. The Minister of Labour knew where to find them if he had more vital work that he thought they should be doing. Meanwhile they had best stay where they were and wait for instructions.

> The success of Mr. Bevin's appeals [commented the *Economist*] depends upon the receptiveness of his audience and, unfortunately for their success, the application of conscription to military enlistment together with the introduction of the many-branched Schedule of Reserved Occupations, has engendered the belief generally that no one need " go " until he is specifically and personally sent for.[1]

Later on when experience had proved the failure of appeals alone the administration of the controls showed a more nicely-balanced relationship between compulsion and freedom of choice. The final decision as to whether the work on which an individual is engaged is sufficiently vital to the national effort as to justify him in remaining in it is taken out of the hands of both the worker himself and of his employer and is made by the Government, who alone has the information on which to make such a judgment competently. But once authority has decided that the worker must leave his present occupation he is given a very large measure of choice in the work to which he is transferred. The range of choice varies according to the needs of war strategy, and at times a considerable degree of pressure may be expended in urging the claims of particular trades where the need is acute. But apart from the conscription of men of certain ages into the Armed Forces, it is rare for the worker not to have reasonably wide limits within which to choose the type of national service or war production that he or she undertakes. The vast majority of civilian workers do not, in fact, have to receive written " directions " when they transfer to war work, but the power to issue a direction and to prosecute those who fail to comply with it remains in the background as a sanction to ensure that the individual does really take up the job that he has agreed to.

The unwillingness of the Government to make use of its powers of compulsion was in part due to a praiseworthy appreciation of the fact that the members of a free community work with greater enthusiasm under a discipline to which they have voluntarily submitted themselves than when they are threatened with penalties. But it was also partly the result of a faulty gauging of the psychological temperature which has shown itself also in certain examples of bad timing. If an appeal is made to the good will and patriotism of citizens to offer themselves for work it is of the utmost importance that the jobs should actually be immediately available for those who respond. To greet enthusiastic volunteers with the news that their names will be put on a waiting list until there is enough accommodation or

[1] *Economist*, March 15, 1941.

E

training apparatus for them causes such a reaction that later appeals are likely to be met with apathy. In the summer of 1940, for example, the Minister of Labour called for a million women for urgent war work. The Employment Exchanges were besieged by long queues of women who answered the call, only to be told that there were not yet any vacancies to which they could be sent. It is true that eventually many more than a million were required, but the factories in which they were to be employed and the machines they were to man had not yet been constructed. If reliance is to be placed on volunteers, the authorities must be careful not to arouse enthusiasm for which there is no outlet or they will later discover that they have called " Wolf " too often. A similar example of bad timing was shown during the same period in the Government's appeal to house-wives to offer themselves for week-end work in factories so as to relieve the strain on the regular workers. But at this time the labour shortage had not yet become general and firms were still able to get fairly adequate supplies of ordinary staff. They were not yet prepared to make the many adjustments that are a neces-sary preliminary to the employment of part-time labour and very few of the housewives who offered themselves found any employ-ment open to them. Later, when part-time female labour was the last remaining reserve available, the Government had learned its lesson and timed its appeal to coincide with vacancies.

Closely connected with mistakes in timing has been the mal-adjustment due to lack of co-ordination. The basic problem of a man-power policy in war-time is the proper allocation of resources between the Armed Forces and industry in the first place, and in the second, between the various branches of pro-duction. Since such an allocation depends primarily on war strategy, it can be determined only by those who are in control of the conduct of the war, i.e. the War Cabinet. The Labour Controls do not decide on the objective ; they can only provide the machinery for reaching the desired end as quickly, as efficiently and as economically as possible. But while the final decision must be made by the highest authority, those who are in control of labour distribution have a very important part to play in all the intermediate stages, for it is their job to calculate how far labour resources are, or could be made, available to implement the various policies that are under discussion. Suppose, for example, that the Cabinet decides that an Army or Navy or Air Force of such and such a strength is needed, it is necessary to estimate whether there would remain in the country sufficient labour of the right kinds and skills to staff the factories to produce the equipment they would require. Or if it is determined to cut down the quantity of shipping used for food imports and rely more on home production, what would be the effect of the resulting increase in the number of agricultural workers on the size of the Forces or the output of aircraft factories ? Or suppose that more tanks are to be produced, what numbers of workers must be induced to train so as to provide the staff for tank factories next year ? As far as it is possible to judge, there seems to have been little successful balancing of priorities against one another so as to dovetail them most economically within the narrow framework of available man-power, and little calculation made in advance of the repercussions of one decision on the remainder of the field.

Even more striking has been the failure to look ahead and provide for future needs that were quite certain to develop. The extraordinary delay in devising an adequate training programme is perhaps the most outstanding illustration, but the short-sightedness which allowed coal-miners to be recruited into the Forces, or to drift off to other occupations, runs it pretty close. On the whole, the manipulation of man-power has been altogether too hand-to-mouth in character. When an acute shortage has actually arisen, the machinery has been set in motion to deal with the situation ; but there has been a lamentable lack of foresight. Little attempt seems to have been made to look even a few months ahead and make such plans as would prevent such acute shortages from developing. In so far as new demands arise from changing policy depending on the course of the war, some emergencies cannot possibly be foreseen or prevented. But as long as a war is being waged at all there are certain needs that will quite definitely have to be met, and preparation for meeting them should be made in advance.

It has been argued [says the Select Committee on National Expenditure] that, even if recruitment had been intensified, the extra labour would not have been required owing to shortages of material. But there is no conclusive evidence that there have been widespread and continuing shortages of this kind. Moreover, if there is a shortage of material at any point, this may itself be due to an insufficient supply of labour at other points in the sequence of production, either in the extraction of raw materials or in constructing or operating means of transport or in earlier processing operations. It indicates too that the fundamental problem of total war, that of employing every person capable of work in the job where he or she is most needed, has not been fully appreciated.[1]

The Ministry of Labour, in answering the criticisms of the Select Committee, claimed that with some minor local exceptions, no essential war production had been held up for lack of labour. But the fact that employers' demands have been met proves

[1] Seventh Report of 1941–2.

nothing, since these are made in relation to the work actually on the order book and departments placing contracts have to estimate the likelihood of the contract being fulfilled, though the needs of the country would have indicated a larger order. One of the most serious labour problems is the amount of absenteeism and, while the causes are complex, there is no doubt that severe overwork has been one of the most important factors in the situation. Workers can manage a long working day and a seven-day week for a short spurt, but they cannot possibly keep up under great strain over a prolonged period. Such overwork would not have been necessary if there had been more labour available, as there might have been if the Government had got more quickly into its task of mobilisation and training.

There have been further wastes of labour as a result of the failure to consider the problem of man-power as a whole. One of the main objects of the concentration of industry was the release of labour for more important purposes. Yet for a long time none of the measures curtailing production ensured that the released workers were actually put into war industries. A great many found jobs for themselves in other local employment which was no more essential than the work from which they had come. Many married women retired altogether from wage-earning ; they had been ready to work at jobs of their own choosing which enabled them to combine work with their household responsi- bilities. But rather than face the difficulties of working out a new routine in unfamiliar employment, perhaps not so well situated in relation to their homes, they claimed household responsibilities to excuse them from transferring. After some time the mistake was realised and there was closer correlation between the release of labour and its placing in essential war work. But this did not prevent a similar mistake from being made in regard to part-time workers. When women with household responsibilities were first urged to undertake part-time duties so as to release full-time workers for munitions and the services, it was considered a matter for general congratulation if the numbers of part-timers increased, no matter what the trades they entered. But when labour is scarce, it is just as wasteful to use part-time labour in non-essential production as it is to use ordinary full-time workers. But it took a full year for this fact to be appreciated, or at least to be acted upon.

Once compulsory allocation of labour has been decided upon, there are other considerations which determine its success. Firstly, the labour directed into a certain occupation must stay there until it is wanted more urgently elsewhere. No purpose is served if workers merely pass through from entrance to exit.

Secondly, the workers must do the jobs assigned to them industriously and efficiently. And thirdly, there must be means for those in control to estimate accurately the relative priorities of different industries and to ensure that there is the utmost flexibility in the response of the administrative machinery to the continuous changes in the situation. On none of these points, however, is it possible to feel complete confidence. Despite the Essential Work Order the labour turnover is extraordinarily high. The efficacy of any statutory decree is relative to the adequacy of its inspectorate. Particularly is this so when it introduces so novel and revolutionary a feature as the abolition of the freedom of the worker to choose his job and of the employer to dismiss an employee. Very little has been done, however, to prevent workers from leaving the employment to which they have been sent. It is true that to leave without permission of the National Service Officer is against the law ; but, in fact, very many discontented workers have simply taken *carte blanche*. Every scheduled firm has on its books a large number of names of workers who, in theory, are still on its staff because they have never been given official permission to leave but who, in practice, have not attended for work for many weeks. In theory, it is impossible for workers who have taken French leave in this way to get other jobs since it is illegal to engage them except through the Employment Exchange. But, in practice, they do get employment and there is nothing to guarantee that it is in essential war work. Many women who dislike the work to which they have been sent fail to turn up at the works and simply fade back into the domestic background. This could only be prevented by constant revision of the registers and persistent following-up of the workers after they have been placed, and in the middle of a war, with an administration that is as subject to labour shortage as industry, this has not proved practicable.

This is only one aspect of the wider problem of discipline inside the factory, amongst those who do stay in the jobs to which they have been sent. Discipline is naturally more difficult to maintain amongst groups of workers, the majority of whom are new to the type of work and many of whom are new to industrial life altogether. It takes time for the workers to be welded together into a community in which they take pride and of whose good name they are jealous. Many have left home for the first time and are feeling lonely and cut off from all that they thought made life worth living. They are not yet used to their billets and feel lost in a strange town. Nervous and on edge, they are ready to flare up at supposed slights and injustices or are bitter and resentful of those in authority over them. It is no wonder if it takes time for transferred workers to settle down into an ordered routine. A more serious problem, because more widespread and more persistent, is the very great amount of absenteeism that is a feature of all war industries. Many factories are situated in rural areas with no local labour supplies or accommodation. This means that all the workers have a good deal of travelling to add to the length of a tiring working day. Often enough the transport is inadequate or wrongly timed, but even if this difficulty is overcome, the sheer fatigue of a long journey induces workers to slip a day occasionally. This is particularly so if the hours of work are long as they are in many factories, or if the shortage of staff leads to the working of a seven-day week. The importance of fatigue as a factor in absenteeism can be seen in the experience of a Filling factory which changed from a two-shift to a three-shift day, and found that its absenteeism, which had fluctuated between 15 and 20%, dropped at once to 10%. For women the burden is especially heavy since the vast majority of them are doing a double job. The difficulties of shopping, cooking and house cleaning add so greatly to the length of their working day that the wonder is that they are able to carry on at all rather than that they take an occasional day off. This is one of the reasons for the fact that the output of the part-time worker is proportionately so much higher and the rate of absenteeism so much less than that of the ostensible full-time employee.

In general, then, absenteeism is caused by an overheavy burden placed on workers who, however willing, are unable to stand up to the strain. But there are other factors which have a serious influence, though they affect only a minority of workers. In many occupations high piece rates coupled with long hours of work enable a worker to earn in a few days a higher wage than he has ever had before. Owing to the shortage of consumption goods there is not much on which he can spend and he feels it is not worth while to go on working with so little compensation. For the first time, too, many wage-earners have been brought within the income-tax paying class and they feel that too much of the pay for their week's work " goes to the Government ". With the majority of workers, patriotism is strong enough to outweigh these considerations, but there is a section whose sense of social obligation is weak and who refuse to over-exert themselves when the material reward they can enjoy is inadequate. Despite the tightening up of the Essential Work Order so as to allow of disciplinary measures in such cases, no adequate method has been found for dealing with this problem. It has been suggested that persistent offenders should be dereserved and sent to the Forces, where they would receive service pay and be subject to military discipline, but the authorities have wisely rejected this proposal. It would be fatal to army morale to lend any support to the theory that recruitment to the Forces was a punishment for the backslider, and also if the man was reserved, presumably his work is needed in civilian production. To prevent him from doing it is no solution to the problem.

Here again the only solution must be sought along moral and psychological lines. The only effective check to idleness and the only successful incentive to increased output is the realisation on the part of the worker of the important part he plays in waging the war. The industrial worker has none of the prestige and glory of the uniformed service man ; he has no opportunity for personal distinction and stands little chance of being singled out as a national hero. Only if his imagination has been fired, so that he understands his share in the national exploits, can it be expected of him to continue day after day with what would otherwise be monotonous and soul-destroying labour. Attempts are now made to link up the industrial worker with the service men whose equipment he makes. Selected work-people are taken to Fighter and Bomber stations to see the planes they constructed in use and men who have been on operations come to the factories to tell the workers what they did with the weapons the factory manufactured for them. The success of such an interchange is seen in the telegram which Yorkshire coal-miners sent to the Admiralty to congratulate them on the *Bismarck* action, a courtesy which the Admiralty promptly returned by sending down officers who had taken part in the action to talk to the men about it.

The third essential for a successful allocation of labour is a procedure for determining labour priorities and a flexible administrative machine to effect the consequent changes in labour distribution. The danger of substituting authoritarian control for wage differentials is that political pressure or skill in stating a case may play too big a part in determining the rate at which workers leave one occupation for another. Each Minister is naturally concerned with the success of his own Department and will press the claims of those for whom he is responsible as hard as he can. In this respect it is not yet possible to make confident judgments, because the facts are not available, but it is probable that even such a vital matter as the relative strengths of the Armed Forces has been largely determined by the different degrees of persuasiveness at the command of the Ministers in charge of them, rather than a careful balancing of military and civilian needs. And there is little doubt that retail distribution could have been cut down drastically at an early stage in the war without any serious adverse consequences to the community, and that clothes rationing could have been more severe, without causing any undue deprivation, had it not been for the political pressure brought to bear by the firms in those industries. Again, the policy of individual deferment has been largely negatived by the blanket agreements made by representative associations with the Ministry of Labour, and it is difficult to say whether the actual release of workers has not been due more to the relaxation of pressure on the part of employers whose supplies of raw materials have been cut off than to the severity of the Man-power Boards in deciding that the work of the firm asking for the retention of its personnel was non-essential.

The Man-power Boards illustrate a general problem in the administration of a national labour policy, which admits of no easy solution, that is, the correct line of demarcation between national uniformity and local discretion. It is essential that law should operate impartially as between one citizen and another ; people in like circumstances must receive the same treatment no matter whether they live in London or Newcastle, Slowcombe-on-Mud or Sleepy Hollow. At the same time, exactly like circumstances are rarely found ; there is an infinite gradation of slight differences dependent on the variations in the details of individual lives, and no general statement can be so phrased as to cover all the possible combinations of differences that might exist. If policy is expressed in general principles and the application is left to local officials it is possible to take into account all the details of each case, but it is impossible for every official to interpret general directions in exactly the same way, so that local elasticity is gained at the expense of variation in the treatment of similar cases, according to the district in which the person happens to live. Such differences rapidly give rise to a sense of injustice and resentment and what commences as criticism of apparently arbitrary inequalities soon develops into opposition to the basic policy itself.[1] If on the other hand local bodies work closely to directions given by national headquarters there must be an inevitable sacrifice of elasticity and a considerable degree of bureaucratic rigidity. Everybody is familiar with instances of individuals whose calling up has been deferred

---

[1] A good example of this is to be found in the public reaction to the Means Test. When it was first introduced in 1930 there was hardly any central direction as to what should or should not be taken into account in calculating resources and needs. It was left to local administration with the natural consequence of wide divergencies of treatment. A very large part of the bitter opposition to the Means Test originated in the angry resentment engendered at this time against inequality and many people, who would have been willing to put up with it if the administration had been just, would have nothing to do with it. It is a case of throwing away the baby with the bath-water.

although the actual work they are doing seems of very slight value to the war. The explanation, of course, is that the official classification of their occupation brings them within a category of employment which is reckoned as too important to be depleted. Theoretically, it is still possible to make a distinction and withdraw a worker who, individually, is not engaged on sufficiently valuable work, even though the category in which he is classified is considered to be so. But in practice, this presents many difficulties. The employer who wishes to keep his staff is likely to claim the support of his association in opposing this different treatment and as it is not a simple matter to collect evidence to show that the individual is really doing work of less importance than other employees in that kind of job, the local official is unlikely to exercise his discretionary power.

To a great extent, then, a national labour policy must necessarily be administered by central direction and this makes it harder for the officials on the circumference to keep that flexibility and rapid adjustment to changing circumstances without which the whole machinery of allocation is apt to become clogged. During this war, for example, when one type of labour after another has taken the front of the stage as of prime importance, those at the centre who have been in close touch with the situation and have been able to get a bird's-eye view, of the whole field, have constantly had to alter their instructions to the local officials who are in charge of the actual executive work of distribution. As they themselves are cognisant of the situation which has necessitated the change, they have not always fully appreciated the fact that the local officials have not the same access to information and that to the latter the frequent alterations are bewildering and meaningless ; "just one damned thing after another ". There is a tendency, therefore, for the sense of urgency to be dissipated during the period of transmission from the centre to the local area ; and very often the administration of the step in policy gets into working order only at the moment when a still further change is immanent. In practice, that is, the administration is always a little out of date and gets to grips with a situation only when it is beginning to dissolve into something else. This difficulty is, of course, intensified during a war, partly because the policy has to shift so rapidly and in directions which it is impossible for any but those at the highest level to anticipate, and partly because the large volume of work to be done requires the employment in administration of a much swollen staff, who have not the requisite training and experience to respond as quickly as they should to directions from their headquarters.

Yet despite the criticisms which can be made of the war-time labour controls the fact remains that, one way and another, a very remarkable feat of labour mobilisation has been achieved. It has taken longer than it should have done ; it has often been jerky and spasmodic ; it has made many mistakes that could have been avoided by a little foresight and a little more adventurous thinking. But no other country in the world has ever accomplished such a high degree of mobilisation, either for war or for any other purpose. Quite apart from the millions of men enlisted into the Armed Forces and Civil Defence, by the spring of 1943, nearly two million men and approximately nine and a half million women had been registered for industrial work. The main work of allocation has dealt with women workers, of whom four and a half millions had been interviewed by April, 1943. It was officially stated that by the summer of 1943, 90% of the 3,250,000 unmarried women between the ages of 18 and 40 were engaged on full-time war work in the Forces, in Civil Defence and in industry ; 500,000 workers had been released by clothes rationing and 250,000 by the concentration of industry. Two million men and women in classes not normally engaged in industrial employment had been mobilised for full-time war work, and 650,000 women, mostly married and with household responsibilities, engaged in part-time work.

Moreover, this colossal piece of work has been carried through for the most part with the consent and with the good will of the workers themselves. From this point of view, the slow rate of development may be justified. Every step has been fully discussed with the workers' representatives, and a real attempt has been made to take account of domestic and personal difficulties and of firmly held social traditions. As a consequence the community has had a chance to get accustomed to one stage before being faced with another. Control has been extended and intensified by almost imperceptible steps so that a revolution has taken place without most people being aware of the fact. The necessity of war has brought about changes in organisation which have been the subject of bitter controversy for generations. There is now a guaranteed week in industries which have fought for decasualisation for half a century. For thirty-five years the Employment Exchanges have been trying to persuade employers to notify them of vacancies. It is now done as a matter of course. The end of the war will leave us with a very differently organised labour market from the one with which we began. From being one among a number of placing agencies, the Employment Exchanges have come to be the dominant institution in the allocation of labour, and the attitude of both employers and workers towards them has altered. But perhaps most important of all, because most subtle in its far-reaching influence, members of the community have been asked for the first time in their lives to evaluate their work by other than economic criteria and to see themselves as a society in which each individual makes whatever contribution he is capable of for the common good.

CHAPTER V

LABOUR CONTROL IN GERMANY AND RUSSIA

I

SYNOPSIS OF CHAPTER

1. Germany's problem is similar to that of Britain, but the machinery for dealing with it was set up before the war. It differs from the British in being imposed by authority instead of with the co-operation of those concerned.

2. The Soviet Union is faced with the same problem of occupational distribution as are capitalist countries. The individual is free to choose his own occupation and is induced to train for skilled work or to transfer to other employment by means of wage differentials. No institutions are allowed to interfere with the operation of wage differentials or to mitigate the results of unwise choices on the part of individuals. But the incentive to work is not purely economic because of the developing sense of community and of social responsibility.

THE question that has been discussed in earlier chapters centres round the problems that arise when a degree of economic security is assured to the members of a community whose political ideology places a high value on the individual's freedom of action and in which the economic system assumes a large measure of individual initiative in the choice of occupation. In Great Britain, limitations on personal freedom and the exercise of authoritarian control of labour have been only slowly and reluctantly introduced in response to the urgent needs of war. In both Germany and Russia, however, the subordination of the individual to the State is accepted as an integral part of political faith rather than as an unwilling concession to war-time necessity ; it requires neither special justification nor apology. Though the objectives of the two countries lie far apart, their Governments are alike in imposing on all citizens the obligation to adjust themselves to a national economy planned from above, and both are prepared, if necessary, to be ruthless in their use of sanctions to compel obedience. It is of interest, therefore, to examine the ways in which these two countries attempt to solve the problem of occupational distribution.

When the Nazi Government came into power in 1933 Germany was suffering from extremely high unemployment. Unemployment insurance, which had been instituted in 1927, had broken down completely under the pressure of six million claims to benefit, and the majority of those who were out of work were existing on a very inadequate poor relief. This fact was undoubtedly one of the most important contributory factors in the triumph of the Nazi Party, and it is one of their chief claims to the gratitude and support of the population that the State accepted the duty of guaranteeing to all its citizens the right to work, either in regular jobs or, if these were not available, in substitute employment created for the purpose. As part of this policy the Government employed nearly a million men on emergency relief work. They did not receive wages in the usual sense of the term, but they got board and lodging (often under canvas) and a small amount of pocket money in return for very hard physical work. After 1935 general employment improved and the Labour Service was no longer necessary to provide relief work, but it was retained to serve a different purpose. It became a course of training for young men in unpaid physical work as an addition and counterpart to their compulsory military training. Although it did, in fact, draw a fair number of men off the labour market, this was not its primary purpose, but it was intended to be a means of fostering national consciousness and of raising the prestige of manual labour. This general purpose of the Compulsory Labour Service was defined by Hitler in a speech in 1934.

> Through the Labour Service we would compel every young German to work at least once with his hands and thus to contribute towards the building up of his people. Above all, we want those Germans who are in sedentary occupations to experience what manual labour is, so that they may feel understanding and sympathy for those of their countrymen whose lives are spent in the fields, the factory or the workshop. We want to abolish for ever that attitude of superiority which unfortunately so many of our intellectuals adopt towards the manual workers, and we wish them to realise that they too will be worth all the more if they know themselves to possess a capacity for physical work. But the ultimate aim behind the Labour Service is to promote mutual understanding between the different classes, and thus to strengthen the spirit of national solidarity among the whole people.[1]

For the most part the work done by young men in the Labour Service was on land reclamation and afforestation and such enterprises as would not usually be undertaken on a commercial basis. But when labour was short for urgent work they could be employed wherever they were sent, side by side with workers employed in the normal way for wages ; and they were, in fact, largely used in this way during the years prior to the war in building the western fortifications.

In accepting the duty to guarantee work the State imposed a far-reaching obligation on the citizen to do what he is told, to work for the length of time and at rates of wages laid down by the State and to engage in any occupation to which he is directed.

[1] Quoted in C. W. Guillebaud, *Social Policy of Nazi Germany*, pp. 67-8.

The Trade Unions and their collective agreements had been abolished as soon as Hitler took charge, but the existing wage rates were kept in force by general decree for the time being. Meanwhile Labour Trustees, State officials appointed by the Ministry of Labour, were established with the duty of fixing minimum wages for the industries under their control. But although the Government had the right to order anybody to do anything, in practice the mass of workers were left to choose their own occupations and places of employment. It was only as the country began to organise on a war economy that, gradually more and more effective control began to be exercised. The first move was made in agriculture, whose labour forces were being depleted by the attractions of the higher-paid jobs in the expanding armament industries. As the maintenance of a thriving agriculture was an important part of the Nazi policy steps had to be taken to prevent this flow. Agricultural workers who had gone into other jobs were compelled to return to the land, and employers were prohibited from engaging agricultural workers in any other occupation without official permit. In addition, a system of long-term contracts was introduced so as to tie the worker to the farm for indefinite periods of time. In urban industries, the shortage of labour showed itself at first principally amongst the skilled categories in the munitions trades, and orders were issued to prohibit advertisement for workers in the metal industries and to prevent the enticement of men from firms in these trades by offers of higher wages. It is evident that these orders were not very effective, for they were soon supplemented by further decrees which forbade employers in the metal and building industries to engage any worker without written permission, and this permission was never granted unless the worker was either unemployed or at work in another occupation of less political importance.

By the late thirties the labour shortage was beginning to be general and it was necessary to look for further reserves as well as make the best use of what was already in industry. The latter aim was made easier by the exact knowledge of all labour resources that was gradually being accumulated. A system of Labour Books had been introduced in 1935 which gave a complete record of the industrial history and qualifications of the worker to whom it referred. When a worker was engaged the book had to be handed to the employer, who filled in the details of the work done and retained the book until the worker was dismissed. The worker had then to register it with the Employment Exchange before he could get another job. The issue of these Labour Books naturally took some time, but as the work in connection with each group of industries was completed it was made compulsory for the workers in these occupations to have their books with them in order to get employment. This provided a very effective check on the power of an employee to leave his work without permission. Unless the new firm to which he applied for a job was willing to take the very considerable political risk of signing him on without seeing his book, he was bound to remain where he was.

. The drawback of such a system from the point of view of economising labour is, of course, that it leads firms to hold on to their skilled workers even when there is not sufficient work for them on hand. A pretence of employment can be made by putting them on to routine jobs or by working them on short time. This is what happened in Germany and to prevent this waste, supervisors were appointed to investigate the relation between the orders on a firm's books and the number of its skilled staff. Further, in 1937, short time was eliminated by making it obligatory on all firms to guarantee a full week's wage to all the workers on their books.

In Germany, as in other industrial countries, the only considerable addition to the total labour supply had to be sought from among the women who were not usually " gainfully occupied ". It was part of the Nazi philosophy that women's rôle should be restricted as far as possible to the home, but as the stringency of the labour situation increased, this policy had perforce to be reversed. A compulsory labour service for girls was introduced in 1933, which compelled all under 25 years of age to do one year's work in agriculture or domestic service, or two years' work as an auxiliary nurse or social welfare worker, before being permitted to go into such occupations as clothing, textile, tobacco or clerical trades. Later this was extended to cover entry into all private and public undertakings. Firms were no longer prohibited from engaging married women in receipt of marriage loans, as they had been before, and all able-bodied women, married or single, were asked to register and give particulars of their occupations and industrial experience. The number of women employed for wages, which had dropped to 4,700,000 in 1933, had risen to 6,300,000 by 1938 [1] and plans were on foot to draw still more into the industrial field.

By 1938 it was fairly certain that war would soon be inevitable, and the pace of production was stepped up. For the first time now general industrial conscription came into force, at first only for limited periods, but by March, 1939, the obligation to perform compulsory labour service had been extended to cover all citizens between the ages of 15 and 70 with the exception of pregnant women, invalids and, under certain conditions, mothers

[1] Franz Neumann, *Behemoth*, p. 279.

of minors. Hundreds of thousands of workers were drafted from their own jobs to work on the West Wall fortifications. In general, workers moved in this way were considered to have been seconded from their own work for jobs requiring their particular skill or strength, and they returned to their former employment when the special need for them was over. But in many cases this power to transfer was used as a weapon to enforce political conformity and to punish those who, in any way, displeased the authorities. When a piece of work of national importance was particularly urgent, certain public bodies had the right to requisition labour as they pleased. The local employment office might object on account of the seriousness of the labour situation in the district but, unless a protest was made and upheld in this way, the employer was compelled to give leave of absence to the requisitioned workers and to reinstate them when they were returned. The only concession made to the employer was in the grant of a hardship allowance to those who could prove that they had been put in financial difficulties by the loss of their staff.

As the reserves of labour began to be exhausted efforts were made to increase the output of those already in employment by changes in working conditions. The Labour Trustees had formerly had the duty of fixing minimum rates of wages and of enforcing statutory conditions of work for the protection of the worker. Their powers were now extended to allow them to fix maximum as well as minimum rates of pay, with the special object of keeping down extra pay for over-time. At the same time hours of work were lengthened so that by 1939 a ten-hour day was general in industry, while in iron and steel, coal-mining and building, twelve and fourteen hours were not uncommon. The Government soon found, however, that it had overshot the mark. Output, instead of increasing, began to show a decline. As no overtime or bonus pay was allowed the workers had not even the stimulus of higher earnings to compensate for the fatigue endured in these long working days ; and the Government was forced to modify the most stringent provisions.

Two further measures were employed to make the best use of labour. Surveys were made of those sections of industry that were thought to be less important from the national point of view, and those businesses which could not justify their existence were compelled to close down. In this way many small shopkeepers, hairdressers and handicraft trades went out of business and released their employees for other work. Secondly, the character of unemployment insurance was altered so that the receipt of an allowance to an unemployed worker depended partly on an estimate of his own resources and partly on his willingness to undertake any work offered him and to undergo any prescribed course of training.   As a result more than a million persons were in attendance at such courses between 1933 and 1937.

Quite apart from this idea of the rehabilitation of the unemployed, training has been given a high place in Nazi labour policy.   When the Four Year Plan for the full utilisation of economic resources was put into operation in 1936, German industry was faced by such a serious shortage of skilled workers, as a consequence of the profound depression of the preceding period, that a comprehensive and diversified system of training was thought to be one of the first essentials.   Courses were established in technical schools, not only for young people who had not yet started on their industrial careers, but also to enable those who were already in work to improve their knowledge. The Labour Front itself (the State organisation which took the place of the abolished Trade Unions) had many thousands of instructors on its staff and ran courses of instruction for skilled trades.   To encourage workers to take advantage of these courses competitions were held all over the country, and, during 1937 to 1939 [1] some two million people were examined.   The winners in the village competitions went on to the district examinations and from those to the province.   Those who had come safely through this weeding-out process competed in a grand final contest from which the national winners emerged, sure of reward and advancement in their chosen occupations.   Even those who had not managed to make the final grade were marked out for further training and posts of special importance if they had done creditably in the earlier stages of the examination.   In this way something of the excitement and public prestige of athletic prowess was carried over into the industrial field and by 1941 the Labour Front was able to claim that over three million people were attending its courses.[2]   The greater part of the instructional work had, however, to be done in the factories and workshops.   The periods of apprenticeship were shortened so as to get quick results, and learnerships which provided intensive training for a shorter time were introduced.   The most drastic step was taken in 1936, when all firms in the metal and building industries employing more than ten workers were ordered to undertake the training of a definite number of trainees, proportionate to their total staff, and employers who were unable to make the necessary provision had to pay a compensatory fee to the National Labour Board.   This decree increased the openings for apprentices so greatly that there were not enough school leavers to fill the vacancies and the exchanges were able to apportion new entrants according to a scale of priorities.

[1] G. W. Guillebaud, *Social Policy of Nazi Germany*, p. 61.
[2] *Labour Supply and National Defence*, I.L.O., p. 106.

By the time that war broke out, therefore, Germany had already established effective and comprehensive labour controls, and all that was needed was to develop further along lines which were tested and familiar. Boards were established to examine each factory and find out what contribution it had made or could be expected to make to the upgrading of labour. The investigation showed that while some firms had taken the problem so seriously that 40% of their staff had been trained in the works, others had relied exclusively on the exchanges to supply them with ready trained workers as they required them. The Boards were empowered to compel such recalcitrant employers to surrender their experienced workers and to take on and train new men. Concentration of production in the bigger enterprises was enforced so as to increase the scope for the employment of women (since the larger units could generally make more use of rapidly trained and semi-skilled labour) ; and the Work Book, which by the beginning of the war covered all the important occupations, was of immense value in providing a record of the industrial experience of the workers needed for transference.

Although the Government had the right of industrial conscription, the authority was kept in the background as a final resource. During 1940, for example, of ten million vacancies filled by the exchanges only one million were filled by conscription. The recruitment of women, on which more and more reliance had to be placed, was almost entirely voluntary. The organisation of part-time work began much earlier in the course of the war in Germany than in this country. Firms were encouraged to offer various amenities to make it easier for women with household responsibilities to undertake industrial work. Some firms arranged to do their women employees' washing in the firm's laundry ; others provided hot meals ready cooked to be taken away for the family dinner ; the Women's Organisation of the Party established thousands of crèches to look after workers' children. The Government urged all concerned to do all in their power to make half-day work " a pleasant change from household drudgery ".[1] The effect of all these measures can be seen in the rapid growth in the number of women employed. Whereas from the outbreak of war to the end of 1940 the number of women workers had risen by only 300,000, between January and September, 1941, a further 700,000 were absorbed.

There is evidence, however, that neither the control machinery nor the voluntary encouragement was working entirely satisfactorily. The control exercised through the Labour Book was so strict and the penalty for leaving a job without permission so severe, that many women hesitated to come into industry for

[1] H. W. Singer, " German War Economy", *Economic Journal*, Dec. 1941.

fear of becoming " slaves of the Labour Book ". To overcome this difficulty temporary entrants were provided with a less formidable type of record. Even so, as household maintenance and shopping became more burdensome with war shortages, many women who were previously accustomed to full-time employment have tried to take advantage of the organisation of part-time work. This means that the total of new entrants noted above does not, in fact, represent altogether an addition to previous labour resources, particularly as the reorganisation of the firm that is made necessary by a number of short shifts adds to the overhead charges in office work, insurance, protective clothing, etc. On the other hand, it is generally agreed that the part-time workers produce more proportionately than full-time employees and are less guilty of absenteeism.

The absentee problem is evidently as serious for Germany as for this country. One decree after another has been issued threatening heavier and heavier penalties. Already in 1940 workers were warned that if they took extra holidays the payment for their legitimate holidays would be stopped, but the trouble continued and suggestions were put forward to use " educational " labour corps as a cure. That even this threat has not had the desired effect is shown by the fact that in the summer of 1942 absentees were told that they would lose a fortnight's rights under health and unemployment insurance schemes.[1] It is unlikely that such a threat would have much influence on workers who know that the labour shortage is so severe that nobody in authority would be willing to risk allowing any worker to be unemployed at all.

Apart from absenteeism, the poaching of labour has been the practice which has proved most difficult to control. Although the enticement of skilled labour from one firm by another was prohibited in many trades even before the war, the practice still continued, as is shown by the decree issued in 1942 imposing very heavy fines on employers convicted of breaking the poaching laws. On the whole the general trend has been towards a more extended use of conscription. The labour controls were already so stringent that there was not much chance to tighten them up further. In the summer of 1942, for example, the agricultural situation was dealt with by the conscription of all residents in the countryside and country towns, on the grounds that the wives of farmers and farm workers had ceased to do their usual jobs because their husbands were earning such unusually high incomes ; and for general employment there were nearly a quarter of a million more conscripts a month than there had been in the early part of the war.

[1] H. W. Singer, " German War Economy ", *Economic Journal*, June–Sept. 1942.

On the whole, then, the German Labour Controls are pretty much the same as those that are being used in England and, indeed, the German papers have had much pleasure in pointing out derisively that this country has found it necessary to copy their methods, only more clumsily and more slowly. There is, however, one fundamental difference between the methods of the two countries, even though the actual machinery in operation has so many features in common. From the outset the legislation giving power to the British Minister of Labour and National Service required consultation, prior to action, with the interested parties ; and even where this has not been expressly provided for by law, there has invariably been the fullest discussion before any step has been taken. This means that every move in restricting the liberty of the individual has been made with the consent of those whose freedom has been thereby curtailed. Not that every employer and worker has welcomed the restrictions, but that the associations representing his interests have had an opportunity of putting forward any special circumstances that ought to be taken into consideration and have finally agreed to the subordination of such considerations to the overriding purpose of winning the war. In Germany, on the other hand, the controls have been imposed from above. Not that this means that the State has been all-powerful and has been able to distribute labour according to plan. Far from it. When working hours were increased at the same time that overtime pay and bonuses were abolished, the resulting passive resistance led to such a reduction in output that the severity of the decree had to be modified. Similarly the unwillingness of women to abandon the rôle assigned to them in earlier Nazi ideology has, in fact, prevented the general use of conscription with regard to female labour. And despite the incessant threats to absentees or those who leave their jobs to get others at higher pay, the workers know quite well that there is no very real danger of " educational " camps or other serious punitive measures while the need for their output is so immediate and so urgent. The distinction between the controls of the two countries, therefore, lies much more in the atmosphere surrounding them and in the ideas on which they are based than in either their machinery or their effectiveness.[1]

II

In Germany, as in England, the control of occupational distribution has been introduced as part of a war economy. The

---

[1] No mention has been made here of the employment of foreign workers nor of prisoners of war, since in neither case is the problem of the occupational distribution of the general population involved.

difference has been one of timing. For in Germany, as in practically all other countries, the productive system is one of private enterprise at private risk. The decision as to what shall be produced, and by what methods, rests with the owners of property, who decide to do this or that according to their estimate of the profits to be gained. In no country is this system universal or unchecked ; there are activities which are undertaken collectively and judged by other criteria than their economic profitability, and the individual in making his own decisions must operate within a social framework which has been designed to fulfil social purposes. But by and large, goods and services are produced because somebody, rightly or wrongly, thinks that it will pay him to make them.

In Russia, on the other hand, the utilisation of economic resources is part of a plan nationally designed and collectively executed. Production is organised in response to an order from authority and not in the hope of rousing and meeting the wishes of consumers sufficiently accurately as to result in gain for the owner of the enterprise. But even though initiative in planning production lies with the State, the Soviet economy is faced with the same problem as one that is based on private enterprise. It has to devise some mechanism for apportioning its human resources amongst the various productive branches. The Soviet Union's experience in this respect is particularly interesting and valuable because of the Russian genius for improvisation. They are sure of their objective, but they are ready to make endless experiments to find the best road to it. No device has the chance to get sanctified by tradition ; unless it meets the need it is scrapped at once and a new method tried out with the same glowing enthusiasm as its predecessor. It is this readiness to cut their losses and speculate afresh, no less than their deliberate attempt to establish a new set of incentives for work in place of those which dominate in bourgeois countries, which focuses on Russia the fascinated attention of the rest of the world.

In the years immediately following the Revolution, Russian workers confidently expected to advance at once into a new world of freedom and plenty. In the first flush of revolutionary ardour decrees were issued giving workers all those things for which they had longed in Tsarist days—an eight-hour day, a month's holiday with pay, a comprehensive scheme of social insurance which provided that the worker should have full wages whether in work or not, etc. But uncompromising economic facts soon forced them to shake themselves free of this pipe dream. Russia had entered the war as a poor country with the greater part of her natural resources still unexploited and with most of her industries still in the embryonic stage of develop-

ment.	She emerged in 1917 poorer still by the loss of her most
highly industrialised regions (Poland and the Baltic provinces)
and with her internal communications so disrupted that large
areas were faced by famine. Though the agricultural regions
continued to produce food, there was no means of getting it
to the towns, nor were the peasants willing to part with their
produce, even where roads, bridges and railways remained in
existence, since the urban trades were not producing manufactured
goods to give them in exchange. Some of the factories continued
to work as they had before under their old owners and management, but the large majority came under either centralised State
control, or, more often, under the management of the local factory
committees representing the workers employed in the enterprise.
Neither of these two methods was effective, partly because there
had not yet grown up a body of trained managers, partly because
the need for such specialised talent had not yet occurred to the
main body of workers. It has always been difficult for the
manual worker, who sees the evidence of his own work in the
growing volume of the material products for which he is responsible, to understand the part played by the man who sits quietly
in the office, talking or writing or issuing instructions. The
Revolution exalted the prestige of the manual worker and taught
him to despise the managerial classes (most of whom were bitter
opponents of Bolshevism). Nor did he feel that there was any
reason to submit to discipline from fear of want, as the decree
assured him an income irrespective of whether he was in a job
or not. The inevitable consequence of this was that the earnings
of the worker came to be a smaller and smaller proportion of his
income. By 1919, the wage represented only 6% of the workers'
income and the rest came from grants from the State.

No amount of State decrees, however, can alter the inexorable
fact that a community cannot share out more than is produced.
Whatever the amount of the wage or however high the State
allowances in terms of money, real incomes must be determined
by the amount that is being produced, and the catastrophic fall in
productivity which characterised the first years following the
Revolution necessarily meant poverty for all. "The radical
defect of War Communism", says Sir John Maynard, "lay, not
in its immediate and removable defects, or in an unorthodoxy
which may be merely freedom from unnecessary obsessions, but
in the low productivity which inevitably ruined it."[1] It came
to be obvious that it was essential to establish immediately temporary machinery for getting the productive system to operate
while a new technique, more appropriate to the beliefs of the
régime, was being worked out.

[1] Sir John Maynard, *The Russian Peasant and other Studies*, p. 111.

There was talk of mobilising labour on military lines and subjecting workers to the same control and sanctions as soldiers, and although a compromise solution was decided on, the discipline decreed was almost as drastic. Gangs of men were conscripted and sent about the country to repair ruined railways, bridges, etc. Managers were no longer elected by the workers but selected by the authorities according to their competence, and "one-man" instead of committee management became the rule. Even this was not enough by itself to stop the rot, and as, for the time, the one most important need was to increase productivity by whatever means, capitalist private enterprise was re-introduced temporarily in order to give the Soviet Government breathing space in which to mature its plans. With this came the same sort of protective legislation with which we are familiar in capitalist countries, and a Trade Union organisation modelled on that of the Western communities.

This was only an interlude, a stoppage of the engine, as Trotsky put it, in order to take in water; but it served to bring the community face to face with economic realities and changed the temper of the revolutionary experiment. No longer did people believe that the walls of Jericho would fall at the blast of the trumpet and they would walk into the Promised Land flowing with milk and honey. Nor was it enough to say that something had happened in the old days, for it to be condemned out of hand as worthless in the new. They had come to realise that the new world had to be built up bit by bit by hard work and dogged persistence, and they were prepared to use any method that helped reach the goal, whether it was borrowed from bourgeois economy or not. It is not intended to convey the impression that this understanding and determination were common property. Far from it. But those in authority were hard-headed and intelligent men. They had come to terms with reality, and their control of all channels of public information and opinion gave them an opportunity to set the tone.

When the New Revolution began, then, with the inauguration of the Five Year Plan, the discipline of work was well established and was more rigorous than had ever been experienced before. The Government had set itself the stupendous task of creating a Socialist State and carrying through an industrial revolution at one and the same time; and for this, a well-trained and well-disciplined labour force was an absolute necessity. There was an almost limitless supply of unskilled labour to be drawn from the agricultural reservoir, but there was an acute shortage of every kind of skill, and no tradition of good workmanship or of industrial efficiency. To some extent, compulsion could be and was employed. In all agricultural communities where there are few who work for wages, communal emergency jobs must inevitably be done by imposing a sort of labour-tax on the local inhabitants. The English Highways Act of 1555, for example, which compelled every man to work four days of eight hours on the roads each year in order to maintain the local highways, was not repealed until the nineteenth century. And, similarly, in Russia compulsion was used to meet a sudden emergency. For example, in 1930 all unemployed workers (including intellectuals) could be used in connection with timber-floating after the thaw ; a crisis in railway transport was met by the compulsory recall of all with technical experience in transport ; the accumulations of loading and unloading grain were dealt with by brigades of shock workers which the labour organisations were ordered to mobilise, and so on. Recently Collective Farms and Town Soviets have been told to select a certain number of young men and women for technical courses, and those chosen are compelled to take up the trade for which they have been trained for a stated period. An early decree made labour obligatory on all citizens of the Soviet Union on the revolutionary principle " He who does not work shall not eat ", and, at first, human nature being what it is, it is no matter for surprise that the nastiest tasks were compulsorily allotted to those who had been expropriated. But experience soon showed, as it invariably has done through the ages in similar circumstances, that compulsory labour does not pay except for the very simplest jobs. And with the exception of the emergency work noted above, the Russian worker was left free to choose his own occupation and offer himself to whichever enterprise is willing to engage him.

Inducements had, therefore, to be devised to persuade people to train for the more difficult jobs and to be efficient and industrious when they were trained. The mechanisms on which the Soviet Union has come to rely are, in fact, exactly the same as those with which we are familiar in capitalist communities, that is, to make as close a correlation as possible between individual effort and individual reward. Wherever possible, piece rates are paid so as to make it worth while for the worker to increase his output ; individual conduct sheets are kept ; differential rations are allowed for " shock " workers (i.e. those doing more than the average amount of work), and the continuous working week, whereby successive shifts of workers worked on the same job with the same tools, was given up because this " depersonalisation " of work, to use Stalin's phrase, made it impossible to have that strict adherence to personal responsibility which is the prime essential of an efficiently run industry.

The effort to increase the number of skilled workers has led to the setting up of ambitious training schemes, supplemented by shorter courses given in factory schools by the foremen and staff.

To persuade workers to take the courses, reliance is placed, in the main, on wage differentials in the occupations for which the training qualifies. Jobs are divided into many categories, each of which carries not only different wage rates but rights to various amenities (e.g. holidays, housing, etc.). Any worker who believes himself qualified to do work of a higher category can demand a fortnight's trial. If he makes good, he remains at that work and receives the higher rate of pay and amenities that go with it. As a result, the number of skilled mechanics increased four times and of engineers seven times within a decade.[1] As all enterprises, even though State run, must get their labour for themselves, and as the worker is free to leave, the different wages are an indication of the relative intensity of the demand for labour.

The grading is not by craft ; nor by age or seniority ; nor yet simply by any estimate of skill ; nor of the length of time necessary to gain the skill. The grading is really determined and from time to time changed, according to the requirements of the enterprise, or of all the enterprises with similar needs, in the various kinds of skill and craftsmanship and to the extent to which these requirements are being automatically met by the supply of workers competent to perform the various tasks.[2]

And when circumstances change and more workers are wanted in one or another occupation, it is by alterations in economic rewards that recruits are directed into the desired channels.

Very interesting is it [comment the Webbs] to find all this manipulation of wage payment for different grades which always assumes a national minimum of desirable personal expenditure, becoming more and more dominated by the principle of payment according to " social value ". This principle is applied alike in the case of particular crafts, or kinds of skill, of which there is, at the moment, a shortage, or for which there is an increasing demand ; and at the other extreme, to a whole district to which it is desired to attract immigrants. When we asked, in 1932, why the work of coppersmiths had been placed in a higher grade than that of other smiths, we were informed that the rapid development of electrification was hindered by the lack of an adequate number of workers who could do coppersmithing with technical efficiency. In order to encourage more boys voluntarily to take to this particular craft in their apprenticeship, and young mechanics to qualify themselves as coppersmiths in evening classes, the craft of coppersmithing was put into a higher grade. In a remarkably short time the supply of coppersmiths was increased.[3]

As would be expected with the rapid industrialisation of the country, the heavy industries producing capital goods and fuel

---

[1] M. Dobb, *Soviet Planning and Labour.*
[2] S. and B. Webb, *Soviet Communism,* Book II, p. 710.
[3] Ibid.

have improved their position *vis-à-vis* the light industries making consumption goods. For a time the difference in wages earned in the heavy and light industries was not sufficient to get an adequate staff into the former.

> In order to put an end to this evil [Stalin told a conference of leaders of industry in June, 1931] we must set up a wage scale that will take into account the difference between skilled labour and unskilled labour, between heavy work and light work. It cannot be tolerated that a highly skilled worker in a steel mill should earn no more than a sweeper. It cannot be tolerated that a locomotive driver on a railway should earn only as much as a copy clerk.[1]

Why " cannot be tolerated " ? Surely only because one is scarce and the other is not, and not for any reason of morals or propriety. If a new technical device made the skill of the steel-worker redundant, it would be equally " intolerable " to continue to pay him the high wage that would attract into the industry a larger number of workers than would be required. In capitalist countries we call it " marginal productivity " or some such phrase, and in Russia it is called " social value "—a different name but the same thing.

There is, however, an important difference in the working of wage differentials in England and Russia. As has been shown in an earlier chapter, the operation of the price economy, in so far as labour is concerned, is prevented from working freely in this country by many institutional factors. Wages retain customary levels and ratios long after the demands for labour which they mirrored have become obsolete ; collecting bargaining slows down changes in rates of pay, and the maintenance of the unemployed through insurance benefits and State allowances postpones the movement of labour from declining to expanding industries. In Russia, however, the system is " plus royaliste que le roi ". In fundamentals it is the same ; in practice it differs by adhering more logically to its nature and by casting off the institutional shackles. From the beginning of the Five Year Plan, the Trade Unions have been shorn of their power to negotiate wages. The official view is that, as there is no longer any enemy class, the Trade Unions cannot exercise the functions for which they rightly exist in capitalist countries. They argue that there can be no fear of exploitation in a Soviet country, nor can there be any sufficiently serious divergence of interest to justify a group of workers striking to enforce their view. While the Trade Unions, then, carry out an immense amount of administrative work with regard to social insurance, employment exchanges, etc., they have no voice at all in what, in capitalist countries, constitutes their main work, i.e. the

---

[1] J. Stalin, *New Conditions, New Tasks*, p. 7, quoted Webb.

negotiation of wage rates.   The wages are settled by authority and can be, and are, altered at will whenever it is thought necessary to attract or discourage additional personnel.   In so far as the Trade Unions are concerned with wages, they are confined to fixing appropriate piece rates on the basis of the time rates settled from above.

There have recently been efforts to establish a rock bottom below which wages in any occupation shall not fall.   In November, 1937, the Government decreed a minimum wage of 115 roubles a month for all workers.[1]   It was estimated at the time that the cost of bringing all wages up to this level would be 600 million roubles in twelve months and that the average increase in wage of those below the minimum would be 19 roubles a month.   This means that before the decree two and a half million workers were earning less than the minimum.   In this country a firm bottom to wages is provided by the amount of the allowance paid to the unemployed.   But it is just here that the difference between the working of wage differentials in England and Russia presents the most marked contrast.   During the early 'twenties, when a modified form of capitalism was in operation in the Soviet Union, there was a considerable amount of unemployment, and an unemployment benefit scheme was introduced in 1925.   It was never at any time, however, complete or comprehensive.   It was strictly limited by a severe means test to those without any resources at all.   The period during which benefit was payable was limited to nine months for a skilled worker and six for an unskilled in any one year, with a total maximum over any period of time of eighteen monthly payments to a skilled worker and twelve to an unskilled.   Applications for benefit were considered only from industrial workers who had been members of a Trade Union for at least a year.   Those who could show good reason for having dropped from membership might receive an allowance if they could prove a qualifying period of three years' previous employment.   Moreover, in contrast with the extreme liberality of the payments to the sick and aged, the unemployment benefit never amounted to anything like full subsistence and usually varied between one-fifth and one-half of the applicant's previous earnings.   Even these inadequate benefits were, in fact, never paid to more than about one-fifth of those who were actually unemployed.

There was here, then, no attempt to provide economic security for those out of work, even during the period of industrial dislocation when the difficulty of getting work was considerable. But when the Five Year Plan began to get into its stride and the demand for urban labour became acute, the whole system of

[1] L. E. Hubbard, *Soviet Trade and Distribution*, pp. 329–30.
(One hundred roubles a month compares roughly with 10s. a week in England.)

unemployment maintenance was given up completely. In 1930 unemployment benefit was abolished on the grounds that there was work for everybody who was willing to do it. The Trade Unions took over the work of the Labour Exchanges, which had previously been separately constituted organisations, and were prepared to find work at Trade Union rates for every able-bodied worker, though not necessarily in his own town or his own craft. As an alternative the Government might pay him or her a maintenance allowance while training for a new skilled job.

It can be seen, therefore, that in Russia, as in this country, there is freedom of choice of occupation, but unlike this country, Russia is prepared to maintain the logical corollary of this freedom —that the individual must bear the consequences of his choice. There is no compulsion to learn a new trade or go to another locality in the sense that legal proceedings would be taken against those who do not comply with State demands. But very serious, though indirect, pressure is exercised by the refusal of an allowance of any sort to those who are out of a job. As a non-producer must thus depend solely on the charity of his friends, and as, moreover, he has no ration-card to entitle him to buy necessaries at controlled prices, he is under very strong persuasion to do the work the authorities want of him. In England, the statement that there is no freedom of choice since the only alternative is starvation has not, for a very long time, been more than a rhetorical flourish ; in Russia it is, on the other hand, a literal description of the actual state of affairs.

There is, of course, one important difference between the two countries : a nationally-planned economy can take steps to avoid large-scale unemployment and if it does, in fact, take such steps can guarantee that there are jobs available for all who are prepared to make the necessary individual adjustments in their qualifications and homes. The Soviet Government claims that since the inauguration of the first Five Year Plan it has been able to maintain full employment, but there are no records from which we can judge the accuracy of this claim. When unemployment benefit was abolished in 1930 there were about a million workers registered as unemployed, but, as has been shown above, only those with certain qualifications were registered. Doubtless a substantial addition would have to be made to this figure to give the total of all those out of work. Since 1930 there are no figures at all and any estimate would have to be guesswork. But if we are to judge from the industrial experience of other countries there is always a fair amount of unemployment even during periods of maintained activity—unemployment due to seasonal or climatic conditions, to time lost in changing from job to job, and to the natural hesitation in making up one's mind whether the loss of one's present work is due to a temporary setback or is an indication of a long-term change in the industry's demand for personnel.   It is worth recalling that the Unemployment Insurance system was established in this country to deal with the privations caused by this type of temporary unemployment rather than the miseries of mass unemployment, and that Sir William Beveridge estimates that, even on the assumption of a successful policy for maintaining full employment, we must reckon on about $8\frac{1}{2}\%$ [1] of the working population being unemployed for these temporary, frictional causes.   It is unlikely that the percentage would have been as high as this in Russia, since the total number engaged in industrial work is a much smaller proportion of the population than in this country, and since the Russian economy is a much more self-contained unit and less dependent on the vagaries of international trade.   But it is reasonable to assume that when the employment situation in Russia presented such a happy contrast to that of other parts of the world, there was still a considerable amount of temporary unemployment, and that the Government preferred to allow the consequent suffering to be endured rather than risk a slowing down in the mobility of workers into the expanding industries on whose staffing the success of the Five Year Plan depended. There is some evidence for this assumption, for in 1932 State enterprises were employing $4\frac{3}{4}$ million [2] persons in excess of the plan and were forced to get rid of these superfluous workers as quickly as possible.   It is certain that, even though there were factories eager to absorb more personnel, there must have been some unemployment before the workers turned out from the State enterprises found themselves in their new jobs—particularly as there was no centralised machinery for bringing together workers and vacancies.

It is, yet, probably true, on the whole, that since 1930 the shortage of skilled labour has been so acute that the periods of temporary unemployment for workers with any technical qualifications have been very slight.   It is with the semi-skilled and the unskilled that the problem has been more serious, and amongst the unskilled, in particular, there has probably been a good deal of underemployment.   Russian agriculture concentrates predominantly on cereal cultivation, which requires a large amount of labour only during certain periods of the year, and there is, consequently, a persistent influx of peasants into the towns in search of a more regular and a higher income.   To some extent this migration is controlled by the authorities.   Many of the collective farms make

---

[1] Sir W. Beveridge, *Social Insurance and Allied Services*, Cmd. 6404/1942, p. 164.

[2] Sir John Maynard, *The Russian Peasant*, p. 353.

agreements with town factories to supply them with a number of unskilled workers for a period of time at given rates of pay. In 1938 there were about one and a half millions employed in industry on this type of contract.[1] In such contracts the individual is definitely under compulsion ; the contract is made over his head. But for the most part the peasant has made his own arrangements, wandering from place to place in search of better conditions. It was partly in order to deal with this constant shifting of workers, with its attendant effects on housing and transport, that the passport system was reintroduced in 1932. This tendency to be perpetually " flitting " from job to job is not confined to the unskilled ; it has been one of the toughest nuts to crack in the whole labour situation. Many factory managers have complained that there is little sense in organising efficient training schemes in the works, as so many of the workers go off to other districts as soon as they are qualified, or even before, and leave the managers with a new lot of " green " labour on their hands. The fundamental difference in the cultural traits of the British and Russian worker is apparent in this. The problem in this country is to persuade people to move from the tiny area, it may be the village, it may, even, be the street, which to them is " home " ; anything outside it is strange, unfamiliar and therefore to be avoided. The problem in Russia is to get people to " stay put ".

> It is natural [says Sir John Maynard] to think of the Russian as a peasant. But he is a peasant with a difference ; a peasant in whom the nomad survived till yesterday. . . . There is something in him of the land-sailor, with a range from Minsk to Vladivostock and with some of that flexibility of mind which a sailor acquires. The land led him on as an inland sea led on the sailor, from headland to headland till he learned to explore the deep and master the oceans ; and at each new advance his mind jumped, till imagination came into existence, and with it those wider sympathies which have no corners for the narrowness of race. It is a part of the nomad spirit which makes it so easy for him to blend with any and every class of humanity. His own thinkers have recognised it and called it his all-humanitarianism. With what tenacity the nomad spirit persists to-day we see in that persistent " flitting " which is a characteristic feature in the comparatively settled life of the factory.[2]

From the point of view of industrial efficiency the " flitting " tendency is as serious as the " stay put " tendency. The Russian worker flits from where he is badly needed, and there is no guarantee that he goes to where he is wanted. The move is often the

---

[1] M. Dobb, *Soviet Labour and Planning*, p. 97.
[2] Maynard, *The Russian Peasant*, pp. 22–3.

result of the restless nomad stirring below the factory worker exterior, though it may be rationalised as a search for better work or conditions.

Stern disciplinary measures have been introduced to try and curb this national restlessness.   Since 1938 a system of Work Books has been in operation.   The Book, which contains a record of the worker's industrial experience, must be presented to and retained by the works manager until the worker leaves. Unless the Work Book showed a record of at least eleven months' employment in the same enterprise the worker did not qualify for holidays with pay, and the various social insurance benefits were also graded according to the length of time spent in one works.   Since 1940, when industry was put on a war footing, flitting has been made a punishable offence.

The other problem with which the Soviets have had to deal in common with all countries with a labour shortage is that of voluntary absenteeism, and here again a rigorous discipline has been imposed.   Since 1932 the management has had the right to dismiss a worker for a single day's absence without leave.   Dismissal ordinarily has little effect when a worker knows there are a dozen other jobs waiting for him, but in Russia it involved the cancellation of his ration books, and as the co-operative shops in all the most important industries were under the control of the works managers, this proved for a time very effective.   There is always the possibility, however, of collusion between the manager and the worker to evade a check imposed from outside.   The harried manager, under orders to deliver a certain output by a certain day and realising the immense difficulty he will meet in getting further supplies of qualified workers, may think it better to turn a blind eye to the peccadilloes of those he has already got.   He has the right to dismiss a worker ; he may decide not to use his power.   Since 1938, however, pressure has been put on him to do so.   Managers have been ordered to count twenty minutes' lateness in commencing work as amounting to absenteeism and have been informed that those who do not dismiss a worker guilty of three unjustified absences in a month will themselves be liable to penalties.

Does all this mean then that in Russia the main reliance is still placed on the threat of starvation to get work done and done efficiently ?   By no means, any more than it is true in this country that men do their jobs solely because they are afraid of starvation.   Men are not as simple as that.   Interest in the work itself, habit, the simplicity of sticking to an established routine, pride in one's capacity, self-respect, the wish to shine before one's fellow workers or family, the boredom of being too little occupied, convention, ambition, desire for the good things of life that money will buy, all play their part. Sometimes one motive is dominant, sometimes another. Rarely is a man dominated always by the same part of his nature. But in Russia there is a further incentive to work—one which does not take the place of these others but which is additional to them : the sense of community and of obligation to society. To the Russian worker has come the revelation that the future development of society is something in which he, as an individual, can play a part. It is on him that devolves the responsibility for building the new world. Whatever sacrifices he may have to make, whatever privations he may have to endure, whatever portion of his own freedom he may have to surrender, are justified as necessary stages in the greatest constructive effort of mankind—the shaping of a new social order. His leaders never hide from him the fact that they are engaged in a great experiment and that serious blunders may be made. The readiness to confess that a wrong direction has been taken, to retrace their steps and start again in a fresh way constantly brings home to their minds that they are all engaged in a stupendous adventure. But equally it keeps vivid the knowledge that it is an adventure in which all are involved and in which each individual must take his full share. A recital of the legal restrictions on the individual may give the impression that the Russian worker has little freedom to do anything else than the work he is told to do by authority. He cannot move without a passport ; he loses his rations if he leaves work without permission ; if he does not get a job he may be left to starve. All these are true but their effect is negative. What the worker gets besides is a positive ideal towards which to strive, a future of hope to justify and ennoble his present sacrifice, a reason for his present endurance which commends itself to his mind as a sufficient and worthy explanation. All who have visited Russian factories have commented on the sense of " ownness ", and of belonging to something bigger than themselves which permeates them. In its extreme form this enthusiasm finds expression in the work of the Stakhanovite movement, whose members set themselves to speed up production, or in the activities of the volunteer brigades who undertake extra tasks in their leisure time. A great deal of publicity has been given to these movements. But, after all, there is nothing very new or revolutionary in such voluntary work. For generations it has been the accepted tradition in England for thousands of men and women to undertake tasks without hope of reward or honour, solely from a sense of public duty. None of our present highly developed social services could have come into being without this unselfish and mostly unrecorded effort. As unpaid magistrates, in local government, as founders of all types of philanthropic society, men and women have given their time and energy and thought to work for which they have received no economic reward and often enough little public recognition. The significance of such organisations as the volunteer brigades in Russia is not that men are willing to work without economic reward, but that the obligation to do so is continually stressed as something which is expected of every citizen, irrespective of his age or sex or position in the community. In England there is still a great deal of class distinction in social obligations. During the war, the responsibility for doing the necessary extra emergency jobs in communal life has been accepted by every individual in all sections of society, from the school child who helps to collect salvage to the superannuated workman who takes his turn at manning the Wardens' Post. But in ordinary peace-times, while there is an immense amount of personal kindliness and neighbourly assistance amongst the mass of the population, it is the middle and upper classes who are the readiest to recognise a duty to give *organised* help to those less fortunately placed than themselves. Although happily there are many sensitive and thoughtful people who can meet those to whose interests they are devoting themselves with humility and friendliness on the basis of their common humanity, it is still true to say, as a generalisation, that there is a good deal of snobbishness in the public work in this country. What makes the Russian experience outstanding is the fact that there it is the ordinary manual worker who is called upon to give, and that as the obligation is placed on all, the giving is reciprocal and equal. " You would think they owned the country ", wrote Mr. Knickerbocker, " maybe they do, maybe they don't, but they think so "; and Sir John Maynard in describing the modern factories writes, " They remind me of great British public schools in their cultivation of *esprit de corps*."

It would be foolish to pretend that this sense of social obligation is the dominating influence in the Russian worker's life. But it is there; and all the combined effort of propaganda, education, public prestige, etc., is concentrated on developing it further. Where the Russian authorities show their realism and sound common sense is that they do not try and build too much on it until it has grown sufficiently strong to be a solid foundation. It takes a long time for men to learn to subordinate their private individual and family interests voluntarily to those of the bigger community. They may do it for a time, but it would be foolish to act as though they have learned to do it always. And so, while building up the new incentives, Russia retains the checks it has found necessary while men are as they are. In this country we have given up one set of incentives without even facing the fact that we need something to take their place.

F

CHAPTER VI

OCCUPATIONAL DISTRIBUTION AFTER THE WAR

I

SYNOPSIS OF CHAPTER

1. The problem stated. Social security weakens the incentive to find paid employment. By common consent, social security must be retained and developed, hence the need to find an alternative mechanism for occupational distribution. There are two alternatives (a) changed incentives, (b) State control of transference.

2. The Beveridge Report proposes compulsory training as a condition of receiving unemployment benefit, but there are reasons for considering this impracticable.

3. The sense of community is not as strong in peace-time as in war, and there is room for more divergence of opinion as to what constitutes the " public good ", particularly in a society in which production is carried on by private enterprise.

4. Much could be done to educate both young people and adults to understand basic economic relationships and to appreciate the value of community. But educational processes are inevitably slow, and until attitudes change education must be supplemented by some degree of control of labour.

5. Peace-time labour control presents knottier problems to solve than that of war-time.

6. Freedom of choice of occupation should be retained as far as possible, but people should have much fuller knowledge of available openings. Youth should be given more guidance in choosing jobs, and adults should have access to fuller information through the compulsory notification by employers of vacancies.

7. Freedom of choice of occupation cannot be maintained indefinitely for those out of work. Unemployment benefit should continue as long as unemployment lasts but after a prescribed period the worker should be offered the alternative of training or direction to another type of work.

8. Labour controls cannot be effective unless (a) the Government is prepared to prosecute those who do not obey, and here trade unions can do much to create a favourable public opinion, and (b) the Government knows enough of economic trends to direct labour into expanding industries. For this, changes in the recruitment, training and organisation of the Civil Service are essential.

WHAT methods of occupational distribution will be needed after the war ? Are we to retain the war-time labour controls or abandon them as soon as peace is signed ? It is worth while to recapitulate briefly the problem facing us.

The self-adjusting character of industry has been profoundly changed by the development of a system of social security. The provision of a subsistence income based on needs weakens the urge to find and keep an independent job. By strengthening those tendencies which already operate to resist changes in work and locality, it slows down the occupational redistribution of labour which is necessitated by changing demands, improved techniques and new raw materials, and in so doing it inevitably reduces the wealth on whose increase the advance in standards of living depends. Yet social security cannot be given up. The building of a secure economic foundation to the lives of the population must be accounted as one of the greatest triumphs of the twentieth century. It can be justified on grounds both of justice and expediency. The individual's control of his economic destiny is now so reduced, in a world of mass production and quick communications, that he cannot be asked to bear the brunt of policies and development for which he has no responsibility, and whose future course he has no means of knowing. But even if justice did not demand that he should be given collective protection, experience has shown that the consequence of leaving him without assistance is an incalculable number of social casualties. The stunting, both physically and mentally, of those who are forced to grow up in poverty, the inability to plan for the future when the very foundations of life are continually shifting, the sense of bitterness and frustration when your world tumbles about your ears through no fault of your own, and the loss to society when its children's potentialities remain undeveloped through lack of food or space, or of adequate educational opportunities, are now so obvious as to need little elaboration. There can be no question, therefore, of the imperative need for further advances along the path that has been marked out during the last forty years. There may be differences of opinion about the details of the schemes of social assistance, there can be none with regard to the objective. Freedom from want can be obtained by the mass of the population only by collective provision. But when we accept this as an aim of national policy it is essential to realise that we are grafting a revolutionary principle on to a social system of an entirely different design. We have the ability, at least in this country, to produce enough wealth to provide for everybody a standard of living which allows for the satisfaction of basic needs. We can produce the wealth and we have devised schemes of distribution, in the various social services, to enable those in want to make a claim on the common pool. But this does not mean that we can dissociate distribution from production. However comprehensive our schemes of social security and however ingenious our methods of distribution, we cannot guarantee freedom from even basic want, and certainly we cannot hope for higher standards of living, unless wealth is, in fact, being produced at the requisite rate. And since the production of wealth depends upon human agency, this cannot happen unless the individual members of society are ready to play their part in the co-operative enterprise.

Before subsistence was guaranteed, the majority of the community laboured under the stern decree, " He who does not work neither shall he eat ", and the goad of hunger fought against natural conservatism. But if the " claim to eat " is upheld as a civic right, it becomes essential to find some new mechanism for getting workers to produce the wealth that the State guarantees to distribute. A price has to be paid for social security as for any other economic good.

There are two alternatives. Either some new incentive must be found to replace the old one of personal gain and the emphasis laid on the right of the citizen, *vis-à-vis* the State, must be balanced by an equal insistence on his duty to contribute to the community ; or else, freedom of choice of occupation, must be abandoned as an anachronistic survival in a world which has given up the principle of individual responsibility.

II

In the *Beveridge Report* the proposals made for securing the basic standard of living during unemployment show the logical conclusion towards which developments in this field over the last twenty-five years have tended. It is there proposed that unemployment benefit should be a weekly sum calculated to provide full subsistence for the needs of the family and that it should be indefinite in duration. Sir William Beveridge has recognised that the provision of an income for an indefinite period may lead to equally indefinite idleness, and a method is suggested for overcoming this difficulty.

> The correlative of the State's undertaking to ensure adequate benefit for unavoidable interruption of earnings, however long [says the *Report*], is enforcement of the citizen's obligation to seek and accept all reasonable opportunities of work, to co-operate in measures designed to save him from habituation to idleness and to take all proper measures to be well. The higher the benefits provided out of a common fund for unmerited misfortune, the higher must be the citizen's sense of obligation not to draw on that fund unnecessarily.[1]

This general principle leads to the following practical conclusions :

1. Unemployed persons cannot be allowed to hold out indefinitely for their accustomed type of work in their home district if there is work they could do elsewhere.

2. Benefit should be unconditional only for a limited period and should then carry with it the obligation to attend a work or training centre " such attendance being designed both as a means

[1] *Beveridge Report*, Cmd. 6404/1942, p. 58.

of preventing habituation to idleness and as a means of improving capacity ".

These recommendations cannot be considered alone, since all the proposals made in the *Report* assume the prevention of mass unemployment. Unconditional benefit cannot be a satisfactory provision for more than limited periods of unemployment. What people really want is not an income but a job, and a job that seems worth doing. But, apart from this, the only adequate test of a claimant's right to benefit is an offer of suitable work, and this offer cannot be made if the incidence of unemployment is high in general. If no job is available attendance at a Work or Training Centre could be made a compulsory condition of receiving benefit, but this is impracticable if it has to be applied to men by the million. An assumption of full employment does not imply, however, absolute continuity of employment. Many industries are subject to unavoidable seasonable fluctuations in productive activity, and the waxing and waning fortunes of individual firms inevitably cause changes in their demand for labour. Moreover a country like Britain which is dependent on the rest of the world for its raw materials and markets cannot hope to remain untouched by economic disturbances in other parts of the world. But the assumption that mass unemployment does not occur does take as its starting point that the Government will be willing to use its authority to stabilise the general demand for labour and will be capable of finding the right method of doing so.

A number of questions here call for consideration. Granted that a high general level of industrial prosperity can be maintained by Government action (and there is reason to believe that a sufficiently bold policy of national investment might achieve this), does this inevitably prevent long-term unemployment on a large scale ? The year 1929 was one of very great prosperity, and the late 'thirties saw a general recovery in trade after the world depression, but in both these periods the hard core of unemployment in the Special Areas was hardly affected. It would be fatal to the welfare of the country to try and use Government authority to prevent the decline of methods or of whole industries that have served their turn and should be replaced by others. Decisions as to what should be produced should be determined by the needs and wishes of consumers and not by the desire to keep the incidence of unemployment low. If not, we get " production for the sake of employment " in the place of " production for the sake of profit ", and wherein lies the advance ? So that however successful we may be in preventing a general economic blizzard, we must still envisage a future in which local changes in economic climate introduce lasting transformations into the industrial landscape. Moreover, the rate of change is gathering momentum. It is true that the adjustments necessitated by the changes in demand and in methods of the post-war years were made infinitely more difficult by the catastrophic depression of 1921–2, but even when the rest of the world was moving rapidly towards boom conditions, this country still showed a percentage of unemployment that would earlier have been taken as the symbol of the blackest depression. And this situation was caused principally by the difficulty of manœuvring large groups of workers from declining to expanding industries. The time has gone by when we could assume that the personnel of one trade could be painlessly reduced by natural wastage while that of another was increased by recruiting the new entrants to industry. If this were so, a state of general prosperity could reasonably be considered as the only essential in preventing chronic unemployment. But the rate of invention has been immensely speeded up by the war. If ships can be built in sections in inland engineering shops and merely assembled at the shipyards, if plastics are to take the place of the traditional raw materials in one industry after another, it is evident that a new industrial revolution is on the way. The world moves faster than it used to do, and changes in materials, methods and products share in this general increase in acceleration. There is every likelihood, therefore, that we shall be faced in the future, as we have been in the past, with the existence of hundreds of thousands of adult, able-bodied, experienced workers who are unable to find work of the type to which they are accustomed and who must, in one way or another, get into industries requiring different knowledge or skill and, perhaps, situated in other localities.

It is with this problem in mind that the suggestion has been made that after a certain period of time the receipt of benefit should be made conditional on attendance at a work or training centre. It is stressed that the " certain period " must vary with circumstances. It is argued that it is unreasonable and extravagant to train a man for a new job if there is ground for believing that he will be reabsorbed into his own industry again pretty soon after whatever period has been specified as the maximum for unconditional benefit. But it is just here, where the discretionary element must, of necessity, enter in, that the difficulty begins. Experience has shown that very few people, whether employers or workers, are willing to recognise that the decline in the demand for their goods or services is more than a temporary setback. They are always anxious to hang on desperately until the " corner is turned ", and though each corner as it is turned shows the same dreary desolation ahead they continue to cling to the hope that a little later it will be different and a bright new world of recovery will be opened out. As was shown in an earlier chapter there are strong psychological factors at work here.

The experience of the war is likely to strengthen resistance in the post-war world. Miners who had been told for twenty years that they must make up their minds to the disagreeable fact that they were no longer wanted and must get out into other industries in other counties have suddenly discovered that mining is once again work of the utmost national importance. Men who, in misery and resentment, finally tore themselves from their homes and familiar environment and made a new niche for themselves in other employments are cajoled and badgered, or even compelled, to return to their former employment in the pits. The same public which formerly rated them for their lack of enterprise in waiting in the coalfields for things to improve now sneers at them for war profiteers because they are unwilling to throw up better jobs in another industry, although it is one which will probably continue to grow and give them a chance of progressive employment after the war. There has been a similar situation in shipbuilding and cotton. It seems probable that after the war these experiences will be remembered and that many of those who refused to contemplate changing their jobs and homes will feel that events justified their obstinacy ; and that those who did change will be determined not to be caught a second time.

It is not a simple matter, either, to decide at what point it is advisable to put pressure on a worker to fit himself for a new job. The inability to recognise the permanent nature of the changes in industry in the 'twenties was not confined to those most directly concerned. It was not until a full decade after the last war that appreciation of the fundamental character of the modifications began to creep into official memoranda and public pronouncements. In an authoritarian country, where production and trade are either owned by the State or under rigorous official control, the difficulty is not so great. The authority which decides the quantities and types of products to be made can estimate the consequent distribution of man-power that is involved. The estimates may be wrong, but the mistakes are not so obvious when the worker's employment is a matter of official decree, as they are when the value of his work has to be balanced against his wage in a profit-making enterprise. Where, as in this country, the bulk of production depends on the interplay of economic forces, and industries expand or decline in accordance with changes in profitable demand, the estimates are neither so easy to make in the first place nor mistakes so easy to conceal later on. Where there is so much room for legitimate doubt as to the need for changing one's job it is unlikely that compulsory training would prove a very practicable method of inducing increased labour mobility. Unwilling trainees do not usually prove very apt pupils. Once compulsion is introduced there is always the likelihood that the man on whom the choice falls is filled with resentment on the score that " they " " have a down on him " or want him out of the way for political or Trade Union reasons, and it is probable that more will be accomplished in the long run, even at the price of greater initial difficulty, if the recruits for training centres remain volunteers.

Even compulsory attendance at a work centre is not a simple thing to achieve. In this case, the aim is not to teach the worker a new trade but to attempt, by means of regular occupation, to retain industrial efficiency and aptitude and to prevent idleness from becoming a demoralising habit. If such a centre is to serve any constructive purpose it is essential that the work to which the men are put should be of real social value and not, as was so often the case in the old relief works, simply a face-saving measure to conceal the fact that money is being given for nothing. The problem that confronts such a centre is, however, the same as that which proved so hard·a nut for the organisers of relief work to crack. It must not be work that would be undertaken as a paying concern in the ordinary way of business, since this would create a new body of unemployment in order to occupy an existing set of unemployed persons. If it is to keep alive industrial efficiency, it must be interesting and educative ; it must be useful ; it must be such that workmen of widely differing experience can take advantage of it and learn something from it, and yet it must not be so attractive (as the unemployed occupational centres of the 'thirties often were) that men in attendance are unwilling to leave it to go back to normal industrial life. The mere enumeration of essentials is enough to show that the organisation of a work centre adequate to the object for which it is designed is far from easy. The difficulty is exaggerated by the impossibility of knowing with any degree of accuracy the number of men and women for whom provision should be made from time to time. The Juvenile Instruction Centres which for many years have tried to do this work for adolescents have already been faced with this problem. The work centre must be comparatively near to the home of the unemployed worker, or time and money are wasted on transport, and the smaller the area taken as the unit the wider are the fluctuations in the number unemployed at any moment. This gives rise either to almost insuperable problems of administration, staffing and equipment or else means that the occupation offered to those in attendance is somewhat makeshift.

At the best, it must be recognised that no amount of compulsion can really force men to work, though conditional benefit may compel them to attend the centre and go through the prescribed gestures. Here again the early relief works have valuable experience to offer. They show that there can be forms of work which can be very much more demoralising than the idleness they try to avoid. Even in paid work men vary in the amount of effort and conscientiousness they put into the job, but here there is a minimum below which the idle dare not go if they want to keep the job. What sanctions can be used in a work centre which men attend merely to qualify for benefit? The majority of men are decent and are ready to do what is required of them, but a minority of idle and worthless people, well versed in the tricks of keeping just the right side, could rapidly lower the standard of all and make those who were pulling their weight feel that they were mugs to be doing so. And suppose a man absents himself from the work centre or persistently arrives late? Nothing could be gained by reducing his allowance, since this would lead to the undernourishment of his wife and children and begin once more the cycle of " poverty-stricken childhood and below-par adult " that it is one of the purposes of adequate maintenance to try and break.

One is led to the conclusion, therefore, that compulsory attendance at a training or a work centre as a condition of drawing unlimited benefit would not solve the problem of immobility of labour unless men and women themselves become acutely conscious of their social obligations. Administrative machinery is a poor substitute for human virtue. Here again, as so often, the problem is fundamentally a psychological one. How can the incentives to work be adapted to a changing world? How far can a sense of social obligation supersede hunger as a spur to effort?

III

In war-time the obligation of the citizen towards the community is so obvious that it cannot be overlooked. For the men of the fighting forces, it is an obligation that knows no limit ; but even among non-combatants it is accepted as overriding almost everything else. The non-economic incentives to work can, it is evident, be made as potent if not more potent than the fear of poverty. Is it possible to carry over this social incentive to peace-time?

It must be admitted that the difficulties are many. A war which is carried on with popular consent always brings with it a heightened sense of community. The divergent interests

which divide society into warring factions in peace-time may
continue to exist but they lose their importance and significance
in relation to the one objective which dominates the minds of
all. The aim to which all effort is directed is definite and obvious.
Though there may be differences of opinion as to the best methods
to be adopted, there is none with regard to the goal to be reached.
The defeat of the enemy must take precedence over everything
else, and, provided people are convinced that the sacrifices they
are asked to make have this in view, they are prepared to make
them. Even though efforts may be made to spread the burden
that the community has to bear as fairly as possible over the
members it is accepted that " equality of sacrifice " in war-time
is absolutely impossible of achievement. The price paid by the
fighting man in the loss of his life or in severe permanent dis-
ability is something which cannot in any sense be equalled by
any other fellow citizen. Yet millions are prepared to risk paying
this price for their citizenship in a war in which they believe,
although the ideals they uphold are the property of all alike
and the victory for which they strive is a general, and not an
individual, reward.

But when men are pursuing their ordinary peace-time occupations there is no such definite common objective to which their
efforts are directed. Very rarely has the attempt been made in
peace as it necessarily has to be in war, to arouse individuals
to the realisation of the part they play in the social effort.
Occasionally during some time of stress when, for example, a
strike in an important industry throws the economic machine
out of gear, the rest of the community becomes resentfully aware
of their dependence on the work of those who are refusing to
carry on as usual and urges the recalcitrant industry to remember
their social obligations. Or sometimes at some local ceremonial
a half-hearted tribute is paid to the workers in an industry on
" whose skill and toil the prosperity of the area depends ",
and so on. But for the most part it is assumed that men do
their jobs for what they can get out of them in material rewards
and not because they make an essential contribution to the
welfare of the community as a whole. And in general this
assumption is correct. Even if one still believes that through the
guidance of an invisible hand the jobs that pay best turn out to
be the things that society needs, it must be confessed that the
social welfare is not the motive that actuates the person doing
it ; it is merely one of the unconsidered by-products of his
actions. The social repercussions, whether good or bad, are
not part of the calculations that men usually make in deciding
their course of action.

This is not an indictment of the selfish and callous nature of man. In ordinary peace-times the constituents of social welfare are neither so narrow nor so clearly defined as in war-time. There may be a wide divergence of opinion in the objectives to be aimed at as well as the methods by which to reach them. There is greater possibility of conflict between short-term and long-term aims. There is the impossibility of finding a common denominator in the comparison of economic and political and social goods. In war-time, however much we may enjoy ourselves as armchair critics of strategy, there is general recognition of the fact that the men in charge have access to knowledge which, on security grounds, is denied to the general public and that they must be allowed a fair amount of latitude in making decisions on behalf of us all. But in a peace-time democracy there is no reason why we should thus subordinate our individual views as to the most desirable courses of action, and this means that the whole concept of the " welfare of the community " loses its sharpness of outline. One of the political advantages enjoyed by the totalitarian states is that they can carry over from war to peace this power to focus public opinion on one objective, defined by the leaders in their own terms and elevated, by skilful propaganda, into a national symbol. But it is of the essence of democracy that each man sees the world with his own eyes and makes his own judgments of what is right and what is wrong. As members of the same community we have a common foundation and some measure of agreement on general moral principles, but we differ profoundly from one another on most immediate issues, and this makes it much more difficult to get any acceptable symbol for the common good. Hitler can din a particular cliché into the ears of his subjects until it is accepted as a national goal worthy of any sacrifice. A democracy does not want this sheep-like following nor could it get it if it did. But the price it pays for a more diffused power of judgment and decision is a lessening of fervour, so that, except during war or other similar crisis, the " public good " is part of a shadowy background rather than a consciously desired goal.

That the main emphasis should be put on self-interest instead of the general good is an obvious consequence of an economic organisation which is set in motion by millions of individual decisions. This would be so even if there were widespread acceptance of the belief that the " invisible hand " is actually at work to reconcile private and public interests. We no longer have this comfortable confidence, however. We are no longer able to believe that because a certain type of production " pays " in the profit-making sense of the term, no further proof is necessary that it is the best possible use of our resources. Nor do we believe the corollary—that there can be no social purpose served by carrying on an economic activity which nobody has found profitable. Experience has shown that it may be more profitable to a section of the community to cut down the making and distribution of certain products than to produce them on the wide scale that the general public might desire. This divergence between sectional and general interest is not confined to a society in which the desire for profit is the dominant factor in determining the use of economic resources. It is idle to pretend that collective ownership or control of an industry is enough to make its personnel forget their individual aspirations and grievances. Self-interest may express itself in other ways than by the fight for a higher income. Even in an industry which is nationalised, we may favour a particular policy because it gives security or greater prestige to the kind of work we do, or oppose a suggestion because we don't want to be bothered with the innumerable detailed adjustments it would entail. But in profit-making industry, the clash of sectional interests is both more obvious and more difficult to overcome. If it is decided to have more Tanks divisions in the army and fewer cavalry, there may be a good deal of angry controversy as to the value of the policy ; there may be much heartburning on the part of those whose stock goes down and sinister suggestions that it is because " old So-and-so has got a pull " and so on. But there is on the whole a belief that the decision is taken with the aim of ensuring greater efficiency even if one does not agree with it oneself. When industry is run primarily for profit there is not this consolation. When, after the last war, it became evident that the cotton and coal industries had to be cut down and it was suggested that the most economical policy would be to concentrate production on the most efficient units, there was bitter hostility on the part of those who would have been squeezed out, on the grounds that their interests were being subordinated to the profits of the bigger firms, and reorganisation was consequently held up for a very long time.

Half a century ago when Socialism was being preached as the panacea of all our industrial ills, there was a naïve belief that everybody would work in quite a new spirit in a collectivised world because they would realise that they were working for the public good and not for private profit. The extension of public enterprise has not confirmed this belief. The man who earns his living in the Post Office or Woolwich Arsenal is not ordinarily more imbued with public spirit than the one who works on the Great Western Railway or as a shop assistant at Barker's. This may be due in part to our great neglect of this aspect of public enterprise. We have not bothered to make vivid to those engaged in the newer forms of public service the rôle they play in society. With the older kinds of service—the Army and the Navy, for example—this necessity is well understood. The new recruit is told something of the history and achievements of his branch of the Service, There are uniforms and bands, ceremonial and pageantry, jokes and old customs, to form and maintain a corporate tradition and to make him feel proud to be a member of that community and ready to do all in his power to make its name shine. Through lack of imagination, we have failed to build up a similar corporate spirit and tradition in the newer forms of public enterprises. The municipal dustman does not think of himself as a private in the army that is waging war in the front line against disease ; he has just a job to be done for so much a week. Yet we have the Russian experience to prove that it is just as possible to make men aware of the social value and importance, the interest and excitement, of the humblest civilian rôle as it is to awaken their pride in their regiment or their ship. There is no doubt that we could do much to strengthen those incentives to effort in the public industries in this country. But with the industries that depend on private enterprise there is a big hurdle to jump. As long as the control of industrial policy is in the hands of those who own the capital, it is impossible for those employed in the industry to be convinced that the changes introduced are dictated by the public good and not by the shareholders' dividends, and it is by so much the more difficult to change the incentives to work.

IV

Does this mean that nothing can be done and that we must accept the situation as it is ? I think not. Democracy has been at a disadvantage because it is nobody's job to explain and justify what is happening. In Russia, the authorities feel they have a mission to imbue in the members of the community a sense of the great enterprise to which they have consecrated themselves. They have before them always the ideal of the new world towards which all their hopes are directed. They are acutely aware of their share in great possessions and the need for their active participation in moulding their destiny ; so that although individuals may be resentful of the effects on their own personal lives they get a vicarious satisfaction from their sense of sharing in the community's welfare. It might sometimes be possible for the critical and detached observer to show that this sharing is illusory. Even if it were so, it would be beside the point. The only thing that matters in such things is what people believe ; as Mr. Knickerbocker said of the Soviet people.   " You would think they owned the country ; maybe they do, maybe they don't, but they think so " ; and it is the effect on their behaviour that counts.

In this country, most working men are so firmly convinced that they are invariably sacrificed to the employer's interest that the difficulty is to persuade them that a decision which is taken by an employer for his own profit might still be equally in the public interest.   And it is, of course, possible that no amount of persuasion would modify so deep-rooted a belief.   But it is worth a trial.   To the majority of the community, of all classes, the elementary principles underlying the economic system are a closed book ; and one is generally inclined to suspect that there is something sinister in the unknown.   The widespread ignorance on the subject is due, to some extent, to the comparative newness of economics as a disciplined study.   The large majority of those who, as teachers or writers or officials, influence ideas have the sketchiest knowledge of economic operations.   But to some degree it is due, too, to the erroneous belief that economics is not only so abstruse and complicated that only the expert can hope to make head or tail of it, but that it is also so highly controversial that no two experts ever agree on any part of it.   The disagreements of economists have become almost a music-hall joke.   It is the unfortunate fact that during the inter-war years when economic controversies first forced themselves brutally into the public consciousness, the main interest was, for practical reasons, in that section of economics—the workings of the currency and banking systems—from which the man in the street feels himself most cut off both in experience and understanding.   It is natural that in the course of these controversies, when economists were trying to find the basis for sound public policy, more emphasis was put on points of dispute than on matters of common agreement.   There thus arose the idea that it is useless for the ordinary person to try and understand such esoteric matters, and that even if he did he had no guarantee that he was learning " the truth ".   But there is no foundation for this fear.   There are, of course, some branches of economic science which require a rigorous mental discipline, and a good deal of what economists discuss among themselves cannot be understood without the necessary training.   But to assume, from this, that there is nothing in the network of economic relationships which can come within the comprehension of the general public is as fantastic as to assert that it is useless to teach little boys and girls that two and two make four because they would not be able to understand the Einstein theory.   There is, indeed, an immense area in economic territory which can be easily traversed by anyone prepared to take a little exercise, provided there is somebody to point out the landmarks and help the traveller to appreciate their significance. Take, for example, the family history of a child in an urban school. Ask any boy in the class what his father does for a living and what his grandfather did, and get him to try to discover what was the work of his great-grandfather. Where did they live ? How did they get to their work ? What sort of things did they make and what tools did they use ? Whom did they make the things for ? Did they work for an employer ? How many children did great-grandfather have ? and how many brothers and sisters has this boy got now ? The answers to such simple questions can make even a child understand something of the dynamic character of economic life and realise, even if dimly, the constant shifting in social and economic patterns. The raw material of economics is so much part of normal everyday experience that it is not difficult for people to understand the simple basic relationships—such seemingly obvious, but often ignored facts, as that we produce things to use, that we do not all produce everything for ourselves, that we sell what we do produce so as to be able to buy the products of others, and so on.

In practice, every one of us is bound to make economic decisions every day of our lives. We buy food and eat it or decide to store it for next month ; or we buy a savings certificate or a shirt or send the children to school on bicycles instead of by bus. Every decision we make is based on certain assumptions, and through ignorance very often these assumptions are wrong. There is a possibility that with more understanding of the elementary principles of the economic system some at least of these assumptions may be right and that consequently the decisions we take may be more rational and more appropriate to the situation.

There are a great many simple economic relationships which are not the subject of controversy and which should form part of the general background of knowledge. The war has taught many of these in a very practical way. There are few adults who would, at this stage in the war, confuse money and real wealth. They have been taught by experience that the heaviest pay packet cannot buy goods that have not been produced. And similarly the part played by this country in world trade has been sharply emphasised by the effects of war on the family larder. During the war various Government Departments have, as a by-product of their main work, spread a lot of sound economic knowledge in the effort to explain and gain consent for their necessarily restrictionist policies. But there is no reason why this should remain a by-product of war. It is just as necessary for people to understand what is happening in peace-time as in war, and it is likely that they would be readier to make personal adjustments in their economic lives if they had some under-standing of why these were demanded of them. Given the English temperament, nothing is going to eradicate completely the bitterness in having to tear up one's roots, in changing one's job or home ; but if you realise why it is necessary you may be able to face it with greater equanimity or at least with less for-midable resistance.

For such understanding to be part of the common possession of the community it is necessary to rouse the interest of the young. Pupils in senior schools (i.e. those over eleven years of age) are not too young to grasp some general and simple ideas of the part played by the individual in the community, both as producer and as consumer. And even more vital is it to stimu-late the child's imagination to realise his membership of a living and growing society. If, as can be assumed, the school-leaving age is raised immediately after the war, room should be found in the curriculum both for some elementary economic teaching (of the simple type indicated above) and for some explanation of the social and political structure of the country, so that the child enters the adult world with some ideas already in his mind of his position as worker and as citizen. But this is no more than a slight foundation. It is to be hoped that some form of con-tinued education will be compulsory for all young people, and it is during this most important and impressionable period in life that an opportunity presents itself for such education as may make citizenship a living reality. Adolescence is a time of generous enthusiasm and aspiration for the future, for which only too often in the past no outlet has been provided. We have failed to assign to youth any recognised place in community life. With the excep-tion of the tiny minority, privileged to enter highly skilled trades or professions, we have made young people into the odd-job-men of society. Their work has often been not merely uneducative and monotonous in itself but has been carried on in such circumstances as to destroy the qualities of pride in good work, the inventiveness and initiative which the schools are at such pains to develop. Nor did we give them any understanding of the meaning of society, nor of pride in its institutions. During the war a tardy attempt has been made to remedy this serious defect and to give to young people the assurance that they count for something vital and precious in communal life. If we build further on this experience after the war it is possible that the next generation may enter on adult status less bewildered and frustrated than their predecessors and may feel that the community is something more than an abstraction. They may come to see it as a living and growing entity for whose welfare and right development they are them-selves responsible.

The war has immensely increased the general interest in civic affairs, and the desire to understand the whys and wherefores has awakened in many adults who before took the social background for granted. The admirable work of Army Education will, by the end of the war, have introduced many millions of citizens, both men and women, to the interest and importance of citizenship ; and it is likely that there will be a lively demand for further opportunities for education. Every facility must be given for this demand to be satisfied through classes and study circles, through the publication of cheap books and pamphlets and through the building of Community Centres in which people of all types and backgrounds can meet on equal terms to make their citizenship a living force. While, in general, adult education must be voluntary, there is one field in which compulsion can be rightly applied. Education in citizenship should be an integral part of the curriculum of Training and Work Centres. It is not suggested that formal courses in economics should be provided, or that " citizenship " should be deliberately taught—it is doubtful if that is possible—but that some time should be spent in the free discussion of affairs on the lines made familiar by the work of ABCA in the Army. So far the valuable opportunity presented by the Government Training Centres has been overlooked. The training has either been purely technical or has accustomed the trainees to the workshop discipline to which they will have to submit when they re-enter a trade. But nothing has been done to give men any understanding of the wider problems in industry nor to encourage them to take their civic responsibilities seriously. The ABCA experiment has proved conclusively how eager the rank and file are to find a clear way for themselves in the affairs of the day and how rapidly they can learn the give and take of friendly argument. Such training is one of the most valuable constituents of education for democracy.

Stress has been laid here on the educational approach to the development of new incentives rather than on any attempt to inculcate a sense of social obligation by direct methods. The problem that faces a democracy is so much greater than that of an authoritarian state because the sort of individual it hopes to develop is so much higher in the human scale. The authoritarian is content if its members are docile and obedient and ready to subordinate themselves completely to the ideal set before them by their leaders. In such a community uniformity is an advantage. But in a democracy, the aim is to develop the greatest diversity of human capacity while at the same time ensuring the willingness of each to modify his individual idiosyncrasy sufficiently to maintain general harmony. The real problem to be solved is the delicate line of demarcation between individual variety and social harmony or, to put it crudely, how to make members of the community feel a strong sense of community without overdoing it. It is necessary to develop in every citizen a realisation of the degree to which his life and freedom depend on the social framework within which he lives, and the seriousness of his responsibility to build and maintain it, and yet not to make him feel an insignificant unit who is of no value in relation to the whole. It is the great virtue of a democracy that the social organisation is held to exist in order that the lives of individuals may be full and diverse, not to act as a Procrustean bed lopping off the individual to make him fit into a neatly conceived social pattern. And it is because of this delicate balancing of values, when the obligation of the individual is to help build the sort of society in which individuals can develop freely, that democracies cannot set forth the social virtues with as loud and brazen a tongue as the totalitarian countries. But better education, though slower in effect, may arouse the awareness of the citizen of his place in society and may lead gradually to a change of attitude. Instead of assuming in times of difficulty that " *they* ought to do something " or " there ought to be a law about it " he may be led to think, " What ought *we* to do about this situation ? " or, " How ought *I* to behave to help in this matter ? "

There are, it must be admitted, certain institutional hurdles in the way. One of the never-ending problems in a changing world is that the institutions which grow up to satisfy the needs of one period harden in outline and fail to adapt themselves as quickly as they should when circumstances alter. They develop certain almost automatic responses to particular situations, and it takes a long time of irritating maladjustment before people begin to consider whether the response is as appropriate as it was when it originated. Indeed, it often takes longer to alter the line of policy of an institution than to change the individuals who compose it. Its constitution and procedure have been framed with a certain purpose in view, and its officials are well versed in methods which cannot readily be adapted to other ends. Like the Maginot Line, its guns point only in one direction. British Trade Unions are a good example of this tendency to a hardening of the arteries in the life of an institution. They grew up to deal with very definite problems in the wage-earners' life. Their chief work has been to protect their members' wages and conditions of employment in a world which perpetually threatened them. As the loss of employment has always been the most dreaded menace, whether that loss was occasioned by a temporary industrial depression, a permanent decline in the size of the industry or a change in the technique of production, the traditional policy of the Trade Union has generally been restrictionist. The " solidarity of labour " is a conception of fairly recent growth in this country and is supported much more strongly in the political than the industrial field. The aim of most Trade Unions has, in fact, generally been to " keep the other fellow out " and inter-union demarcation disputes are often more bitter and rancorous than the quarrels of a Trade Union with an Employers' Association. Most Unions try to make agreements to secure to their members the monopoly of work on particular machines or with certain materials and jealously guard their frontiers from invasion. When skill and training are required there is justification for such a policy; but the restriction continues long after changes in method have made it an anachronism, and it then degenerates into nothing more than the efforts of a Trade Association to kill all competitors in its chosen market. Many unions follow the policy of big business when they say in effect to employers, "Always look for the name of this union on your worker and refuse all substitutes."

As long as the hold on a job is precarious and the misery and poverty of unemployment severe, there is good reason for workers to use every device in their power to monopolise their jobs: But a policy of full employment and social security completely changes the situation. If we are successful in avoiding mass unemployment in the future, it follows that any prolonged unemployment on the part of members of the community must be due to long-term changes in technique or consumers' demands, necessitating a change in occupational distribution. Such a change cannot be made if the unions continue to use their power to guard their members' monopoly of certain areas of employment or to enforce restrictionist measures which have ceased to have any economic justification. If unemployed workers had no other resources than union funds the urgency of the situation would compel union officials to come to terms with the new position. But the more adequate the social provision for the unemployed, the greater the strength given to conservative tradition to resist change, and in this case a change in policy must depend on a deliberate effort on the part of those in control of the unions to alter their attitude.

But a change in attitude takes a long time to mature. Even in a country which uses the whole of its propaganda machinery— radio, newspapers, meetings, popular slogans, the schools—it takes at least one generation to bring about a change in reactions which is strong enough to stand a strain. It is significant that in Russia, which has done more in this way than any other country and over a longer period of time, and where there is no doubt whatever of the loyal enthusiasm felt by the mass of the population for the Soviet régime, the hard-headed and realistic authorities take cognisance of human frailties and do not risk building a structure on an incomplete foundation. The authorities have put gigantic efforts into changing the incentives to work and have stressed the social obligation of the citizen. They have done this in a particularly favourable environment, for the Russian is by temperament or culture congregation-minded and ready to respond to the idea of community. Moreover, Soviet rulers are free from any inhibitions about the deliberate attempt to mould the minds of their subjects ; and they can prohibit the propaganda of any alternative ideas. And, most important of of all, they are free from the conflict which is inevitable in a society in which production is carried on by private capital at private risk. As was argued earlier, it is by no means certain that every decision taken by the manager in a collectively owned enterprise is dictated solely by public interest. There is little doubt that human nature will keep on butting in. But the influence of personal interest is much less obvious and is less easily recognised. Yet even where all the circumstances are the most favourable, as they are in Russia, the authorities are careful to make economic incentives run parallel with social ones. It may be true that the Russian worker whose skill is redundant in his usual trade would readily recognise the need to learn something entirely different, even if he were able to claim full subsistence as long as he remained unemployed. It may be so, but there is no means of knowing. The Soviet Union does not take the risk. The worker is taught that his duty to society demands that he should do the job that is required whatever his own preferences may be, but the lesson is enforced by the knowledge that unless he complies he will get neither food nor lodging.

In this country the attitude to work is likely to take longer to alter than in the Soviet Union, since the circumstances are neither so favourable nor the direction of ideas so deliberate. Nor are we prepared to do as the Russians do and use the economic whip to spur on the laggard social sense. Of all social ideals, social security is the most definite and the most widely supported. The population is determined to retain what it has already got and to build further on this foundation. It follows then that until the change in incentives is effected and until the sense of social obligation is as powerful, and as unconsciously accepted, as an underlying principle of conduct as self-interest is now, we must choose the other alternative and restrict the freedom of choice of occupation. That is, we must pay the price of social security by instituting in peace-time as in war some degree of State control over occupational distribution.

V

State control of the movement of labour is in some respects easier in peace-time than in war, and in other respects it is more difficult. It is impossible to envisage any other circumstances in which such a wholesale redistribution of personnel could be needed as has had to be undertaken during the last few years, and peace-time control would therefore be more manageable. And yet, in a sense, the very comprehensiveness of the reshuffle makes it easier to carry out. When such large numbers are on the move and the new activities of one's family and friends are so general a topic of conversation, there is almost a sense of guilt experienced by those whose ordinary work is considered of sufficient importance to continue unchanged despite the war. But whether the extensive control makes it easier or more difficult, it is certain that in war-time the time element is more serious. It is rarely that peace-time changes in the numbers engaged in different industries must be brought about with the same speed as is required by the urgent demand for munitions. Changes in consumers' demands or in productive techniques do not usually take place quickly and may indeed take a very considerable time to establish themselves sufficiently to cause an appreciable difference in the relative demands for labour. But it must be remembered that there is one fact which makes an increase in mobility essential even if the rate of change is not very rapid— As a result of the alteration in the age-composition of the population, the proportionate number of new young recruits to industry has decreased and will continue to decrease further for some time. No matter how successful any new policy may be in inducing parents to have a larger number of children, the adolescent population of the next decade will be small. The young people who will enter industry during 1945–55 have already been born, and nothing can now alter the fact that the birth-rates of 1930–40 must result in a comparatively small entry of youths into the industrial world.[1] And it is very unlikely that any rise in the birth-rate will be either so rapid or so marked as to make an appreciable difference for some decades to come. Even without rapid changes in the relative sizes of industries, therefore, their expansion and contraction could not be brought about painlessly by the deaths of redundant workers and the recruitment of youths to expanding trades. For a very long time to come, whatever the later changes in the birth-rate may be, a high degree of adult mobility will be an essential of industrial pros-

[1] Allowing for the decline in the birth-rate and the raising of the school-leaving age after the war, the young people under 18 available for employment 10 years from now will probably be not more than half the present number. (*Times*, Nov. 26, 1943).

perity. It must be faced that this adds considerably to the difficulties of the post-war period. The older the population, the more settled it is in its habits and the less elasticity it shows in adaptation. It may well be that part of the Russian adventurousness we so much admire, the readiness to scrap an unsuccessful experiment that has not panned out as well as was hoped and try another line with undiminished zeal and hope—all this may be a function of youth. Nearly half the population of Russia is under 21 and two-thirds are under 30. But the British population is middle-aged. By 1945, 38·6% will, it is estimated, be over 45, and it can hardly be expected that they should have the same spirit of adventurousness and the same readiness to start out on unexplored paths.

Mobility will be difficult, then, even without a speeding up of change. But there is, in fact, likely to be an acceleration in this respect. With the increase in the scale of the productive unit, the new knowledge made available by scientific research is more quickly applied to industrial uses and soon becomes the general practice. In the days when an industry was made up of a large number of separate businesses of modest size, the more conservative firms could continue with the methods to which they were accustomed for a generation after the pioneers had introduced a new technique. Their goodwill and the reputation of their name with their long-established market was probably adequate to provide them with an outlet for their goods. And so their employees could hope that the methods in which they had been brought up would last their time. But the typical business unit in highly mechanised industry is now so large and the number of independent firms so few that a new technique quickly becomes universal. The war is acting as a forcing house alike in emphasising the advantage of the large firm and in familiarising producers with revolutionary changes in methods and materials. Industry after the war will be very different from what it was in 1939. The great development in the uses of plastics is likely to revolutionise many trades in the near future and to call for very different types of skill and manipulative dexterity.

But there is one respect above all in which post-war industry will present a knotty problem to be solved. In war-time there is not much room for speculation and prophecy about the expanding trades ; the range of war industries is comparatively small. You may need to produce more shells at one time and more bombs at another, but the variation is definitely one of emphasis within branches of the armament industries. More important, as the Government is the sole purchaser of the products of most industries during a war, it can know in advance where expansion is likely to take place and make plans accordingly. Provided there is proper co-ordination between Government Departments there should be no need for guesswork as to where pressure should be applied or could be relaxed. But in ordinary times the demand for labour is the result of decisions made by millions of individuals in the spending of their incomes, and it is probable that in the future these decisions will be even less predictable than they have been in the past. It is true that social security schemes, by stabilising basic standards of living at a higher level, will bring many present-day amenities within the sphere of conventional expenditure in which variations are usually only slight ; but every increase in our wealth-producing capacity raises incomes above the minimum and widens the margin within which individual, rather than conventional class choice, has the bigger influence. One person spends the extra bit in the pay packet on a motorbike, another on giving the children a better chance, a third on dressy clothes, a fourth on a vacuum cleaner to help the wife, and so on. There is not only the gamble of guessing how many people will do one and how many another, but the added difficulty that the same person is not consistent and varies from one time to another in an erratic and completely unpredictable way. The prime distinction between basic expenditure and the rest is that the first is dictated by custom, which changes usually fairly slowly and can, therefore, be estimated over a long period, while the second is determined by individual taste and is subject to the vagaries of personal idiosyncrasy as well as to temporary and fast-changing fashion.

Once the war is over and the control of industry reverts to private owners, the decision as to what shall be produced and the rate at which new techniques and materials which are available are actually used in production, will come once more to depend on the judgments of large numbers of owners and managers, each of whom makes up his mind by that amalgam of rational estimate and personal prejudice on which individual judgment usually rests. Their judgments may be better or worse than those reached by similar persons in control of similar operations during the war, who are acting on behalf of Government. The point is, however, that they are less easy to foretell since they are responsible to nobody but their shareholders and are under no compulsion to explain their actions or to get authority for their decisions. This means that any State department which tries to direct labour into the channels where it is likely to be needed is faced with the necessity of predicting the trends of coming events and of foreseeing the effects of decisions before they are taken.

There is, on the other hand, one factor which may lighten this task. The Government has already undertaken the obligation to prevent mass unemployment, and it is widely accepted that this can only be accomplished by a fairly comprehensive control of national investment. There is a very strong probability that a larger area of future industry will be under the direct control of the community, either through the extension of the system of the Public Corporation or by some other mechanism of public enterprise. And even where there does not exist so direct a relationship between production and Government, there must be a wide influence over general development if the policy of Full Employment by control of investment is to be implemented. To the extent that these developments take place the Government will be less in the dark about the demands for personnel and will have a good deal of data on which to base its estimates.

VI

War-time labour controls, comprehensive as they have grown to be, have yet left as much freedom of choice to the individual as possible. As the urgency of economising labour has exerted an ever-increasing pressure, the area in which choice can be exercised has naturally narrowed. But from the first it has been recognised that a voluntary worker is likely to be happier as a citizen and more useful as a worker than one who has been forced unwillingly into a job. If this is so during a war, when the overriding obligation to serve the State is universally accepted, it is even more essential to retain as much liberty as possible to choose one's own work in times of peace. To say that the necessary concomitant of social security is State control of labour does not mean that it should become the function of the State to apportion to each individual in the community his place in the productive system. That has been necessary during the war because we have deliberately forced an economic organisation, whose peculiar shape and institutions have been fashioned to respond to price differentials, to adapt itself to a temporary system in which price changes are the least important of considerations. During war certain things *must* be produced irrespective of the demands of individual consumers for anything else. Only the Government can know what those things are and in what order of priority they must be placed ; and, therefore, only the Government can know where, and in what quantities, workers are needed. But when the war is over the satisfaction of consumers' demands must once again become the final arbiter of the relative urgency of work to be done. Industry is carried on to produce the things that consumers want to have— whether the consumer is a public body expressing a collective want or an individual voicing a personal desire. And price differentials must again exercise their magnetic influence to determine the use to which our resources shall be put. There is no reason, therefore, why wage-earners should not choose their own work, guided thereto by a comparison of the relative pay, regularity of employment and attractiveness of the jobs available to them. It might be possible to devise a paper scheme whereby the correct numbers of workers were apportioned to different productive uses with the neatness and despatch of a mail-order office ; but men want different things of life, and a machine-made efficiency is likely to be a much less successful way of dealing with human beings, who are not mechanical robots, than one which adapts itself to the innumerable variations on the human pattern. There is no reason why a man should not continue to do a job he likes in a place that suits him, even though he could draw a higher income at something else that happens not to appeal to him or which involves leaving a place he is fond of. But there is no real freedom of choice unless the person making the choice is fully cognisant of the alternatives open to him and has the opportunity to qualify himself for those for which he considers himself suitable.

Before the war, the freedom of choice of the vast majority was narrowly restricted by ignorance of the possibilities. They had no ability to gauge the probable future course of industries which had jobs to offer at the moment and but slight opportunity to get whatever training was a necessary prerequisite. When young people are making their first choice of employment it is particularly important that they should be given the chance to choose wisely. Though circumstances may compel adults to show a greater readiness to move, there is little doubt that a radical change in employment will continue to cause a good deal of psychological distress to workers who have grown accustomed to one kind of work, and it is all the more necessary that the initial employment into which a child goes on leaving school should not only be such as to be suited to his tastes and capacity but should also be likely to offer him progressive employment for a reasonable time in the future. There are many humane and social reasons in favour of raising the school-leaving age, but, in addition, there is the strong economic one that the older the child when he leaves school, the greater the likelihood that he will know what type of work attracts him and the more possibility there is that others will make a correct estimate of his capacity. But even at sixteen, beyond which age it is not at present practical politics to contemplate the extension of universal full-time education, he has only a narrow vision of the world and can have little appreciation of what might be possible. There seems a place here for the use of such aptitude tests as have been widely developed in the army in the placing of recruits. The boy who has a sense of spatial relations will do well in one kind of job, while the boy who shows manual dexterity or the one with an ability to handle words or one with particular quickness of movement will be better placed in work which requires, and which gives scope to, these various qualities.   The present agencies for guiding the young are too rough and ready in their estimate of capacity and too blundering in their advice to be of much value.   It is right to consult the teacher about the child's general characteristics ; a teacher may know a good deal more about a child than simply his scholastic attainments.   But he has not the detailed familiarity with industrial processes to realise which category of employment is likely to offer the best opening, much less to advise in a more specialised way.   A carefully devised test may often reveal qualities that were quite unsuspected and give at least an indication of the direction in which the pupil would be advised. to turn.   How many of the young men and women who are now performing efficiently all sorts of new and adventurous jobs in the Forces would ever have suspected that they possessed the power to develop such aptitudes and skills ?   Some have eagerly seized the opportunity to try out new types of work and have been grateful for the chance that they might have been denied in civilian life ; but many others, and these not the least successful, were full of apprehension and diffidence when they began their new life and have been filled with delighted surprise at the discovery of their latent powers.

Before the war aptitude tests were very little used in vocational guidance, but experiments had been made, in London and Birmingham, which gave evidence of the value they might have.   In the London experiment 300 elementary school children were tested by the staff of the National Institute of Industrial Psychology and advised as to the type of work they should try to get.   At the same time, 300 other children from the same schools in the same area received the guidance of the normal agencies.   The subsequent careers of these two sets of children were then followed, in some cases for two years, in other cases for four, in order to see whether those who had been tested psychologically were more or less successful in their industrial lives.   The problem here, of course, is to decide what are the criteria of success—happiness in work, or the employers' satisfaction, perhaps ?   But these do not lend themselves to accurate comparison. Rates of wages and promotions gained are more capable of quantitative measurement but do not necessarily prove that the test has guided the worker correctly, since there are so many other factors involved than simply suitability for the job.   No one yardstick taken by itself is really conclusive, but probably length of tenure of a job may be taken as the most truly indicative.

of suitability, since the employer is unlikely to retain a young employee who is not shaping to some extent, and the comparative ease of changing for the young worker makes it unnecessary for him to endure a job he dislikes or feels unable to do. From this standpoint the value of psychological guidance seems certain. More of the guided children followed the advice given them than did those advised in the ordinary way, and more of the guided children who followed the advice were in the same jobs at the follow-up than were those who had taken the advice of the normal agencies.

The Birmingham experiment, which was carried out on the same lines, was somewhat larger in scale and provides more detailed results. Four hundred and twenty-six children were tested and advised by industrial psychologists while 394 received advice in the ordinary way. Of the first group, 56% of those who took the advice were found to be in the same post after two years and 43% after four years, while of the second group the comparable figures were 39% and 26%. Further, 91% of the tested children who followed the advice reported themselves as happy in their jobs while only 30% of those who did not take the advice were satisfied. The very significant corresponding figures in the case of the control children were 69% and 76%.[1]

These experiments are on too small a scale to do more than show that further trials are worth making, but the data now being accumulated in the Forces should provide very valuable material when it is possible to make it public. At the same time, it must always be remembered that more than psychological advice is necessary in guiding young workers into occupations. The psychologist may be able to devise very accurate tests of the child's capacities and may be able to correlate these to various industrial processes, but he does not necessarily know anything of the future economic position of the industry. However suitable a child may prove to be for a particular occupation, it is no use to guide him into a trade whose personnel will soon have to be reduced. Nor is it much use to test and advise children unless they and their parents are sufficiently aroused to the importance of making a good initial choice to be prepared to give the advice a trial. In fact, guiding young people into jobs requires a good deal of co-operative effort. Most parents are anxious to do as well as they can for their children and would be prepared to give some thought to the question if they could get the information necessary to enable them to compare different types of work. A series of simple leaflets

[1] M. B. Stott, " The Appraisal of Vocational Guidance ", *Occupational Psychology*, Jan. 1943. A more detailed account of the Birmingham experiment can be found in E. Patrick Allen, and Perceval Smith, *The Value of Vocational Tests as Aids to Choice of Employment*, published by the Birmingham Educational Committee, 1932.

dealing with the regional industries should be prepared, giving details of wages and prospects, any training necessary, how to get into the trade and so on. These leaflets should be sent to the parents a full year before the child is due to leave school, and stress should be laid on the need for giving the matter careful thought, so that by the time the child came for advice he might already have some idea, both of the kinds of work he would like to do and the future prospects of different occupations. All that the psychologist can hope to do is to prevent misfits and to cut down the waste of the " trial and error " flitting from job to job until the worker finds something he can settle down to.

But while aptitude tests may reduce the quantity of square pegs in round holes, practical experience is necessary for the real test of the individual's powers. In present-day industry, when a high degree of technical skill is no longer needed in most industries, the line of promotion is more likely to be taken by those who show the personal qualities which are so much more in demand than manual skill—readiness to take responsibility, flexibility and adaptability to allow one's knowledge to be used in changing circumstances and so on. All these qualities can be developed only by experience, and there is something to be said for the young person who · has no very decided bent trying out a number of different jobs during his adolescence before he undertakes the responsibilities of family life, which must inevitably tie him down somewhat. The fault in the present system, which makes it easy for young people to move quickly from job to job, is not the restless change in itself, but that the jobs are chosen and left so casually and because the care given to the conditions and types of employment of the young worker is so inadequate that the kind of work done is only too often harmful to his physical, mental and moral development. The jobs are chosen haphazard ; and as soon as the whim takes him the young worker moves off to another employment equally worthless in its training. But if the successive jobs were carefully chosen, this period of adolescence might be used as a sort of trying-out time during which the young recruit to industry could discover his bent and the type of work which is likely to provide him with satisfactory employment. If adolescent workers are in attendance at a Young People's College there will be more opportunity to guide them and make industrial experience more constructive.

The arguments which can be used to oppose compulsory attendance at Training Centres for unemployed adults have not the same force in regard to the young worker who is out of a job. The adolescent can be considered as still partly in tutelage, and regular attendance at some form of organised educational institution should be required of him. If Continuation Schools or Young People's Colleges become an integral part of the education system there will not be the same problems of staffing, equipment and administration as have proved so difficult to solve when provision was made solely for the unemployed. At any time and in any locality, the number of young people out of work forms only a tiny proportion of the total age group, and arrangements for their care can be more easily fitted into the wider organisation.

For the adult worker the problem of freedom of choice is something different. However his initial choice of a trade has been made, whether by deliberate design or by the chance of being offered a job, that choice is now behind him. His capacities have been canalised; he has grown to associate himself with a particular group of trades; he is probably a member of an occupational trade union, and by these ties and others he is constrained. But he ought to be able to get from the State accurate information over a wider field than is open to him by his own efforts. There is no doubt that the comprehensiveness of labour controls during the war has caused a radical, and probably permanent, change in the organisation of the labour market. It is likely that by the time the war is over, every type of employment will be legally negotiated only through the Employment Exchanges or through some body to which they have delegated their power. Employers who obstinately refused to make use of the Exchanges before the war, because of difficulties they had encountered a quarter of a century earlier, have been compelled to rely on them exclusively for their labour supply and have learned to notify their needs as a matter of course. The national system of unemployment insurance, with its obligation on the insured person to report to the Exchange, but with no corresponding obligation on the employer to notify vacancies, resulted in a lopsided arrangement, which is likely now to be adjusted. Even if the notification of vacancies is not compulsory after the war, it is probable that the procedure has become so common that most firms will continue to use it. In the future, therefore, the Exchanges will have much fuller data from which to build a picture of industrial trends than they had before the war and should be able to offer the worker more information about alternative employments.

VII

There is no suggestion, then, that there should be any general control of the flow of labour into industry. It is the duty of the State to provide full information so that the choice may be made intelligently and with full knowledge of the facts; but it is the privilege of the individual to choose for himself what he will do with his life. As long as he is able to meet the obligations demanded of him as a citizen—the maintenance of himself and his dependants on the scale of decency accepted by society as proper—he has the right to live according to his own scale of values. But when he is *not* able to meet his civic obligations, and demands that the community should maintain him, it is a different matter. As long as his inability to maintain himself is temporary his claim on public funds can be regarded as a retaining fee so that he will be able to resume his work when he is needed. But the more prolonged his unemployment, the more likely that he has become redundant in his industry and must change to a new one. It is at this point that compulsion should be exercised. If a policy of full employment is implemented, it may be taken that a period of six months' continuous unemployment (or, say, nine months of very intermittent employment) is an indication that the worker is unlikely to be fully reabsorbed in his own trade. At this point, he should be offered an alternative—to enter a training course or to be directed to a new occupation. He may submit to an aptitude test to establish whether he is likely to do well in an expanding industry and, if successful in passing the test, go to a Training Centre for training. The pay at the Training Centre should be higher than the unemployment allowance so as to offer an added incentive. If he refuses to enter a Centre or is unable to pass the tests for industries which will probably expand sufficiently to offer progressive employment, he should be directed to a job which is either unskilled or of the type that can be picked up in the factory. As is done with the war-time controls it is not essential that every worker should in fact be " directed ". He may be offered a choice of jobs to which to make a voluntary application, but the right to direct must be there as a sanction for those who refuse to make the choice or, having made it, fail to act on it. It should be no reason for refusal that the work offered him carries a wage which is less than he has been getting in his own trade, provided that it is paid at the trade union rate for the job or, if there is no trade union, at what is customary for the industry or locality. Nor should it be ground for refusal that the job is in an industry or area with which the worker is unfamiliar, since it is to get just this type of transference that compulsion is proposed. But if a man is obliged by the State to take a particular job, it is an obligation on the Government to make certain that the conditions of employment are reasonable and that adequate welfare, travelling and removal arrangements are in existence, on the lines of those that have been developed during the war.

But to get a man to apply for a job does not solve the problem. From our war-time experience it has proved much simpler to direct workers into the front door of a factory than to prevent them slipping out at the back. Even if a worker does not walk out, he can make a lot of trouble by frequent absenteeism or by unruly behaviour when at work. If he feels resentful of his enforced transference he is less likely to settle down quietly and pull his weight in the factory. He does not much care if he is dismissed, since he would not have chosen, of his own free will, to be employed. So that compulsory direction needs to be supplemented by some method of reducing voluntary absenteeism and indiscipline. It must be admitted that there is no watertight solution to this problem, because there is no sovereign prescription for virtue. But there are means of mitigating its seriousness. A great deal of such conduct is due to a sense of grievance. A man who feels that " he's been put upon " or that he has been singled out for compulsory transference because somebody has a " down " on him, has no other outlet for his outraged feelings than indiscipline. It is essential, therefore, to reduce the compulsory element to the minimum. Wherever possible, the unemployed man who has exhausted his standard rights should be offered a choice of jobs in different localities. He should be under compulsion to accept one of them within a specified time, but not compelled to take one particular one, chosen for him by authority. And when he has reached his new sphere of employment he must be helped to adjust himself. Here is a specially valuable piece of work for the Joint Production Committees to undertake. During the war these Committees, which are elected bodies representing management and wage-earners in one enterprise, have done very valuable work in dealing with affairs of common interest to the whole body of employees of the firm. Workshop discipline seems a matter with which they are peculiarly fitted to cope. Their detailed activities must necessarily depend on the nature of the problems thrown up by the firm in which they work, but one of their most important functions should be the creation of a public opinion in the factory. In the long run, there is no other really adequate solution of the problem of absenteeism or of general lack of discipline.

VIII

To be fully effective, State labour control must have two qualities. It must take steps to see that its directions are obeyed, and it must know what directions to give. Judging from the experience of controls during the war, the knowledge that the Government " can put you where it wants you " has often caused hesitant workers to make up their minds to move voluntarily much more quickly than they would have done otherwise.

Whenever the Government has announced that a further group of persons was to be brought under control, or that more extensive powers were to be exercised, there has almost invariably been a rush of volunteers who hope that by getting in on a voluntary basis they may enjoy a greater freedom of choice than would be their lot if they waited to be called up. For this, as much as for any other reason, the sanction of compulsion is needed. The proportion of workers who have got into their war jobs by " direction " is a comparatively small proportion of those who have been transferred. But it is quite certain that a large number of those who moved voluntarily, either before or after their calling up notice, would not have done so had they not known that their delay or refusal would have been followed by their compulsory removal. The acceleration of voluntary mobility does not take place unless workers feel fairly sure in their minds that they will not be permitted to flout their legal obligations with impunity. The history of Unemployment Insurance provides a good illustration of this fact. During the whole time that National Unemployment Insurance has been in existence, the wage-earner has had no legal right to benefit if suitable employment was offered to him and refused, and it was expressly stated that he could not legally refuse simply on the grounds that the job was unfamiliar to him, if there was no reasonable hope that he would soon be reabsorbed into his customary employment. In practice, the value of such a check turns, of course, on the interpretation of the term " suitable ", and, for political reasons, the meaning given to the word has been such as to allow applicants for benefit to continue to refuse any job other than the sort in which they had been previously employed or one very closely related to it. No Minister was willing to risk the hostile criticism that he knew awaited him if he allowed his administrative officials to give the word the meaning that had been intended. During the inter-war period there was some excuse for this moral cowardice because the unemployment figures rarely fell below the million mark and were generally above it. It might be argued that some, at least, of this unemployment was caused by the very lack of elasticity and mobility for which it was claimed to be the justification ; but it is not to be wondered at that a Minister should hesitate to try to get this over to the unemployed, even supposing that he himself had enough understanding of economic reactions to be aware of it. As long as the unemployment figures were so high, it seemed obvious that any man forced into another trade would simply be taking the bread out of another man's mouth. But if general unemployment is successfully prevented, this difficulty should disappear. There should then be no excuse for the refusal of a Minister to make use of his powers of compulsion. It is for this reason that it is suggested that the statutory duration of standard benefit should not be discretionary but should be a fixed period of definite length—six months or whatever may be decided. It is, of course, true that any period at all that is fixed upon is purely arbitrary. It may well be that in certain cases it is obvious from the start that a trade's ability to offer employment is on the decline, while in others, the combination of circumstances is such that it is quite likely to expand again in the future, though after a longer time than the duration of standard benefit. In the first case there is no reason for delaying the transference of the employees even as long as the statutory period ; in the second, there are strong reasons for postponing it beyond the limit allowed. But while it is improbable that anybody will cavil in the first instance, it is quite certain that they will in the second. The unwillingness of people to face the facts of industrial change, which have been fully discussed in earlier chapters, is likely to lead to the attempt to pull all the political strings ; and if a Minister is afraid to stand by the necessity for compulsion and to face opposition in the House and in the constituencies, no amount of efficient administration on the part of his Department can prevent the compulsory sanction from becoming ineffective. It is not proposed that the administration should be so rigid that the possibility of exceptions is completely excluded. No successful political machinery can ever hope to be so " neat " as long as human beings retain sufficient vitality to refuse to fit into a carefully composed pattern. But if the knowledge that compulsion exists is to have any real effect in increasing voluntary mobility, it is essential that the onus of proving exceptional circumstances should rest on those who claim them and that such exceptions should be admitted by the authorities with the greatest reluctance.

During the war, more extensive compulsory powers than anybody would have believed possible in this country have been exercised with a minimum of political friction and with a very wide degree of acceptance by those affected. The community's unity in face of danger and its determination to bear whatever sacrifices may be necessary to beat Hitler, have undoubtedly been the principal cause ; but it has also been the result of the wisdom which has ensured that no step should be taken without the fullest consultation with and the active co-operation of the Trade Unions. After the war, the same active co-operation is even more essential, even though the policy has a very much smaller element of compulsion in it. If wage-earners are to relinquish so important an ingredient in liberty as the right to refuse a particular job, their interests must be carefully safeguarded by their collective organisations ; and this is a further reason for stressing the vital influence that can be exercised by the attitude of the unions.   If the Trade Unions have the wisdom to realise that a combination of full employment and social security creates an entirely novel situation, they can do much to commend to their members the view that a measure of labour control is an inevitable corollary of adequate main-tenance of the unemployed.   Their readiness to co-operate in solving the administrative difficulties that inevitably arise from such a policy as compulsory transference of labour could be one of the most potent factors in creating a public opinion about the duty to increase mobility.   In the absence of such a public opinion labour control would not prove very effective.

But the second and more important matter remains to be discussed. Compulsory transference is not suggested primarily as a penalty on those who, through lethargy, idleness or con-servatism, are willing to rest contentedly dependent on public funds.   Its main object is to improve the occupational dis-tribution of the working population so that the most valuable asset the community possesses—the strength and skill of its members—shall not be wasted.   Even if wage-earners become accustomed to the idea that their industrial milieu is not settled once and for all at the commencement of their earning lives, and if the administrative machinery functions with expedition in getting workers into employment, nothing very much has been gained unless employees are, in fact, guided into just those channels where their labour can be most usefully employed.   It remains to be considered, therefore, whether public control is likely to be successful in directing workers where they are needed.

It is here that the problems set by war and peace differ most widely.   In war, the principal buyer of most products is the Government, and only short-term requirements are of prime importance. Most people who have been transferred to other jobs during the war expect to go back to their original employ-ment when the special needs of the war have no longer to be met. They have been moved, not because there is no work for them in their own trades, but because temporarily, and only temporarily, they are needed more urgently elsewhere.   The Government has simply to decide which of two jobs can be of more value in winning the war.   But in peace-time the problem is very much more complex, because it is the long-term trends that are the most vital to discover.   It would be necessary to determine which types of employment were likely to be reduced over a period of years and which new ones would probably supersede them.   The change in the relative emphasis of employments might be due to changes in taste on the part of the consuming public, to new scientific developments, to the discovery of new materials, to changes in the general criss-cross of world trade or to a host of other factors. But unless the directing authorities had the skill to interpret the signs so as to foretell the course of the currents in the economic seas, they would not be very useful pilots.

It must be admitted that in this respect the experience of labour control during the war gives least ground for confidence. There has been much less skill in anticipating needs, even those that seem most obvious, than in devising means to satisfy them once they have become clamant. The dilatory manner of organising a training programme has been, perhaps, one of the most conspicuous examples of this fault, but the impression one gets of war-time control in general is of somebody always running breathlessly after the bus and never catching up with it, instead of anticipating its route and taking a short cut so as to be able to meet it. The problem in war is exaggerated in some ways by its comprehensiveness and by its urgency, but inherently it is much simpler than it would be in peace. If there has been so little evidence of constructive foresight during the war, it is likely that this defect may be even more glaringly obvious after the war unless steps are taken to combat it.

The Civil Service has come in for a lot of hard knocks during the last few years, as is to be expected in a period of rapid change when the members of the community are much more aware of the impingement of the administrative machine on their daily lives than is normal in more placid times. There is, too, a probability that quite a lot of the criticism derives from sources which would be passionately repudiated by the critics. For if you have always been part of that privileged section of the community which is not used to receiving orders, your indignation at being treated as if you were " just anybody " can easily mask itself as an objective estimate of bureaucratic inefficiency. Moreover, much of the criticism is beside the point and springs from an insufficient appreciation of the respective rôles of the civil servant and the politician. The name of the " civil servant " is not an instance of mock humility. He is indeed the servant of his Minister, and if we value the principle of representative government it is absolutely essential that he should remain so. The Minister is responsible to Parliament and, therefore, to the country, for every act, however insignificant, on the part of his Department. However far-sighted and constructive the administrative officials may be, they cannot act unless the Minister agrees ; and the Minister is unlikely to agree if he fears that such action may have unfavourable political repercussions. It is very rarely that really constructive policies are brilliant improvisations, conceived and matured on the instant. They usually require a long hatching period, during which time what is being done cannot be properly understood by the mass of the population who have neither the habit of mind to look far ahead nor the necessary knowledge to build up a picture of future developments. As the preliminary preparations for any such policy are sure to have immediate effects on some section of the community, there is certain to be a good deal of articulate protest. The associations representing those whose interests are concerned write letters to the Press, pointing out the evils they suffer from the actions of an inefficient bureaucracy ; members of Parliament, in whose constituencies the people affected happen to live, gain local popularity, on which they hope to cash in at the next election, by asking questions in the House ; a rival Minister, whose departmental interests are adversely affected, makes objections behind the scenes, and so on. It takes a man of strong personality and with great confidence in his public rating to fight for a policy whose disadvantages are immediate and obvious, while the advantages are a matter of faith and cannot be estimated until time has allowed for maturity. The growth in extent and complexity of Government functions has resulted in so highly specialised a departmentalism that it too often happens that the advantages of a policy are principally the concern of one Department while the consequent adjustments demanded by it are the concern of another. Such a situation does not lead to a dispassionate balancing of pros and cons. The Minister of Labour may believe that young men and women can make a more effective contribution to the war effort than by continuing their work as retail salesmen ; the President of the Board of Trade is more likely to fight the battle of the shop-owners who look to him to protect their trade. Or the Minister of Mines may realise that the maintenance of a high output of coal requires the retention of a large number of young men in the coalfields even if they are not at that moment fully employed while the Treasury is unwilling to sanction the expenditure of funds to guarantee their wages or the Secretary of State for War fulminates against their reservation for civilian duties when his army needs manning. No matter how farsighted and construc-tive the Civil Service might be, these qualities cannot find expres-sion if the Ministers in charge of Departments have narrow vision or are moral cowards. A high standard of Ministerial statesmanship is the essential foundation of successful Govern-ment control, whether of labour mobility or of any other com-munal activity.

But when all this is granted there remains a great deal of

criticism that is justified. The training of the civil servant has not developed with the growth in the range of his functions, and an education which was admirably fitted for its original purpose fails to foster the qualities that are now demanded of him. Most administrative officials, whether they had their preliminary training in a University or through many years of experience in the Department, have been schooled to make detached and objective judgments. Present them with a proposal and they are prepared to state soberly and cogently the arguments for it and the arguments against. This is an admirable and valuable capacity, and as long as, so to speak, " the situation is given ", it is the capacity that is principally required. But it is definitely not enough when the situation is not " given " but must be foretold or created. When the function of the State was limited to the passing of laws which were for the most part an expression of the commonly accepted basic principles governing property rights and the relationship of citizens to one another, the power to make a logical analysis and to give a dispassionate judgment was the chief quality required by the civil servant. In administering the law he had to apply a general principle to a particular instance. But now that the State controls detailed day-to-day economic activities the position is entirely different. A law which gives the State the power to order any man or woman in the community to do any job is in quite a different category from one which says that a person convicted of stealing will receive such and such a punishment ; and it requires a different type of ability and training for its competent administration. There are some fairly obvious requirements—flexibility of mind, ability to relate cause and effect, the power to foresee a chain of developments so that future events may be discounted by present action, quickness of decision and readiness to take action. But there are two particular respects in which the qualities needed by the modern civil servant differ from those of his predecessor. The application of a general principle to a particular instance demands mainly qualitative thinking ; but if a law confers powers but does not state the principles on which they are to be used, it is necessary to supplement this by quantitative thinking. It is of the utmost importance that not one single individual be wrongly convicted and punished for theft, since a general principle is thereby involved. But it is by no means of the utmost importance that every man and woman should, in fact, be told off by the State to do a particular job, since it may not be worth the trouble of ordering him and seeing him obey ; it is a question of expediency, not of principle. It may be that the administrative cost of registering, interviewing and classifying a small group of people in certain circumstances is so high in view of the yield of available labour to be got from them, that the decision might be taken not to make use of the power conferred by the law. The ways in which the general powers given by the law are exercised demands a constant balancing of costs and results. Only by continuous and accurate assessment of the effects of his actions can the official get a correct idea of the value of what he is doing and alter his method accordingly. But although so much of his work is now very similar to that of the management of a big industrial enterprise, he has not yet learned from the business man the importance of the quantitative check. In too many Government Departments, those who are responsible for making decisions are untrained in the collection and use of statistics and are inclined to ignore their importance.

The second difference which results from the wide extension of Government control is that the modern civil servant requires a great deal more knowledge of the ordinary activities of the workaday world ; and he does not get this either from his education or from his experience as an official. The principle of the interchangeability of officials—that an official of one grade can be put to any job in the Department which carries that rank—has a good deal to be said for it. It gives the official the opportunity to see many different facets of the work of the Department and so to gain a better understanding of their mutual relationship ; it develops his mind by giving him situations of widely varying type to cope with, and it greatly simplifies the staffing of new spheres of administrative work that result from increased State activity. But it has the very serious defect of assuming that certain *qualities* of mind in the official are adequate for his job, irrespective of what may be the *contents* of the mind. When the official has to control day-to-day economic activities this is definitely not true. It leads to the erroneous belief that the official can learn as much as he need know of the problem from the files. The extraordinary gaps in the libraries of most Government Departments are evidence of how little it is thought necessary to acquaint oneself with the wider aspects of the problems with which one is supposed to be dealing. Serious blunders are made because the officials simply do not know enough about the subject. They are too often ignorant of the basic economic relationships and of the social institutions which form the fabric of the life of the community and which play so large a part in determining the reactions of individuals. This is one of the reasons that they so often act too late. Given their present training, it is almost inevitable that they should be more inclined to deal with situations as they arise rather than know how to create the situation by looking ahead and preparing for it. And this has the unfortunate result that, as their efforts are more generally concerned with events that have happened than with envisaging the adjustments necessary for the future, much of what they do is already a little out of date by the time that they do it.

If the State is to undertake still further control of economic activity, as it must if social security and full employment are to be implemented, it will be necessary for changes to be made in the training and recruitment of the Civil Service. It is absolutely essential that the official should have more knowledge of the ordinary world. This might be achieved in a number of ways. It should be possible for men and women to enter the Civil Service after they have already had some experience of employment in the industrial or professional field. Except in war-time, when enormously swollen staffs have to be recruited, this is rare, and while it is not suggested that it should be the normal avenue of entry, it should not be regarded as so exceptional as to require very special justification. For the man who enters the service at the beginning of his professional career, it should be the custom to interrupt his duties periodically to allow attendance at refresher courses at which he can study the wider aspects of the problems he is dealing with. It is probable that a good deal more will be got from such study if the official has already had some years of experience of administration in the Department than if he takes it as a preliminary to his appointment, and it can then also be better adapted to qualify him for the particular work to which he has been assigned. For it is likely that in the future it will be found necessary to restrict, at least to some extent, the general interchangeability of officers and develop certain more specialised sections within the general framework of the service. Such a task, for example, as that of the control of the occupational distribution of the population requires a breadth of vision, a quickness of judgment, a fund of knowledge and a sensitiveness to the situation that could be acquired only by long experience in one field. But all these proposals touch on wider topics than can be dealt with in this study of labour mobility. They are mentioned merely as indications of the problems to be solved if labour control is to be efficiently administered.

But when all is said we come back to the more fundamental matter. The good occupational distribution of the working community is not at bottom a result of administration, however efficient this may be and however essential to the smooth functioning of an industrial society. At bottom it depends on the actions of the individual and what he thinks about life. No amount of pushing and prodding is going to make the unwilling or the insensitive citizen play his part in the world. It is only if we come to accept the fact that the community is what we make it, and that as members of a democracy we have a responsibility to society as well as a claim on it, that we can develop those incentives to individual endeavour that will enable us to enjoy both security and prosperity.

SUMMARY OF PROPOSALS

FOR the sake of convenience the positive recommendations made to increase the mobility of labour are summarised.

1. Greater use should be made of Employment Exchange machinery than was customary before the war. Probably the best way to achieve this would be to retain the war-time compulsion to notify vacancies and withdrawals even if workers are not necessarily engaged through the Exchanges.

2. Care should be taken that young people are helped to choose occupations which are likely to suit their capacities and to provide progressive employment. Further experiments should be made in the use of aptitude tests to determine the kind of work for which school-leavers are suitable.

3. It should be compulsory for unemployed adolescents to attend full-time courses at the Young People's Colleges.

4. Courses designed to give young people some understanding of the economic and political structure of the country should be an essential part of the curriculum in Young People's Colleges.

5. Some elementary teaching of fundamental economic relationships should be introduced into the curriculum of senior and secondary schools.

6. Freedom of choice of occupation should be maintained for all capable of finding employment.

7. The right to unconditional unemployment benefit should be strictly limited in duration.

8. Admission to a Training Centre should not be made a condition of unemployment benefit. Training should be voluntary, but applicants should not be admitted unless the results of aptitude tests and medical examination show that they are likely to possess the requisite capacity and physical fitness. Those admitted should receive higher pay than the unemployment benefit.

9. The Training Centre course should not be purely technical, but should aim also at giving trainees some understanding of their civic rights and responsibilities. Probably the best way of doing this would be by making discussion groups on the lines of ABCA a compulsory part of the course.

10. The Minister of Labour should have the power to direct applicants for benefit who have exhausted their unconditional benefit rights to any employment, even if this entails a change in locality or occupation. Whenever possible the worker should be given a choice of jobs with the compulsion to accept one within a specified period of time.

11. Similar arrangements for welfare, travelling and lodging allowances should be made for transferred workers as have been instituted as part of the war-time labour controls.

12. Joint Production Committees should be encouraged in all types of employment. Part of their duty should be to help transferred workers to adjust themselves to their new employment.

13. Unemployment benefit should be given beyond the statutory period only in very exceptional circumstances.

14. Changes should be made in the recruitment and training of Civil Servants so as to ensure that those in charge of the occupational distribution of labour, whether as advisers to young people and adults or as administrators of powers of direction, should be able to foretell production trends and guide workers into the appropriate channels.

15. Specialist sections should be developed within the general framework of the Civil Service. Narrow specialisation is not desirable, but the administration of the economic functions of Government requires experience and knowledge which can only be accumulated over a prolonged period of service in closely related fields.

16. Administrative Civil Servants should be periodically released from their duties to take special courses in subjects connected with their duties or to have opportunities to get first-hand knowledge of the workaday world.

BIBLIOGRAPHY

CHAPTER I

COLIN CLARK, *Conditions of Economic Progress.* Macmillan, 1940.
J. L. GRAY, *The Nation's Intelligence.* Watts, 1936.
J. and S. JEWKES, *The Juvenile Labour Market.* Gollancz, 1938.
J. R. HICKS, *The Theory of Wages.* Macmillan, 1932.
M. DOBB, *Wages.* Nisbet and C.U.P., 1938.
Abstract of Labour Statistics. 1938.

CHAPTER II

Report of the Royal Commission on Unemployment Insurance. 1932.
H. CLAY, *Problem of Industrial Relations.* Macmillan, 1929.
——, *Post-war Unemployment Problem.* Macmillan, 1930.
A. LOVEDAY, *Britain and World Trade.* Longmans, 1931.
Edited by JOHN HILTON and Others, *Are Trade Unions Obstructive?* Gollancz, 1935.
J. F. ROWE, *Wages in Theory and Practice.* Routledge, 1928.
T. S. CHEGWIDDEN and G. MYRDDIN-EVANS, *Employment Exchange Service of Great Britain.* Macmillan, 1934.
A. G. B. FISHER, *The Clash of Progress and Security.* Macmillan, 1935.

CHAPTER III

Annual Reports of the Unemployment Assistance Board.
Ministry of Labour Gazette.
Economic Journal.
Oxford Economic Papers. Oxford Univ. Press, 1938.
E. WIGHT BAKKE, *The Unemployed Man.* Nisbet, 1933.
Pilgrim Trust Report, *Men Without Work.* C.U.P., 1938.
GERTRUDE WILLIAMS, *The State and the Standard of Living.* King, 1936.

CHAPTER IV

Ministry of Labour Gazette. 1939–43.
Labour Supply and National Defence. I.L.O., 1941.
Wartime Transference of Labour in Great Britain. I.L.O., 1942.
Reports of the Select Committee on National Expenditure. 1940–3.

CHAPTER V

C. W. GUILLEBAUD, *Economic Recovery of Germany, 1933–38.* Macmillan, 1939.
——, *Social Policy of Nazi Germany.* C.U.P., 1941.
F. NEUMANN, *Behemoth.* Gollancz, 1942.
H. W. SINGER, " Germany's War Economy " (Series of articles in *Economic Journal*, 1941–3).
L. E. HUBBARD, *Soviet Trade and Distribution.* Macmillan, 1938.
M. DOBB, *Soviet Economy and the War.* Routledge, 1941.
——, *Soviet Planning and Labour.* Routledge, 1942.

S. and B. Webb, *Soviet Communism : A New Civilisation*, 2 vols.
Longmans, 1941.
Sir John Maynard, *The Russian Peasant and Other Studies.* Gollancz,
1942.

CHAPTER VI

Beveridge Report on Social Insurance. 1942.
F. M. Earle, *Methods of Choosing a Career.* Harrap, 1931.
Joint Productions Committee in Great Britain. I.L.O., 1943.
Alec L. Macfie, *Economic Efficiency and Social Welfare.* Oxford Univ.
Press, 1943.
H. E. Dale, The Higher Civil Service of Great Britain. Oxford, 1941.
A Civil General Staff. *Planning No. 214.* PEP, 1943.

INDEX

For Product Safety Concerns and Information please contact our EU
representative GPSR@taylorandfrancis.com Taylor & Francis Verlag GmbH,
Kaufingerstraße 24, 80331 München, Germany

Printed and bound by CPI Group (UK) Ltd, Croydon, CR0 4YY
08/05/2025
01864422-0003